READING BACKWARDS

Reading Backwards

An Advance Retrospective on Russian Literature

Edited by
Muireann Maguire and Timothy Langen

https://www.openbookpublishers.com

All external links were active at the time of publication unless otherwise stated and have been archived via the Internet Archive Wayback Machine at https://archive.org/web

Digital material and resources associated with this volume are available at https://doi.org/10.11647/OBP.0241#resources

ISBN Paperback: 9781800641198
ISBN Hardback: 9781800641204
ISBN Digital (PDF): 9781800641211
ISBN Digital ebook (epub): 9781800641228
ISBN Digital ebook (mobi): 9781800641235
ISBN Digital (XML): 9781800641242
DOI: 10.11647/OBP.0241

Cover image: Nadezhda Udaltsova, *Mashinistka* (1910s). Wikimedia, https://commons.wikimedia.org/wiki/File:N._Udaltsova_-_Typewriter_girl,_1910s.jpg, Public Domain.

Cover Design by Anna Gatti.

Contents

Contributor Biographies

Michael Bowden is a postgraduate researcher and teaching assistant at the University of Leeds. His dissertation topic explores Dostoevsky's influence over novels by J. M. Coetzee, David Foster Wallace and Atiq Rahimi, with a particular focus on the ethical implications of the polyphonic novel form. He received his BA and MA from the University of Manchester.

David Gillespie taught Russian to BA and MA students at the University of Bath, UK, from 1985 to 2016, when he retired as Professor of Russian Studies. He also taught Russian language to UK Ministry of Defence interpreters on a part-time basis at the University of Bristol from 1986 until 2011. He is currently Honorary Professor of Linguistics at Tomsk State University, and Honorary Research Fellow at Queen Mary University of London. He has published ten monographs, including *Iurii Trifonov: Unity through Time* (1993), and *Russian Cinema* (2003); over seventy peer-reviewed book chapters and journal articles, and presented over 100 papers at conferences in the UK, USA, Canada, Germany, Belgium, Holland, France, Croatia and Russia. He recently completed editing and updating the fourth edition of Terence Wade's definitive *A Comprehensive Russian Grammar*, xxxiii + 601 pp., published by Wiley-Blackwell (USA and UK) in May 2020. He is currently working on a monograph (*A History of Russian Literature on Film*), to be published by Bloomsbury in 2023.

Marina Korneeva gained her Candidate of Sciences degree in 2018 and is currently studying for her doctorate in foreign language teaching methodology at Tomsk State University. Since 2017 she has published over twenty peer-reviewed articles. Her monograph, based on her Candidate of Sciences thesis *Teaching Foreign Languages to Students of*

Applied Mechanics through the Case Study Method, will be published by Tomsk University Press in 2021.

Timothy Langen teaches Russian language, literature, and cultural history at the University of Missouri. His research interests include the writings of Nikolai Gogol, Andrey Bely, and Sigizmund Krzhizhanovsky, and the intellectual history of late nineteenth- and early twentieth-century Russia. He is author of *The Stony Dance: Unity and Gesture in Andrey Bely's "Petersburg"* (2005) and co-editor and co-translator, with Justin Weir, of *Eight Twentieth-Century Russian Plays* (2000).

Muireann Maguire lectures in Russian Literature at the University of Exeter, UK. She is the principal researcher on 'RusTrans, The Dark Side of Translation: 20th and 21st Century Translation from Russian as a Political Phenomenon in the UK, Ireland, and the USA' (2019–23), an academic project funded by the European Research Council. Her academic specializations include Gothic-fantastic literature, the fictional representation of pregnancy and childbirth, and the nineteenth-century Russian novel. Her book *Stalin's Ghosts: Gothic Themes in Early Soviet Literature* was published by Peter Lang in 2012. She has published articles on Russian literature in *Modern Language Review, Slavic Review,* the *Slavonic and East European Review,* and other journals.

Eric Naiman teaches Russian and Comparative Literature at the University of California, Berkeley. He is the author of *Sex in Public: The Incarnation of Early Soviet Ideology* (1997) and *Nabokov, Perversely* (2010), as well as many articles on nineteenth- and twentieth-century Russian literature.

Steven Shankman holds the UNESCO Chair in Transcultural Studies, Interreligious Dialogue, and Peace at the University of Oregon. His work in the Western classical tradition includes *Pope's Iliad: Homer in the Age of Passion* (1983) and *In Search of the Classic: Reconsidering the Classical Tradition, Homer to Valéry and Beyond* (1994). His Penguin edition of Pope's *Iliad* appeared in 1996. Some of his later scholarly work, including *The Siren and the Sage: Knowledge and Wisdom in Ancient Greece and China* (co-authored with Stephen Durrant, 2000) and *Early China/ Ancient Greece: Thinking through Comparisons* (co-edited by Stephen Durrant, 2002), compares classical traditions. He is a co-editor of *The*

World of Literature (1999), an anthology of world literature from a global perspective, which contains some of his own poetic translations from Chinese, Greek, and Latin. His original poems have appeared in a number of journals including *The Sewanee Review, Literary Imagination, Literary Matters, Poetica Magazine,* and *Tikkun Magazine.* Two of his books that explore the work of Emmanuel Levinas are *Other Others: Levinas, Literature, Transcultural Studies* (2010) and *Turned Inside Out: Reading the Russian Novel in Prison* (2017).

Inna Tigountsova holds degrees in Romano-Germanic Philology and Translation (Russian/English/German/Polish) from the Federal Baltic State University (Kaliningrad) and in Mediaeval Studies from the Central European University in Budapest. She received her PhD in Slavic Languages and Literatures at the University of Toronto, held a postdoctoral fellowship at Memorial University, and has taught in Canada, the US, and the UK. Her first book *The Ugly in Russian Literature: Dostoevsky's Influence on Iurii Mamleev, Liudmila Petrushevskaia, and Tatiana Tolstaia* (2009) was well-reviewed, and her second—*Death and Disorder: Dostoevsky in the Context of Petrushevskaia and Goethe*—is under contract with Academic Studies Press' Studies in Comparative Literature and Intellectual History series, edited by Galin Tihanov. She has also published in *The Dostoevsky Journal: A Comparative Literature Review; Modern Language Review; Slavic and East European Journal; Canadian Slavonic Papers; Ulbandus: The Slavic Review of Columbia University; Studies in Slavic Cultures; Canadian-American Slavic Studies,* and elsewhere. Tigountsova's translations include works by Dmitrii Prigov, Liudmila Petrushevskaia, and Alexander Piatigorsky.

Ilya Vinitsky is a Professor of Russian literature in the Slavic Department at Princeton University. His main fields of expertise are Russian Romanticism and Realism, the history of emotions, and nineteenth-century intellectual and spiritual history. His books include *Vasily Zhukovsky's Romanticism and the Emotional History of Russia* (2015), *Ghostly Paradoxes: Modern Spiritualism and Russian Culture in the Age of Realism* (2009) and *A Cultural History of Russian Literature,* co-written with Andrew Baruch Wachtel (2009). His most personal book, *The Count of Sardinia: Dmitry Khvostov and Russian Culture* (2017; in Russian) investigates the phenomenon of anti-poetry in the Russian literary tradition from the eighteenth through the twenty-first century and focuses on the literary biography and cultural function of the "king" of Russian poetasters, Count Dmitry Khvostov. Vinitsky is currently working on a book about the cultural values of forgers and mystifiers.

Svetlana Yefimenko is a PhD candidate in Russian Studies and Classics at the University of Exeter (United Kingdom), researching Tolstoy's diachronic reception of Homer. She is founder and editor-in-chief of *Xanthos: A Journal of Foreign Literatures and Languages*.

Acknowledgements

The editors are indebted to all those who gave moral support or good advice when this volume was still at the planning stage, including Justin Weir and William Mills Todd III. We are grateful to Adam Horsley (University of Exeter) for timely *traduction*, and to Jacob Emery (Indiana University) for an inspiring critique of our volume which was simultaneously astute and empathetic. The memory of Gennady Barabtarlo's deep, playful erudition warmed our work and emboldened our search for unexpected patterns and meanings.

We would also like to thank Alessandra Tosi and Melissa Purkiss, of Open Book Publishers, for their exemplary work on behalf of this volume. The University of Missouri Research Council and the University of Exeter's Institutional Open Access Fund provided invaluable financial support.

We are grateful to our families and colleagues for their forbearance and good humour.

And finally, we thank posterity, for their patience with our plagiarism.

Introduction: Countersense and Interpretation

Muireann Maguire and Timothy Langen

....[W]ho said that the logic of life is compulsory in art?
— Daniil Kharms and Aleksandr Vvedenskii, 'The Oberiu Manifesto'[1]

In the 1960s, the 'Oulipo' group of French writers and philosophers developed, as part of their playful pseudoscience of 'pataphysics', a concept they called 'le plagiat par anticipation' (plagiarism by anticipation). And while we will have much more to say about anticipatory plagiarism, a few words about this brilliantly inventive and peculiarly disciplined group are necessary to distinguish them from other, notably Russian, twentieth-century literary innovators. The Oulipo (Ouvroir de Littérature Potentielle) movement proved productive and long-lived, publishing manifestos well into the 1980s, surviving the deaths of its founders (Raymond Queneau and François Le Lionnais) and of its most famous member, Georges Perec. Like the Russian avant-garde movements of the early twentieth century, the Oulipo writers proposed a radical reconstruction of literary technique in the pursuit of creative freedom, and an equally sweeping re-evaluation of what constitutes a literary text. But the Oulipo was no second OBERIU; Queneau and Le Lionnais were not plagiarizing Kharms and Vvedensky.[2] Like their Russian predecessors, Oulipo favoured artistic experimentation; unlike them, they privileged process over product. The Oulipo writers were not primarily interested in creating literature or performances; instead, they were preoccupied by the development of new *contraintes*—constraints, or systems of rules—which would force writers to compose within strict limitations. While their results might

 https://doi.org/10.11647/OBP.0241.10

appear absurd—for example, Le Lionnais wrote poems consisting of a single letter, or of a sequence of numbers and punctuation marks; Perec designed rhyming acrostics—the constraints underpinning these creations were tightly plotted and internally coherent. Their approach to literary production is epitomized by Queneau's *A Hundred Thousand Billion Poems* (*Cent mille milliards de poèmes*, 1961). This set of ten sonnets where each of the lines could be physically cut out and re-inserted in place of any other lines, giving a potential maximum of 10^{14} unique fourteen-line poems, was in fact structured according to the mathematical operation of permutation.[3] We might add that the use of mathematics as a literary trope had been plagiarized well in advance of the Oulipians' efforts by Dostoevsky's Underground Man, with his nonconformist insistence that 'two-times-two-is-five is also sometimes a very lovely little thing'.[4]

Also unlike the Russian avant-garde and absurdist tradition, the Oulipians did not reject their antecedents. On the contrary, they celebrated their own immersion in literary tradition, especially where Greek classics and French medieval poetry and prose were concerned; and they revelled in identifying past examples of *contrainte* in literature, particularly if it happened to foreshadow an Oulipian technique or if it had been exercised unwittingly. Hence connection, rather than rupture, was a core tenet of the group's philosophy. A favourite *contrainte* was the lipogram, a text missing at least one letter of the alphabet. The most famous example of this is Perec's 1969 novel *The Disappearance* (*La Disparition*), which omits the letter 'e'; three years later he published *Les Revenentes* [sic], which omits every vowel *except* 'e'. The lipogram is in fact an ancient form; the sixth-century AD Greek poet Tryphiodorus wrote a twenty-four-volume version of the *Odyssey*, in each successive volume of which he contrived to leave out one letter, following the order of the Greek alphabet.[5] Tryphiodorus and other ancient lipogrammatists were much admired by the Oulipians, although the casual reader might be more inclined to sympathize with De Quincey's opinion that the ancient poets who 'gloried in dispensing with some one separate consonant, some vowel, or some diphthong' resembled 'that pedestrian athlete who wins a race by hopping on one leg, or wins it under the condition of confining both legs in a sack'.[6] Extended *ad absurdum*, as the Oulipo writers often did extend their conceptions, any sentence can be qualified as lipogrammatic: the one you are reading is a lipogram on the letters *j*, *k*, *v*, and *z*.

Lipograms also open up the Oulipians' concept of anticipatory plagiarism. Our use of *contrainte* in the final sentence of the last paragraph was unintentional: we had no plan to embargo those four consonants. But should a future author deliberately compose a sonnet or a novel excluding *j*, *k*, *v*, and *z*, our essay could be hailed (at least by Oulipian critics) as an example of anticipatory plagiarism of that precise *contrainte*. Both Perec and Le Lionnais mischievously alleged that writers commonly plagiarize, not their antecedents, but their posterity, by anticipating—and, from a certain perspective, stealing—the subjects, styles, and even the precise words of writers not yet born. This idea turns Harold Bloom's concept of the 'anxiety of influence' on its head: instead of worrying about the originality of their creative ideas, writers should evidently be anxious to ring-fence their copyright from predatory predecessors. A latter-day Oulipian, the writer Jacques Jouet, claimed to have exposed the Romantic poet Alfred de Musset as a proto-Oulipian—in effect, a plagiarist of the group—because Musset allegedly practices an Oulipian *contrainte* in his 1832 poem, 'A mon ami Édouard B'. Here the poet enjoins his aspiring poet friend to discover genuine inspiration in his own heart ('frappe-toi le coeur') rather than by reading others' verse (here, Lamartine—the hint of plagiarism may have drawn Jouet to this particular poem by Musset). But, as Jouet points out, Musset's instructions to his friend are composed in alexandrines, which function as a hidden *contrainte*.[7] Musset explicitly instructs his friend to find poetry in his heart; yet, by delivering this advice in a specific metre, he implicitly suggests that metre, not chest-beating, is the key to creativity. Or further still, that the heart itself—manifestly governed as it is by its own metre—demonstrates the inextricability of expression from constraint. The use of concealed constraint like this appealed to the paradox-loving Oulipian mind. Whether or not Musset had plagiarized one of their methods, Jouet and his fellow Oulipians elaborated that any literary or stylistic technique, whether unintentionally deployed (like our lipogram above), or used without formal acknowledgement (like Musset's alexandrines), can be classified as anticipatory plagiarism if it is later more fully and explicitly expressed in the work of a different author. Instead of suggesting that the successor writer had committed conventional plagiarism of the first, the Oulipo authors read this connection backwards as evidence that the earlier writer had plagiarized his or her descendant—by anticipating them. Like the lipogram, anticipatory plagiarism is of potentially universal application: *La Bibliothèque oulipienne* reminds us, 'Tout texte est un plagiat par anticipation d'une contrainte inconnue' ('Every text is an anticipatory plagiarism of an unknown constraint').[8]

The notion that every text may have multiple, recognized literary offspring suited the provocative Oulipo aesthetic. In a 1979 short story, Perec traded the paradoxical notion of anticipatory plagiarism for the even more radically unbelievable suggestion that the entire cohort of French Symbolist authors had collectively suppressed all traces of a precursor whom they had plagiarized in the conventional manner, by stealing from his published work. The crime comes to light when a young literary historian chances upon an obscure 1864 novel by the unknown Hugo Vernier. After originally accepting the novel's evocations of Verlaine, Rimbaud, Lautréamont, Huysmans and others, even reading a direct quote from Mallarmé as contemporary pastiche, he suddenly realizes that the novel's publication pre-dates all of these writers and that they must, therefore, have plagiarized Vernier. But all attempts to research Vernier's life or even to preserve the last remaining copy of his book fail, forcing the scholar to conclude that most of the print run 'had been intentionally destroyed by the very people who had been directly inspired by it'.[9] Unlikely as it is that France's leading writers would club together to suppress evidence of a shared crime of plagiarism, even this audaciously paranoid idea may just be more rational than the basic paradox defining anticipatory plagiarism. After all, the notion that every text is a plagiarism of another not yet written (where both employ the same *contrainte*, implicitly or explicitly) threatens to shift the entire concept of plagiarism towards something like existential guilt. How, then, is it possible to argue meaningfully that specific writers plagiarize their posterity, and how can any such argument hold academic or methodological value?

—

It is our contention in this collection, as our contributors elegantly prove, that anticipatory plagiarism has in fact many insights to offer to scholars, and to readers, and not only in the fields of French—or indeed Russian—literature. We propose that the apparently nonsensical 'advance retrospective' approach provides a new way of understanding reception studies, cultural translation, and even our most hallowed classics. It is what we might call *countersensical*, in that it runs against the patterns of normal experience but reveals new patterns of surprising coherence and scope. It crosses languages, cultures, and genres as readily as it does time. While we do not seriously suggest (nor did the Oulipians) that past authors plagiarized their descendants, the task of thinking about our cultural heritage in this upside-down way forces us to realize that patterns of inspiration are cyclical; that no idea is ever completely original; and that influence flows in many directions (even if not, actually, backwards). In his monograph *Anticipatory Plagiarism* (*Le Plagiat par anticipation*, 2009), the contemporary French philosopher Pierre Bayard has modified the radical Oulipo notion to filter out some of its most marked absurdities, and to leave us with arresting new insights into the continuity of technical and aesthetic constraints between generations and literary epochs. He tames the chronological paradox by setting textual parameters for anticipatory plagiarism and thus eliminating the problem of ubiquity. Anticipatory plagiarism is not, according to Bayard, a process; it is a question of perspective, a way of re-evaluating the influences between writers. By assuming that influence is one-directional, we can fail to see the more subtle connections linking the same idea in different generations. When we reverse the direction of influence, we learn more about the overlap between past and present—which is often a valuable lesson for the future. It is just such an inventive, even Borgesian, and intellectually rewarding interplay of ideas that readers of this volume will find in such essays as Shankman's study of proto-Levinasian ideas in Tolstoy, Langen's suggestion that Gogol borrowed ideas from both Sigizmund Krzhizhanovsky and the Irish satirist Flann O'Brien, Vinitsky's deliberately absurdist investigation of the artist Raphael's plagiarism of Gogol, or Bowden's re-reading of Dostoevsky through the lens of Coetzee. Beyond this volume, our analyses find an echo (unsurprisingly, in the field of Nabokov studies), in the work of Eric Naiman, a champion of 'reading preposterously'; in previous articles, he argues for reading Nabokov's *Lolita* 'as if it were as intricate as a Shakespeare sonnet' and even more counter-intuitively, for Dostoevsky as a pupil or epigone of Nabokov.[10] Naiman argues forcefully for a rejection of linearity in our approach to literary criticism: 'Every understanding of a particular work of fiction is somewhat preposterous, coloured by works written after it but which its readers have already read. Why not make aggressive, productive use of our inescapably contaminated sense of temporality? Can't we read and write history from our own, disciplinary position of strength?'.[11] In his afterword to the present volume, Naiman explores just what such a position might offer, and look like, from a Bayardian perspective.

The Oulipian approach extends to authors the holiday from linear temporality which Naiman recommends for scholars. 'On ne cesse d'évoquer l'influence des écrivains et des artistes sur leurs successeurs, sans jamais envisager que l'inverse soit possible et que Sophocle ait plagié Freud, Voltaire Conan Doyle, ou Fra Angelico Jackson Pollock,' writes Bayard ('We never stop invoking the influence of writers and artists upon their successors, without ever imagining that the reverse might be possible and that Sophocles might have plagiarized Freud, Voltaire Conan Doyle, or Fra Angelico Jackson Pollock').[12] While one might object that Voltaire did not literally plagiarize Arthur Conan Doyle's famous Sherlock Holmes, Bayard demonstrates through close reading that the eponymous hero of Voltaire's *Zadig* undeniably anticipated (in 1747) the deductive techniques of Doyle's detective in the short stories 'The Adventure of Silver Blaze' (1892) and 'The Hound of the Baskervilles' (1901).[13] Bayard is not alone in connecting Holmes and Zadig; but he may be the first scholar to plot this genealogy in reverse. He makes a similar, textually supported argument that Maupassant plagiarized Proust's celebrated reminiscent, multi-clause style before Proust had even commenced writing the *Remembrance of Things Past* (*À la recherche du temps perdu*, 1913–1927) heptalogy.[14] In an effort to make anticipatory plagiarism less arbitrary, Bayard's book isolates four criteria that must be fulfilled: similarity (the original and the plagiarism must resemble each other), dissimulation (the plagiarist must not acknowledge the theft—a condition presumably easily fulfilled if the plagiarist predeceases the birth of his victim), temporal inversion (the plagiarism must pre-date the original, sometimes by decades or centuries), and dissonance (the plagiarism must appear distinct, in style or content, from the context of the work in which it appears—as, for example, the eponymous Zadig's deductive episodes clash stylistically with the remainder of Voltaire's novella).

An Oulipian, countersensical reading can be understood more generally as a kind of play—specifically, the playing of a game with explicitly formalized rules. Apart from whatever pleasurable (or annoying) properties they may have, such games are a valuable and perhaps in some sense unavoidable component of interpretation. A New Critical reading, at least in its archetypical or stereotypical form, proceeds *as if* the text itself could have an intelligible existence outside its context. A Russian Formalist reading, again in its most extreme form, operates on the manifestly unsustainable assumption that a text's literary elements could be separated from its non-literary ones. A psychoanalytic reading may adopt the premise that a text or story could itself experience something like desire. While in polemical contexts these games may appear or claim to be self-justifying (structuralism therefore structuralism), they justify themselves to outsiders by the insight—close enough to the intellectual equivalent of 'fun'—that they yield.

Insight and understanding are of course the aim of the humanistic tradition of interpretation represented by Mikhail Bakhtin and Hans-Georg Gadamer, both of whom argued for a conception of understanding based in some essential way on dialogue. And in this way the hyper-formalism of the Oulipo-game, seemingly so alien in spirit, proves itself to be perfectly suited to the humanistic project. Here the game involves supposing there could be a *fully* dialogic relation between texts from different eras, such that the earlier and later ones could both read each other. This interpretive game, then, is not only (or even mainly) an exercise in paradox; it is also a game designed to exercise, perhaps to exhaustion, a foundational assumption of dialogical hermeneutics itself, *unconstrained* by any preemptive commonsensical timekeeper. There is no thought without constraint, any more than there can be vision without perspective: this is the common ground of our thinkers, and it means that interpretation must remain open to the possibility of new perspectives, new constraints, new thought experiments.

Before and after the French theoreticians, there exist alternative and relatively pragmatic ways of conceptualizing anticipatory plagiarism, which this volume will also explore. Perhaps the foundation-stone of anticipatory plagiarism was its use as a defence of true religion by the early Christian philosopher, Justin Martyr. Early Christian thinkers thus attempted to anchor their faith in God to reality by insisting on its miraculous proofs, while struggling to retain the intellectual achievements of their pagan predecessors. When Justin admits in his *First Apology* (AD 155–57) that the miracles associated with Christ offer 'nothing new or different' from Roman mythology, he could do so because he had found an 'out' that excused the New Testament's apparent lack of originality while definitively humbling all previous faiths.[15] Elsewhere in the *First Apology*, Justin appeared to concede:

> If we state that He [Christ] was born of a Virgin, this may be comparable to what you admit of Perseus. When we say that He cured the lame, the paralytics, and those blind from birth, and raised the dead to life, we seem to attribute to Him actions similar to those said to have been performed by Aesculapius.[16]

Some writers ventured on logistically improbable terrain to resist this charge, proposing that Platonic thought might have developed along proto-Christian lines because Plato visited Egypt, where he read (and plagiarized) the Mosaic Pentateuch.[17] Almost two millennia later Lev Tolstoy would, in his letters and in the 1885 biography of Socrates which he co-wrote with Aleksandra Kalmykova, deliberately depict the Greek thinker as a lesser forerunner, although not a plagiarist, of Christ.[18]

Justin's solution, in his *Dialogue with Trypho* (AD 160), is bolder still:

> ...[W]hen they say that Dionysus was born of Zeus's union with Semele, and narrate that he was the discoverer of the vine, and that after he was torn to pieces and died, he arose again and ascended into heaven, and when they use wine in his mysteries, is it not evident that the Devil has imitated the previously quoted prophecy of the patriarch Jacob, as recorded by Moses?[19]

Here Justin defends the primacy of Christian miracle through a theodicy strangely akin to album or video piracy. According to this view, the Devil exploited his pre-lapsarian VIP access to divine revelation to pre-release a sort of mix-tape of God's teachings: slightly distorted, pagan copies of Christian figures. Thus Aesculapius pre-empted Christ's miracles of healing, Hercules his strength, Perseus his virgin birth, because 'some, namely those previously mentioned demons, foretold through the poets as if already accomplished those things which they invented'.[20] By extension, all the pagan sages' writings were effectively pirate copies of the apologia of future Church fathers; their insights, while not intrinsically sinful, were incomplete or deluded because they were founded on revelations leaked by Satan. Genuine revelation could only come through Christ. This was anticipatory plagiarism by demonic intervention, and it allowed Justin Martyr to argue that the legends of the Christian Church were not, as they might appear to the unenlightened, merely the latest accretion on an intellectual stalagmite of mortal accomplishment: in fact, they were the first *correct* expression of God's divine insight; effectively, the director's cut.

Justin's method would be followed by a succession of later writers keen to identify their work as the only true expression of an underlying truth or the core aesthetic of a genre; while they acknowledge the existence of predecessors, these are redefined as mere advance plagiarists who try to pre-empt the true word, but get it slightly wrong. In this way, Soviet-era socialist realism might be read (and to a certain degree scripted itself) as the authentic fulfilment of the critical tenets of the radical naturalism first expounded by Belinskii in the early-nineteenth century. Dostoevsky, Belinskii's first and most significant protegé, was simply a false prophet along this path, misled by bourgeois ambition and naïve psychology. Perhaps even the superfluous man, that archetype so beloved of Russian literature courses on Pushkin's *Evgenii Onegin* (1833) and Lermontov's *A Hero of Our Time* (*Geroi nashego vremeni*, 1840), is superfluous because he is an incomplete and therefore aberrant forerunner of the human ideal fully expressed by Pavel Korchagin in Ostrovskii's *How the Steel Was Tempered* (*Kak zakalialas' stal'*, 1934). Analogously, in this volume, Inna Tigountsova suggests that Liudmila Petrushevskaia's female protagonists may be a fuller expression of the Underground Man trope than Dostoevsky's original disenchanted narrator; the latter is merely an advance plagiarism of the Underground Woman. David Gillespie and Marina Korneeva question whether it is possible to plagiarize an entire genre, examining whether Dostoevsky's *Notes from the House of the Dead* (*Zapiski iz mertvogo doma*, 1862) is merely a foreshadowing of Guzel' Yakhina's immensely popular 2015 novel of the Soviet criminal justice system, *Zuleikha Opens Her Eyes* (*Zuleikha otkryvaet glaza*). In all these cases, the early Christian philosophers' argument for the originality of their own faith makes a useful analogy for how contemporary writers have chosen to deny or qualify the influence of certain predecessors. In different ways, they each present their work as the only true fulfilment of their chosen aesthetic, or genre, thus relegating their forerunners to the status of proleptic copycats.

After the Oulipian and Justinian systems, there exists a third kind of anticipatory plagiarism, perhaps the one most readily adaptable for the literature classroom. This system is outlined in David Lodge's instructive satire about academic ambition, *Small World* (1984). The naïve protagonist, annoyed that his thesis on Shakespeare's influence on T. S. Eliot is considered too pedestrian, ad-libs that his real topic is T. S. Eliot's influence on Shakespeare. '"...[W]e can't avoid reading Shakespeare through the lens of T. S. Eliot's poetry. I mean, who can read *Hamlet* today without thinking of Prufrock?"'.[21] His reward for 'thinking in reverse' is a publisher's instant invitation to submit his manuscript for review. Lodge may have crafted this anecdote as a satire on the cynicism of publishers, but it confirms the fact that modern writers ineluctably influence our perception of their predecessors; or, to misquote a favourite phrase of Lodge's, every reading is another re-writing. Hence, when we read Voltaire's *Zadig*, we recognize its foreshadowing of nineteenth-century detective fiction; yet instead of reading the Voltairean text by its own standards, we now judge it by our aesthetic reaction to a chronologically later genre. We read *Zadig* post-Sherlock, as a variant of Doyle, rather than the other way round. Must we accept that Shklovsky wrote *War and Peace*, or that Nabokov penned *The Double* (*pace* Naiman), because we inevitably read Tolstoy and Dostoevsky today through a hermeneutic filter of later critical impositions?

Considered more generally, our reception of the classics is clouded and complicated by the layers of derived texts and subtexts, critical commentaries, and even translations which interpose between their original publication and our reading and reception of them. By 'reading backwards', 'reading upside-down', or by positing anticipatory plagiarism, we re-start the hermeneutic timer; we consciously strip the original text of its interpretative accretions. This kind of reading may teach us that great minds think alike and that particular ideas (and aesthetic notions) recur cyclically; but even these simple lessons are important today, when the news headlines remind us constantly of the recurrence of dangerous historical trends. If writers can independently develop the same idea at widely separated points in time, so can politicians. The value of a critique based on anticipatory plagiarism is that it teaches us to read these ideas contextually: why did Doyle's Sherlock become a global cult figure (not least as interpreted on-screen in

Soviet Russia), while the detective capabilities of Voltaire's *Zadig* remain known to relatively few French literature specialists? In this volume, several essays engage with the cultural hermeneutics of influential texts. Maguire's chapter re-reads novels by the forgotten Victorian novelist Hall Caine as aspirational Tolstoyan philosophy, while re-evaluating Tolstoy's *Resurrection* (*Voskresenie*, 1899) as a melodrama in the spirit of one of Caine's bestsellers. Caine's unrequited admiration for Tolstoy justifies these overlapping values. Yefimenko uses analytic techniques from contemporary critical readings of Tolstoy's *War and Peace* (*Voina i mir*, 1869) to study the moral inadequacy of *molodechestvo*, or male heroism, in Homer's *Iliad* (8th Century BC), and to reveal what Achilles can learn from Tolstoy's warrior-prince Andrei Bolkonskii.

This anthology focusses on Gogol, Dostoevsky and Tolstoy, three great Russian writers interpreted here—in three discrete sections—as both victims and perpetrators of anticipatory plagiarism. We open with Gogol, who is both sinner (as Timothy Langen's chapter argues, he steals from the Irish writer Flann O'Brien and the little-known Russian experimentalist Sigizmund Krzhizhanovsky) and sinned against (the distorted physiognomy of Gogol's nose was illegally scanned by Raphael and other portraitists, as Ilya Vinitsky alleges).

Three chapters are devoted to Dostoevsky, whose well-known moral weakness has evolved from gambling to copyright infringement. Inna Tigountsova argues that Dostoevsky's notion of the Underground Man was filched from Liudmila Petrushevskaia's contemporary female embodiment of this narrative archetype in her novel *The Time: Night* (*Vremia: Noch'*, 1992). Michael Bowden explores Dostoevsky's debt to Coetzee and also to Kurt Vonnegut Jr; while David Gillespie and Marina Korneeva return to Dostoevsky's supposedly least-read book, *The House of the Dead*, in order to evaluate its thefts from a contemporary novel recently released in English translation and also set in a Siberian prison, Yakhina's *Zuleikha Opens Her Eyes*.

The book's next-to-final section looks at thefts from and by Tolstoy. Muireann Maguire's chapter studies the paradox of how Tolstoy stole the plot of *Resurrection* from the bestselling British romance novelist Hall Caine (remembered today, when recalled at all, primarily as the dedicatee of Bram Stoker's *Dracula* (1897)). Her essay analyses the critical interactions between Tolstoy and the popular Western writer he famously despised, exploring both Tolstoy's reception in late nineteenth-century Britain and the reception of socially tendentious bestsellers at the time. Svetlana Yefimenko examines Homer's debt to Tolstoy—the overlap in style, plot, and characterization between *War and Peace* and the *Iliad*—in the context of a detailed study of Tolstoy's knowledge of the Greek classics. Steven Shankman performs a Levinasian reading of the last sentence of *Anna Karenina* (1878), interpreting the latter as an anticipation of the radical philosophical speculations of the French Jewish philosopher and also as a means of connecting *Anna Karenina* conceptually with *Resurrection*. In his witty and discursive 'Afterword' to the present volume, Eric Naiman ranges from Bayard to Bakhtin, Gogol to Freud, Proust to Tolstoy, and, of course, back again, to contend that anticipatory plagiarism not only illuminates past literature for present-day readers, but may amount to an art form in itself.

Our focus on Gogol, Dostoevsky, and Tolstoy provides a much-needed *contrainte* on the wide-ranging, speculative critical operations with which we are experimenting. An even wider-ranging experiment, from which most of the essays in this volume emerged, occurred in 2018 at the University of Exeter during a conference called 'Plagiarizing Posterity: Reading the 19th Century Backwards', organized by Muireann Maguire, one of the present co-editors.[22] We therefore want to take this opportunity to renew our thanks to all participants and in particular to acknowledge the stimulating papers read by Roger Cockrell, Anna Ponamareva, Olga Soboleva, Elena Tchougounova-Paulson, and Margarita Vaysman—papers which, though their topics lie outside the constraints of the present volume, helped to shape our understanding of its underlying conception.

This anthology is aimed at scholars and students of literature and culture alike. Our dynamic and challenging system of re-readings and cross-readings of canonical and other texts constitutes a fresh assessment of Russian literary influences, but could be applied to any other national (or indeed global) literature with equally stimulating results. And of course, 'anticipatory plagiarism' is entirely our own original notion—albeit, unfortunately for us, already plagiarized by David Lodge, Pierre Bayard, Georges Perec and other 'ancestors'.

Notes

1 Daniil Kharms and Aleksandr Vvedensky, 'Oberiu Manifesto' (1928), in *The Man with the Black Coat: Russia's Literature of the Absurd*, ed. and trans. by George Gibian (Evanston, IL: Northwestern University Press, 1987), pp. 245–54 (p. 248).

2 The OBERIU were a Leningrad-based group of futurist artists and writers, founded in 1927, whose aesthetic allegiances spanned surrealism, futurism, the Russian notion of *zaum* (or trans-sense) and other kinds of avant-gardism. Their group name is formed from the initials of the phrase 'Ob'edinenie real'nogo iskusstva' (the Association for Real Art). They were known for practising radical artistic experiments in alogism, public pranks, and experimental theatre performances. The OBERIU ceased to exist as a collective in 1930.

3 Raymond Queneau, 'A Hundred Thousand Billion Poems', in *Oulipo Compendium*, ed. by Harry Mathews and Alastair Brotchie (London: Atlas Press, 2005), pp. 14–15.

4 Fyodor Dostoyevsky, *Notes from Underground*, trans. by Natasha Randall (London: Canongate, 2012), pp. 42–43.

5 Henry Benjamin Wheatley, *Of Anagrams: A Monograph Treating of Their History from the Earliest Ages to the Present Time; with an Introduction, Containing Numerous Specimens of Macaronic Poetry, Punning Mottoes, Rhopalic, Shaped, Equivocal, Lyon, and Echo Verses, Alliteration, Acrostics, Lipograms, Chronograms, Logograms, Palindromes, Bouts Rimés* (Hertford: Stephen Austin, 1862), p. 21.

6 Cited by Wheatley in *Of Anagrams*, p. 44.

7 Pierre Bayard, *Le Plagiat par anticipation* (Paris: Les Éditions de Minuit, 2009), pp. 25–26.

8 As cited in Bayard, *Le plagiat*, p. 26. Note: all translations are our own unless otherwise acknowledged.

9 Georges Perec, 'The Winter Journey', trans. by David Bellos, *Conjunctions*, 12 (1988), 81–86 (p. 85).

10 See Eric Naiman, 'What If Nabokov Had Written "Dvoinik"? Reading Literature Preposterously', *The Russian Review*, 64:4 (2005), 575–89, https://doi.org/10.1111/j.1467-9434.2005.00375.x; and even more counter-intuitively, for Dostoevsky as a pupil or epigone of Nabokov, see Naiman,

'A Filthy Look at Shakespeare's "Lolita"', *Comparative Literature*, 58:1 (2006), 1–23, https://www.jstor.org/stable/4122338.

11 Naiman, 'What If Nabokov Had Written "Dvoinik"?', p. 577.

12 From the cover blurb of Bayard's *Le Plagiat*.

13 Bayard, *Le Plagiat*, pp. 30–35.

14 Ibid., pp. 40–48.

15 Justin Martyr, 'The First Apology', in Justin Martyr, *The First Apology, The Second Apology, Dialogue with Trypho, Exhortation to the Greeks, Discourse to the Greeks, The Monarchy or The Rule of God* (Catholic University of America Press, 1948), https://doi.org/10.2307/j.ctt32b2bk.4.

16 Ibid.

17 Henry Chadwick, *Early Christian Thought and the Classical Tradition* (Oxford: Oxford University Press, 1984), pp. 14–15. https://doi.org/10.1093/acprof:oso/9780198266730.001.0001.

18 See Muireann Maguire, 'Tolstoy and the Greek Teachers: The Pre-Socratics and Socrates in Tolstoy's Prose and Educational Writings', *Tolstoy Studies Journal*, XXVII (2015), 17–30, esp. p. 24.

19 Justin Martyr, *Dialogue with Trypho*, trans. by Thomas B. Falls (Washington, DC: Catholic University of America Press, 2003), p. 107.

20 Justin Martyr, 'The First Apology'.

21 David Lodge, *Small World* (London: Random House, 2012), p. 52.

22 We thank the University of Exeter, particularly the Open Research Fund, and the British Association for Slavonic and East European Studies for the funding which made this event and, later, this book, possible.

I. GOGOL

1. Something for Nothing: Imagination and Collapse in O'Brien, Krzhizhanovsky, and Gogol[1]

Timothy Langen

But the other thing—his having been born on the 1st of April—is true.
Vladimir Nabokov, on Nikolai Gogol[2]

He died, aged fifty-four, on April Fool's Day, 1966.
Hugh Kenner, on Flann O'Brien[3]

This essay explores several connections among the imaginary worlds of Flann O'Brien (pseudonym of Brian O'Nolan, 1911–1966), Sigizmund Krzhizhanovsky (1887–1950), and Nikolai Gogol (1809–1852). For each writer, the imagination offers the possibility not just of inventing people, things, and events, but also, and more fundamentally, of altering the basic properties of causation, temporality, and proportion that govern existence. This much puts them in the company of a great many other 'experimental' writers, such as Borges, Beckett, or, to take an earlier example, Laurence Sterne, but I will try to use Pierre Bayard's notion of 'anticipatory plagiarism' to show some closer, more specific connections. My conceit will be that Krzhizhanovsky interpreted certain key ideas of O'Brien's, and that Gogol took some of these ideas and adapted them to the concerns of his age. The most important of these ideas is that imaginary worlds can function as a sort of force-multiplier with powerful but destabilizing effects on the real world.

 https://doi.org/10.11647/OBP.0241.01

Ibid.

The premise of anticipatory plagiarism is particularly attractive in the case of O'Brien, of whom it has been observed that the sources he *could be imagined* to have read are more instructive than the sources he *is likely* to have read. J. C. C. Mays writes that

> Brian O'Nolan's art lives in a literary area of his own invention to the extent that, while he never read more than a fraction of the writers he might be compared to, comparisons to these same writers are more illuminating than to the sources of his writing in his own life [...]. The list of parallels and antecedents could be extended, and they would be no less illuminating because Brian O'Nolan was most likely unaware of them.[4]

If ever there were a place to try out the idea of anticipatory plagiarism, this must surely be it: for if O'Brien was unaware of his antecedents, perhaps they were aware of him.[5]

We might start with O'Brien's novel *The Third Policeman*, written in 1939–1940. 'Not only did he not publish it', writes Hugh Kenner; 'he spent the rest of his life going back from it, not forward'.[6] It eventually came out in 1967, a year after Brian O'Nolan's death, seventeen years after Krzhizhanovsky's, and a hundred and fifteen after Gogol's. The narrator of *The Third Policeman* commits murder so he can acquire the funds to publish a definitive treatise on the works of a certain de Selby, and the novel is full of footnotes reporting the latter's various obscure opinions and attempting to track down their origin and veracity. As M. Keith Booker points out, though, 'the narrator seems to have spent a great deal more time reading de Selby's critics than reading de Selby himself'. Further, 'De Selby's commentators seem to spend more time commentating on (and generally reviling) each other than on explicating the works of de Selby. And the depths of this cross-examination are as bottomless as those presented by de Selby's own texts'.[7]

The meta-commentary extends even further, for the footnotes have proliferated into the world of books *about* Flann O'Brien. One thing O'Brien scholars like to debate is where the name and character of de Selby come from. In *Looking for De Selby*, Conan Kennedy proposes that the name derives from the De Selby quarries, source of the stones used for roads in Blackrock, County Dublin, around 1912. As for the character de Selby, he may, Kennedy argues, have been based on one

Walter Conan, a tailor, inventor, chairman of the De Selby company ... and Kennedy's own great-uncle.[8] The weight of scholarly speculation, though, seems to lie neither with the De Selby quarries, nor with Walter Conan, nor, for that matter, with the English town of Selby in North Yorkshire, but rather with the German *Selbst*, or self. Keith Hopper offers the following in a footnote to his own discussion of de Selby's name, which he associates with the concept of 'self', while scrupulously noting a critique by Rüdiger Imhof, all in response to an idea proposed by Mays.

> In more recent correspondence with the present author (8 December 2006), Prof. Imhof elaborated further:
>
> 'Selby' may indeed be derived from the Old High German pronoun 'selb,' which seems to have the same root as the English 'self' (the exact etymological determination is unclear). The substantive of the pronoun is 'Selbst,' which corresponds to the English 'self.' So, J. C. C. Mays may have been partly right, after all.
>
> Where Mays is wrong is to suggest that 'de Selby' is a variation of 'der Selbe.' As far as 'der Selbe' is concerned, my critical remark still stands: it can only mean 'the same person.' It would seem that either Mays or Flann, or indeed both of them made a mistake, namely this: that in order to derive 'the self' from a German expression to do with 'selb,' 'Selbe' or 'Selbst,' this expression would have to be 'das Selbst' and not 'der Selbe.' If Flann meant us to see the connection between 'de Selby' and 'the self,' he got his German derivation in a twist.
>
> I am grateful to Prof. Imhof for his gracious and erudite scholarship (and apologise for co-opting him into such a de Selbian-style commentary).[9]

Here writing itself, nearly unmoored from any particular reference or source because it grazes lightly against so many of them, achieves an almost Nirvanic state of self(*Selbst*)lessness in the recursive comments and meta-comments of real and fictional scholars. For as Imhof points out, the *Selbe* that can be inferred from de Selby cannot without lexical violence be made to mean 'the self'. A name derived from *der Selbe* must mean not 'the self' but rather 'the same one', a reference hardly less opaque than the name itself.

As strange as it may seem, though, the reference is in fact perfectly clear; it merely took a Krzhizhanovsky, the equal of Flann O'Brien in both fantasy and pedantry, to point it out. 'Known for being unknown', as he said about himself, Krzhizhanovsky remained so for two decades after his death, until his work was tracked down and championed by Vadim Perel'muter. Following a posthumous trajectory familiar to readers of Mikhail Bulgakov or Mikhail Bakhtin, Krzhizhanovsky is among the last of his generation to be "rediscovered" at home and then discovered abroad.[10] What has not yet been discovered, though, is that some ten years before O'Brien wrote *The Third Policeman*, Krzhizhanovsky produced not just a reworking of, but rather the most brilliant commentary on, the later work. The explication came in a story called 'Materials for a Biography of Gorgis Katafalaki' (*'Materialy k biografii Gorgisa Katafalaki'*, 1929). Like O'Brien's narrator, Katafalaki is an intellectual searcher, and he pores through bibliographic material hoping to find a universal mind comparable to Aristotle, Descartes, or Leibniz. Before long he comes across a certain Derselbe, who seems to have published major works in every field, and part of the story concerns his misguided attempts to track down this improbably erudite person. The search can never succeed because its object is not a person at all: *Derselbe* is, after all, 'the same one', referring in German footnotes to the most recently cited source. Herr Derselbe is Mr Ibid.

After reading Krzhizhanovsky's story, it becomes clear that this is the origin of de Selby's name as well. *Derselbe*, a verbal shifter in a language foreign to the characters, is mistaken for a name, and thus for a real person to be found or researched, a nothing imaginatively transformed into a something, even a someone. The Katafalaki story, then, is what we could call an 'anticipatory gloss' by Krzhizhanovsky, and the most acute commentary on O'Brien's character of de Selby, but in the form of a story written a decade earlier. It would seem that Krzhizhanovsky read O'Brien's *Third Policeman* and, frustrated that no one else got the de Selby joke, retold it with a more explicit backstory. If on the other hand we preclude the possibility of some sort of backwards-reaching action in the universe of literary texts, we will be forced to assume (keeping in mind that Flann O'Brien seems to have had no Russian) that our two authors independently came up with exactly the same trick, to turn a bibliographic term in a different language into a proper name, as a pretext for a wild goose chase. Moreover, they chose the *same* different language, German. What are the odds of that?[11]

The covert, backwards-reaching significance of O'Brien's and Krzhizhanovsky's de Selby/Derselbe does not stop there. For Gogol too is an artist of linguistic shifters—one thinks here of the 'words with no particular meaning at all' that comprise so much of Akaky Akakievich's speech in Gogol's story 'The Overcoat' ('Shinel'', 1842), or of Khlestakov in *The Government Inspector* (*Revizor*, 1836), a human cipher onto whom others project their own ambitions, anxieties, and preoccupations. And if O'Brien and Krzhizhanovsky turn a convention of writing into a character, Gogol gives the complementary gesture when the postmaster stands in the pose of a question mark during the famous mute scene at the end of the play, a character transformed into a specimen of punctuation. For all three writers, then, the *means* of depiction and reference (bibliographic terms, letters, punctuation) become thematized *elements within* the depicted world.[12]

Spacetimes of Reading

The premise that earlier texts may borrow or steal from later ones, or—as we might add, somewhat less drastically, that they may interpret them—rests on what Pierre Bayard calls a *dual chronology*. 'While full-fledged citizens of their age, creators are equally participants in another temporality, that of literature or art, which obeys its own rhythms'.[13] Indeed, literary texts could hardly function without complex rhythmic and temporal interactions. For example, the reader of a text may, more or less at will, arrest forward progress and move back to review earlier material—or even look ahead to find particularly informative or juicy parts, only to circle back once again. Separate from the reader, the text itself can enact retrograde motion relative to any posited unidirectional sequence of events depicted within it. This is part of the work of what Russian Formalists called 'siuzhet', the artistic manipulation and distortion of the pre-existing narrative substrate, or 'fabula', that can be imagined to proceed evenly from A to B to C and onward. Siuzhet, by contrast, can accelerate, skip ahead, slow down, and even go backwards, before resuming its progress. Even at the most elementary, phenomenological level of reading, then, literature operates in a universe with spatio-temporal properties different from our own ordinary entropic universe.

Texts encode other texts, of course, and if we want to conceptualize the universe of texts, we must do so in a way that accommodates the sort of retrograde motion I have been describing. T. S. Eliot, for example, suggested that each new addition to the canon subtly changes the relations among all the other texts. 'Events' in this universe, the universe of what Eliot called 'tradition',[14] would appear to move not only in the direction Pushkin→Tolstoy→Nabokov, but also the reverse, from Nabokov→Tolstoy→Pushkin. Or, in our case, from the twentieth-century writers Flann O'Brien and Sigizmund Krzhizhanovsky to the nineteenth-century Nikolai Gogol. This is the universe in which Bayard's 'anticipatory plagiarism' may be imagined to operate.

Our authors were all interested in this broader question: the properties of imaginative space-time itself, of which the notion of anticipatory plagiarism describes only a subset. To posit a phenomenon of retrograde influence, interpretation, and even plagiarism means to imagine a world that functions in a way that is radically different from the paradigms and models that (tacitly or explicitly) shape ordinary discourse. A glance at the history of astronomy may be useful here. Retrograde motion (albeit through space rather than time) was first observed by the ancients in the wandering of the planets, which did not follow the steady fabula-like course of stars across the sky but seemed to mark out their own individual siuzhets, moving forwards and then pausing, moving backwards for a bit, and then resuming their forward progress. The eventual solution to this puzzle was to reimagine the underlying geometry: the motion of those planets makes sense if we imagine them to be circling something, and after centuries of mutually refining observation and imagination (contending, of course, with social, political, religious, and other forces), the solar system was eventually conceived to have the shape we now ascribe to it. As new physical problems arose, scientists began to posit new shapes and dimensions, not just for things *within* the universe, but for the universe itself. If we are to entertain the idea of retrograde action among our three authors, then, we ought to ask what sorts of universe-geometries they construct.

Sausage, Crack, Egg

With O'Brien, the answer is explicit and easy to find. The earth is shaped like a sausage, according to de Selby, who 'likens the position of a human on earth to that of a man on a tight-wire who must continue walking along the wire or perish, being, however, free in all other respects'.

> Movement in this restricted orbit results in the permanent hallucination known conventionally as 'life' with its innumerable concomitant limitations, afflictions and anomalies. If a way can be found, says de Selby, of discovering the 'second direction', i.e., along the 'barrel' of the sausage, a world of entirely new sensation and experience will be open to humanity. New and unimaginable dimensions will supersede the present order and the manifold 'unnecessaries' of 'one-directional' existence will disappear. (pp. 94–95)

'I would have given much for a glimpse of the signpost showing the way along the "barrel" of the sausage' (p. 95), the narrator goes on to remark, unaware that he is travelling around the barrel of the sausage that very moment. For *The Third Policeman* itself is a sausage-shaped imaginary universe, full of what its author called 'back-chat and funny cracks'.[15] The funniest and most horrifying is that the narrator turns out to have been dead all along, the weird disorienting story being his special form or experience of perdition. Thus the strange, looping chronology of this story engulfs the very teller, who continuously tries and fails to chart a rectilinear path out of the perverse curvatures of his sausage-shaped text and universe, a universe where the very atoms of bicycles and their riders intermingle and merge, like sausage ingredients passing through a meat grinder. De Selby seeks a way to the 'second' dimension; the narrator finds only death and damnation.

It is tempting to suppose that Krzhizhanovsky, polyglot in abilities and sensibilities, picked up on O'Brien's 'back-chat and funny cracks' and re-interpreted them in his early story 'The Collector of Cracks' ('Sobiratel' Shchelei', 1922). The inter-lingual pun would have appealed to both writers: O'Brien's 'Chapman and Keats' series is unimaginable without puns, and Krzhizhanovsky attributed great theoretical significance to wordplay.[16] Krzhizhanovsky's main character in 'The Collector of Cracks', Lövenix, describes to the narrator how he became interested in the little bits of nothing all around us. He appeals, for example, to the physiology of vision when one watches a film, and through various experiments, manipulating the length of intervals between frames, he trains (in himself and in one other gifted subject) the ability to perceive the interstices through the apparent continuity of motion. Alas, he gets too close to the void, steps on a shadow on his way to meet his beloved, and suffers the loss of his capacity to feel. He believes (referring here to Descartes) that existence itself flickers into and out of being, and he wants to find a way to persist through the blank spots where everything else disappears. Instead the narrator finds Lövenix dead at his desk and throws his manuscript into the fire—negating nothingness, or at least one dangerous way of flirting with it. If in O'Brien's sausage-verse every path leads to the same place, in Krzhizhanovsky's crack-verse every instant conceals a trap-door to infinite loss. In both cases a character suspects that his universe contains ubiquitous unperceived domains, and he discovers them, and he experiences not liberation but doom.

Combining O'Brien's characteristically terse figure of the sausage with Krzhizhanovsky's characteristically expansive figure of the crack, Gogol arrived at an even richer analogy for the space-time of the imagination. It comes near the end of *Dead Souls* (*Mertvye dushi*, 1842), when Gogol is trying to explain how people should read his novel. In the course of his explanations, he invents a certain Kifa Mokiyevich and gives a sort of transcript of the latter's speculative musings. 'Well then', Kifa Mokieyvich thinks, 'what if an elephant were to be born in an egg, then the shell, I guess, would be so strong and thick that you couldn't break through it with a cannon-ball; some new firearm would have to be invented'.[17] 'Don't be like Kifa Mokievich', seems to be what Gogol may be saying: tend to your responsibilities and use stories like *Dead Souls* as an instrument to examine yourself critically, rather than as an occasion for idle fantasy about elephant eggs and similar nonsense. Here the ontology of the text is something like that of the mirror, an analogy Gogol had used explicitly in his epigraph to *The Government Inspector*: don't blame the mirror if your face is crooked.

Taken another way, though, the imaginary elephant egg is a microcosm of the whole novel. Eggs have come up before—the governor's daughter's pretty face that so captivates Chichikov, for example, is compared to an egg—and once we allow that Gogol may have been thinking of O'Brien and Krzhizhanovsky, it becomes apparent that this egg is the shape of space-time in *Dead Souls*. For hell really is sausage-shaped in *The Third Policeman*, the narrator given just enough of a hint of linearity that he feels things might be moving somewhere, when really he keeps traversing the same topoi over and over again. And hell really is a collection of cracks for Krzhizhanovsky, each interpersonal or existential void threatening infinite expansion at every instant.[18] Likewise, hell in *Dead Souls* is really an egg that never hatches, promising no progress in any direction either along the surface, or from the inside out, or from the outside in. In Gogol's world every Kifa Mokievich will beget a Moka Kifevich, every Nozdryov adventure will lead to another Nozdryov adventure, and no one will ever learn anything. The necessity of inventing new firearms to pierce the elephant-egg space-time is, as Gogol suggests, idle fantasy—but in his world it is desperately necessary idle fantasy. Sensible carriages that could get to Moscow but not Kazan' will never be able to leave this dreary hellish chronotope, and it is dubious whether even the wild Russia-troika at the very end of the novel can reach escape velocity. But the combination of Krzhizhanovsky's analogy with O'Brien's allows Gogol to imply a solution: crack the egg, cut the sausage, change the very topology of space and time. And in each case it is the imagination that must lead the way.

Inception[19]

For all three writers, the creation of spaces by and for the imagination is itself a major and explicit preoccupation, and one that requires effort and risk. Krzhizhanovsky's short novel *The Letter Killers' Club* (*Klub ubiistv bukv*, 1926) devotes a good deal of space to the preparatory work that goes into telling a story, and the reason why that work is necessary. The narrator meets a former writer who has discovered that committing his conceptions to writing uses up his imagination. He has gathered a group of like-minded 'conceivers' to meet on Saturday nights. Each meeting is devoted to one member's conception, described to his listeners as something like a plan for a story or a play but never written down by any of the members nor disclosed to anyone in the outside world. The 'letter killers' are anonymous and referred to by made-up syllables like Zez, Fev, and Rar. The talk-about-talk or story-about-story structure penetrates the work of the individual tellers as well; most of them describe their work—what it is, or, more precisely, what it *would* or *could* or perhaps *will* be—either before or interspersed throughout the telling. What we might think of as the 'content' becomes a kind of shimmering possibility whose existence seems ideal and only provisionally incarnated in the actual telling. It is this ephemerality that the president tries to preserve by 'killing' letters, with the goal of protecting the conceptions from exhaustion by narrating only the possibility of each future could-be text. It is as if the space of imagination can be approached only obliquely (just as de Selby's work can be apprehended only via its deflections through the critical scholarship)—the thing itself is too delicate to touch.

Or too dangerous. A similar predilection for hypotheticals can be observed on the level of rhetorical diction when the narrator of O'Brien's *The Third Policeman* asks the policeman MacCruiskeen, 'before I go back to the day room [...], would it be right to ask what you were performing with that small little piano instrument, the article with the knobs, and the brass pins?'[20] This is a question asked by asking whether the question could rightly be asked, a nervous recursive space-clearing that Krzhizhanovsky's 'conceivers' re-enact week after week with their stories about the stories one *might* imagine telling.

Gogol's treatment of the theme, of course, is the most familiar and fully developed.

> In the department of... but it would be better not to say in which department. There is nothing more irascible than all these departments, regiments, offices—in short, all this officialdom. Nowadays every private individual considers the whole of society insulted in his person. They say a petition came quite recently from some police chief, I don't remember of what town, in which he states clearly that the government's decrees are perishing and his own sacred name is decidedly being taken in vain. And as proof he attached to his petition a most enormous tome of some novelistic work in which a police chief appears on every page, in some places even in a totally drunken state. And so, to avoid any unpleasantness, it would be better to call the department in question *a certain department*.[21]

Here Gogol replicates the same thematic-stylistic cluster that O'Brien hinted at and Krzhizhanovsky elaborated: profuse discussion of the *terms and conditions* of discourse; indirect, hypothetical, or vague discussion of the *content* of discourse; and reference (only implied, in Krzhizhanovsky's case) to political/legal authority as a *context* for verbal nervousness. Here, at the beginning of 'The Overcoat', Gogol self-consciously and explicitly marks out space where his imaginary creations can operate without getting tugged downward (and getting the speaker/narrator/author into trouble) by excessively literal connection with the real world.

It is not only social-rhetorical space that writers have to clear for themselves; they must also find a way to suspend the demands of the physical world so they can launch their fantasies. Characteristic here is the beginning of O'Brien's novel *At Swim-Two-Birds* (1939):

> Having placed in my mouth sufficient bread for three minutes' chewing, I withdrew my powers of sensual perception and retired into the privacy of my mind, my eyes and face assuming a vacant and preoccupied expression. I reflected on the subject of my spare-time literary activities. One beginning and one ending for a book was a thing I did not agree with. A good book may have three openings entirely dissimilar and inter-related only in the prescience of the author, or for that matter one hundred times as many endings.[22]

The narrator, a college student who applies himself sparingly at best to his studies, is negotiating something like a rate of exchange between the temporality of ordinary life and that of the world of his stories. The former is sequential and governed by time's arrow in the ordinary entropic world. Here bodily needs must be satisfied according to their own schedule, and when they are, the resulting imaginative freedom can be measured in minutes or mouthfuls. Mental escape is from this perspective necessarily temporary: the organism will reassert its needs again and again, like clockwork. Each time those needs are placated, though, another temporality can take over, a kind of lateral arrangement that begins with the narrator's mental 'withdrawal' while his mouth keeps on chewing. Consciously or not, he is invoking something like Bayard's dual chronology.

Force Multipliers

In each of the passages above, the writer's project can be conceived as an optimization exercise in which the objective is to minimize input (ink on the page, hours writing or reading, bread in the narrator's mouth) and risk (from readers who might get offended) while maximizing signification and narrative potential. The recursive structure of talking about talking or writing about writing, in turn, operates as a kind of force multiplier in the universe of literary imagination. By discussing the supposed hazards of specific reference, for example, Gogol can expand his realm of signification from the characters' world to a world which also includes writers and readers. Moreover, the arithmetic is not merely additive but rather compounding, since any event in one world may reverberate in the other, perhaps oscillating between the two and accreting volume with each pass. O'Brien is more explicit about the phenomenon. We might return here to de Selby/Derselbe. The special merit of a footnote reference (of which the shorthand *derselbe* is only the most concentrated example) is that it compresses entire passages, arguments, even whole works into a compact form that can be incorporated in a new text. The implication, that a text may encompass indefinitely many other texts, had already gripped Flann O'Brien in *At Swim-Two-Birds*:

> The entire corpus of existing literature should be regarded as a limbo from which discerning authors could draw their characters as required, creating only when they failed to find a suitable existing puppet. The modern novel should be largely a work of reference. Most authors spend their time saying what has been said before—usually said much better. A wealth of references to existing works would acquaint the reader instantaneously with the nature of each character, would obviate tiresome explanations and would effectively preclude mountebanks, upstarts, thimbleriggers and persons of inferior education from an understanding of contemporary literature.[23]

The 'wealth of references' made possible by literary recursiveness is by no means limited to footnote citation, but instead extends to allusions, imitation, and perhaps outright theft. If Krzhizhanovsky and Gogol were looking for an excuse to plagiarize, they could surely have found it here.

There is an unmistakably utopian aspect to the 'modern novel' as conceived by the narrator of *At Swim-Two-Birds*: characters can be invoked, explanations implied, audiences purified, and all 'instantaneously', with the use of a few well-chosen references. By this means, the signifying power of the literary work expands far beyond what might have seemed possible in earlier times. Indeed, the narrator's conception of modernity seems imbued with early-mid twentieth-century utopianism. For if this was the epoch of world wars, totalized oppression, and triumphant vulgarity (according to an impressive variety of cultural critics who agreed on this much and little else), it was also the age of the Olympic movement and of theories of liberation in nearly every sphere of human experience.[24] The USSR itself, in its early years, witnessed—and tried to harness—many expressions of this expansive utopianism. At the end of his 1924 book *Literature and Revolution*, for example, Leon Trotsky, not yet exiled and anathematized, argued that the new social arrangement of communism would boost the creative powers of each individual to unheard-of levels.

> Man will become immeasurably stronger, wiser and subtler; his body will become more harmonized, his movements more rhythmic, his voice more musical. The forms of life will become dynamically dramatic. The average human type will rise to the heights of an Aristotle, a Goethe, or a Marx. And above this ridge new peaks will rise.[25]

Key to Trotsky's image is the fact that the new 'peaks' of human excellence are not at present visible to us. It is only the imagination, nudged in an alpine direction, that can enlist those peaks into a present-day discussion. And even so, what we can imagine in the present is not the substance of those future peaks; if we could do that, we would already have been transformed. Rather, we can evoke the motion from our present cultural position to the 'ridge' of famous names, and then imagine continuing the trajectory.

Similarly giddy claims were made on behalf of various transformational artistic or meditative disciplines. The individual was understood to possess enormous untapped inner resources, and one common way to express this idea was to claim that people typically use only ten percent of the brainpower available to them, and that the proper mental, physical, or social adjustment could liberate the remaining ninety.[26] In this context it would have been easy to conceive of the imagination itself as a kind of force-multiplier, something that can take the paltry present and transform it into the magnificence it always had in potential; it can be a device for stealing a glimpse of the peaks that rise beyond the ridge, or of the potential of creative minds boosted, as it were, from ten to one hundred percent of capacity. Typical here are the musings of the narrator of *The Third Policeman* about a mysterious substance called 'omnium'.

> Sitting at home with my box of omnium I could do anything, see anything and know anything with no limit to my powers save that of my own imagination. Perhaps I could use it even to extend my imagination. I could destroy, alter and improve the universe at will.[27]

In this sort of work, to imagine an imagination-extending substance is to imagine the removal of any and all limitations. 'Omnium' is in this sense the ultimate force-multiplier, potentially generative, with any imaginative input, of any output. In a 1987 essay called 'Quantum Physics and Thought', Roger Penrose observes that 'the totality of all possible universes may be thought of as a single structure', a structure he proposes calling the *omnium* (a name suggested to him by the classicist Peter Darow). It may strain credulity to claim that O'Brien plagiarize the term (anticipatorily) from Penrose and Darow, but the superposition of possible worlds is in any case crucial to the imagination of all three of our writers.

They were aware, too, that their imaginary chronotopes encompassed at least as many dystopian potentials as utopian ones. An important point of entry to the hyper-world of *At Swim-Two-Birds* is the story of Dermot Trellis, a preternaturally lazy writer producing a morality tale full of licentious characters and acts, the better to sell the product. His characters, drawn from various sources, are put through a number of torments and can do nothing about it until he falls asleep, at which point they highjack the story and subject him to a range of hideous tortures inflicted by a demon called Fergus MacPhellimey, or 'The Pooka'. Narrative has become nearly detached from the world that generated it; it is almost free of the need for an author, Flann O'Brien or anyone else, to keep himself fed and able to work. But the potentials liberated by this narrative table-turning are frankly demonic and horrifying. O'Brien's light tone, and that of the Pooka, serve only to intensify the ghoulishness.

> It is my mission here this morning [says the Pooka] to introduce you to a wide variety of physical scourges, torments, and piteous blood-sweats. The fullness of your suffering, that will be the measure of my personal perfection.[28]

The Pooka proceeds to detail the woes that betide poor Trellis, admonishing him all along to put on his coat because it's cold outside. The room starts rearranging itself phantasmically, and in the course of Trellis's appalling bodily torment he flies out of the window and falls on the cobblestone street.

> To inquire as to the gravity of your sore fall, would that be inopportune?

> You black bastard, said Trellis.
>
> The character of your colloquy is not harmonious, rejoined the Pooka, and makes for barriers between the classes. Honey-words in torment, a growing urbanity against the sad extremities of human woe, that is the further injunction I place upon your head; and for the avoidance of opprobrious oddity as to numerals, I add this, a sickly suppuration at the base of the left breast.
>
> I find your last utterance preoccupying to my intellect, said Trellis, and I am at the same time not unmindful of that last hurt upon my person.[29]

Honey-words are the torturer's artistic flourish, a utopianism of form wedded with power to maximize the experience of suffering.

In this connection we might think of Das's story in *The Letter Killers Club,* where the mechanism of control is not recursive narrative but technological refinement. A machine is built to control the actions of human beings, who become automatons, save for the agony that we know their spirit—whatever that vanishing entity might really be—is experiencing as their bodies move independent of their will. As with O'Brien's Dermott Trellis, they are all forced to suffer, do, speak, and feel without having any say in the matter.

The technology of control in Das's story depends on the action of microscopic vibrophages that enter the body of every person, and there is something about fineness itself that evokes nauseating terror in our authors. O'Brien's *The Third Policeman* gives a kind of emblem for the horrors of artistic overreach when Officer MacCruiskeen shows the narrator an exquisite box he has made. 'I do not often look at boxes or chests', says the narrator, 'but this is the most beautiful box I have ever seen and I will always remember it. There might be something inside it?' 'There might be', answers MacCruiskeen,[30] and shows him a smaller version of the same box inside the first one. This second one has another inside it, and so on past twenty-nine of them.

> At this point I became afraid. What he was doing was no longer wonderful but terrible. I shut my eyes and prayed that he would stop while still doing things that were at least possible for a man to do. When I looked again I was happy that there was nothing to see and that he had put no more of the chests prominently on the table but he was working to the left with the invisible thing in his hand on a bit of the table itself. When he felt my look he came over to me and gave me an enormous

> magnifying-glass which looked like a basin fixed to a handle. I felt the muscles around my heart tighten as I took the instrument.[31]

More boxes follow, inevitably, so small that the very tools needed to make them are invisible. The scene suggests something like a craftsman's utopian dream, the production of a thing so fine that it shades from the improbable to the impossible to the inconceivable, and O'Brien's increasingly horrified narrator feels physically ill as MacCruiskeen moves to open the smallest of them.

The demonic potential of art is a major theme of Gogol's story 'The Portrait' ('Portret') as well, a work written under the unmistakable influence of German Romanticism and appearing in a collection of essays and stories, *Arabesques* (*Arabeski*, 1835), with no shortage of breathless, one might say utopian, claims on behalf of art (as well as history, geography, and other concerns). A whisper of the twentieth century might come through when the artist and main character Chertkov first begins to betray his talent and is rewarded with a stream of wealthy visitors, 'all wishing to see their likenesses doubled or, if possible, increased tenfold'.[32] The tenfold increase is, of course, not an exclusive property of twentieth-century dreams, but it may sensitize readers to other parallels with O'Brien and Krzhizhanovsky: the extraordinary fineness of detail in a depicted artwork, the story that eventually moves to an explanation of its own origins, the main character whose very passion—philosophical in 'The Collector of Cracks', scholarly in *The Third Policeman*, artistic in 'The Portrait'—damns him.

In 'The Overcoat,' Gogol takes the theme still further, adding conceptual nuance to what he might have found in his own earlier work or in his later sources. Much of the story is taken up not just with Akaky Akakievich's dream of a new overcoat, but with the process of planning and making it. It is thus another story concerned with making, both its own making and the making of its eponymous garment (a point elaborated in Boris Eikhenbaum's 1919 essay 'How Gogol's Overcoat Is Made', or 'Kak sdelana Shinel' Gogolia'). Akaky Akakievich does not have the money to replace his threadbare overcoat, which is itself beyond repair. By dint of heroic economizing and the mobilization of the tailor Petrovich's full range of skill and imagination, though, a near-nothing set of resources is mobilized to produce something really nice, an overcoat that immediately raises Akaky Akakievich in the eyes of his co-workers and, perhaps, in his own eyes as well. Once again, a story of improbable leverage gained by craftsmanship.

In another unmistakable echo of O'Brien and Krzhizhanovsky, the craftsman himself is depicted in subtly demonic terms.[33] But here we can see that Gogol distributes his themes among many characters: Akaky Akakievich himself, after all, is an intricate craftsman, a copy clerk who forms letters at home for the sheer joy of it, perhaps the one character in literature equipped to appreciate MacCruiskeen's miniscule inventions. The latter is also refracted in the *important person* whose virtuosic tongue-lashing scares Akaky Akakievich to a feverish death. Yet this important person himself suffers in the larger social-narrative mechanism where he plays his oppressive part. Among subordinates and inferiors 'he kept silent, and his position was pitiable [...] in his eyes there could sometimes be seen a strong desire to join in some interesting conversation and circle, but he was stopped by the thought: Would it not be excessive on his part, would it not be familiar, would it not be descending beneath his importance?'[34]

It is the important person's lot to oppress others, or so he understands it (his motto is 'strictness, strictness—and strictness'),[35] but in so doing he oppresses himself in a more dialectical, less sequential way than a character like O'Brien's Dermott Trellis, who abuses *and then* suffers abuse. Likewise, the nominal enforcer of order in 'The Overcoat'—the policeman described near the end of the story—is subject to the same fear and confusion as any other character. Finally, the hypothetical police chief in Gogol's famous digressive opening is yet another refracted image of O'Brien's MacCruiskeen, this time lodging a petition of complaint against his depiction in *The Third Policeman*. By distributing the themes and qualities of craftsmanship, generative potential, oppressive capacity, and terror more broadly among his characters, Gogol deconstructs, as it were, the polarized artistic worlds of O'Brien and Krzhizhanovsky.

Collapse

Apart from the fear that artistic powers may have demonic origins or intentions, our three authors share another anxiety as well: that the gains may be lost at any moment. In 'The Portrait', Gogol gives Chertkov a prodigious force-multiplier in the form of inauthentic, uninspired art, the kind of art that makes him rich—and in the end, Chertkov uses all his money to buy up and destroy real art. Some irresistible law of ethical or aesthetic symmetry converts rapid, unearned gains into catastrophic destruction. There are other ways for the whole thing to crash as, for example, Das's dystopian world eventually falls apart in apparent obedience to some accelerated entropic principle. In O'Brien's work the prospect of imminent collapse often becomes apparent with the humorous reassertion of the physical, as when the narrator of *At Swim-Two-Birds* comes to suffer the predictable consequences of his slothfulness.

> It was in the New Year, in February, I think, that I discovered that my person was verminous. A growing irritation in various parts of my body led me to examine my bedclothes and the discovery of lice in large numbers was the result of my researches.[36]

The author's imaginative constructs avail him nothing against the indignities of the real world; the dream of bootstrapping one's way to an artistic paradise, or even some sort of oasis, is subject to refutation by lice at any time.

The theme of collapse is more complex and total in Krzhizhanovsky's story 'The Unbitten Elbow' ('Neukushennyi lokot'', 1940), which recounts the attempts of an unnamed protagonist to bite his own elbow. The treatment is frankly philosophical, with direct references to Kant as well as to a philosopher called Kint and a columnist named Tnik. Biting one's own elbow is to be taken as a physical version of the more general and abstract notion of doing what can't be done. And the story itself is part of this project, as is clear from the very beginning.

> This whole story would have remained hidden inside the sleeve and starched cuff of a jacket, if not for the *Weekly Review*. The *Weekly Review* came up with a questionnaire (Your favorite writer? Your average weekly earnings? Your goal in life?) and sent it out to all subscribers. Among the thousands of completed forms (the *Review* had a huge circulation) the sorters found one, Form No. 11,111, which, wander as it would from sorter to sorter, could not be sorted: On Form No. 11,111, opposite 'Average Earnings', the respondent had written '0', and opposite 'Goal in Life', in clear round letters, 'To bite my elbow'.[37]

We thus start at zero in both story (which would never have been told) and money (zero earnings). Subsequent narration is as much about how the events were reported and discussed as about the elbow-biting quest itself. 'The Unbitten Elbow' is therefore in large part a story about a story, where words chase the possibility of something new and end up chasing each other, destined for collapse like O'Brien's circular *Third Policeman*, the hypothetical construction of a deceased narrator.

Near the end of the story, Krzhizhanovsky offers an image that might reasonably be understood as a parable within a parable about force-multipliers and collapse.

> An avalanche, they say, may begin like this: A raven, perched high on a mountain peak, beats its wing against the snow, a clump of which goes sliding down the slope, gathering more and more snow as it goes; rocks and earth go crashing after it—debris and more debris—until the avalanche, goring and gouging the mountainside, has engulfed and flattened everything in its path.[38]

The raven has attained the unattainable, altering the landscape out of any proportion to its physical capabilities. A miniscule input can, under the right conditions, turn into a huge commotion—as happens with the story of the elbow itself.

Speculative economies are especially vulnerable to avalanche-like crashes. In 'The Unbitten Elbow', a bankers' trust, including both government officials and leading capitalists, uses the spectacle of No. 11,111 (as the protagonist is known in the story) trying to bite his elbow as a way to raise money. Citizens can buy a ticket and get a huge payout if he ever does get to the elbow.

> One day the fractions of an inch separating mouth from elbow so diminished (triggering yet another surge in ticket sales) that at a secret government meeting the ministers began to fret: What if the impossible were to happen and the elbow were to be bitten? To redeem even a tenth of all the tickets at the advertised rate of 11,111 to one, the finance minister warned, would leave the treasury in tatters.[39]

Here again, the essential dynamic is a form of leverage, involving a tiny input to gain a colossal output. In the financial world as well as the world of narrative, speculation carries the potential for freakish growth and the danger of sudden collapse.

Recursive financial speculation, moreover, recapitulates the same kind of problem we saw with narrative recursiveness in *At Swim-Two-Birds*: it brackets the material world from consciousness and encourages a forgetting of the fact that materiality—whether in the form of lice or debt collectors—will inevitably return and demand its own compound interest. In 'The Unbitten Elbow', the speculative and enabling functions of investment are cut off from one another: buying a ticket does not help No. 11,111 get to the elbow the way that buying a share in a bakery helps the oven get bought in a simplified version of capitalism. Even buying shares in the banks that buy those bakery shares can be said to enable construction. But with each layer of speculation the connection becomes more dubious, until the main things getting constructed are the instruments of financial leverage themselves. The stock market becomes a complex lottery drawing resources from the world of human values and returning only the whiff of hope that a given individual might profit fabulously. While the most obvious context for the lottery episode is the early Soviet campaign against speculation and economic 'parasitism',[40] the theme was spread as wide as modern economic life itself. One thinks here of the particularly fraught case of Ezra Pound's obsession with banking.[41] More recently, in the aftermath of the financial crisis of 2007–2008, John Lanchester argued that finance,

> like other forms of human behavior, underwent a change in the twentieth century, a shift equivalent to the emergence of modernism in the arts—a break with common sense, a turn toward self-referentiality and abstraction and notions that couldn't be explained in workaday English. In poetry, this moment took place with the publication of 'The Waste Land'. In classical music, it was, perhaps, the première of 'The Rite of Spring'. Jazz, dance, architecture, painting—all had comparable moments.

For Lanchester the 'modernist' moment in finance came in 1973 with Fischer Black and Myron Scholes's groundbreaking paper on the pricing of derivatives. But derivatives themselves, which had been around long before the paper, already imply something like the alienation of discourse from its referent.

> With derivatives, we seem to enter a modernist world in which risk no longer means what it means in plain English, and in which there is a profound break between the language of finance and that of common sense. It is difficult for civilians to understand a derivatives contract, or any of a range of closely related instruments, such as credit-default swaps. These are all products that were designed initially to transfer or hedge risks—to purchase some insurance against the prospect of a

> price going down, when your main bet was that the price would go up. The farmer selling his next season's crop might not have understood a modern financial derivative, but he would have recognized that use of it. The trouble is that derivatives are so powerful that—human nature being what it is—people could not resist using them as a form of leveraged bet.[42]

The underlying objection to financial leverage in this sense is that it becomes functionally disconnected from any productive activity or meaningful discourse: it's just money talking to money. From this perspective, the lottery is simply the realization of the recursive utopianism of financial markets, their desire to liberate themselves from the friction of reference and materiality, to inhabit a realm as 'pure' as that of the imagined imaginary—and as unsustainable.

Here it becomes easy, perhaps irresistible, to see Gogol's *Dead Souls* as something of a compendium of Krzhizhanovskiana and O'Brien leavings. Chichikov is one more in a line of people, characters, writers, ideas, trying to make something out of nothing, trying to make *themselves* out of nothing, using the special metachronotope of paper—the de Selby codex in *The Third Policeman*, the lottery slips in 'The Unbitten Elbow', the deeds for dead serfs in *Dead Souls*. Chichikov's scheme is to utilize the instruments of mortgage and the census to get papers to talk to papers in a way that can eventually generate an actual, material estate. Gogol's stated intention was to build the narrative itself into something positive, to turn the spiritual emptiness of the first volume into substance—just as he wanted the products of his pen to be of positive use to the fatherland. But the second volume collapsed under the weight of these expectations, never escaping its origin in Gogol's fantasy or its destiny in his fireplace. The hellish expanding and collapsing geometry of such speculative places, whether generated by stories about stories or by analogous financial meta-processes, had been O'Brien's and Krzhizhanovsky's great theme, and in *Dead Souls* Gogol brought that part of the tradition to its culminating annihilation.

Notes

1 I would like to thank Muireann Maguire, Jacob Emery, Justin Weir, Caryl Emerson, Carsten Strathausen, Mike Barrett, and Trudy Lewis for valuable comments on this essay and some of the ideas behind it.

2 Vladimir Nabokov, *Nikolai Gogol* (New York: New Directions, 1944), p. 150.

3 Hugh Kenner, *A Colder Eye: The Modern Irish Writers* (New York: Alfred A. Knopf, 1983), p. 261.

4 J. C. C. Mays, 'Brian O'Nolan and Joyce on Art and Life', *James Joyce Quarterly*, 11:3 (Spring 1974), 238–56 (pp. 240–41).

5 O'Brien's interest in the work of J. W. Dunne, specifically the latter's ideas about precognitive dreams, suggests another reason he might have embraced the idea of anticipatory plagiarism. See J. W. Dunne, *An Experiment with Time* (London: Faber and Faber, 1927). Dunne's ideas were fruitful for another writer, Vladimir Nabokov, who took them beyond the scope of this essay. See Gennady Barabtarlo, *Insomniac Dreams: Experiments with Time by Vladimir Nabokov* (Princeton, NJ: Princeton University Press, 2018), https://doi.org/10.1515/9781400888962, and Eric Naiman's afterword to this volume.

6 Kenner, *A Colder Eye*, p. 257.

7 M. Keith Booker, *Flann O'Brien, Bakhtin, and Menippean Satire* (Syracuse, NY: Syracuse University Press, 1995), p. 52.

8 Conan Kennedy, *Looking for De Selby* (Killala: Morrigan Books, 1998).

9 Keith Hopper, *Flann O'Brien: Portrait of the Artist as a Young Post-Modernist* (Cork: Cork University Press, 2009), p. 243, fn. 19, https://doi.org/10.5860/choice.47-0718.

10 For some stimulating examples of English-language scholarship on Krzhizhanovsky, see Muireann Maguire, 'The little man in the overcoat: Gogol and Krzhizhanovsky', in *Russian Writers and the Fin de Siècle*, edited by Katherine Bowers and Ani Kokobobo (Cambridge: Cambridge University Press, 2015), pp. 180–96, https://doi.org/10.1017/cbo9781139683449.011; Karen Link Rosenflanz, *Hunter of Themes: The Interplay of Word and Thing in the Works of Sigizmund Krzhizhanovskij* (New York: Peter Lang, 2005), and articles by Rosenflanz, N. L. Liederman, Alisa Ballard, and Caryl Emerson in a special issue of *Slavic and East European Journal* [*SEEJ*], 56:4 (Winter 2012), https:// doi.org/10.30851/seej. Especially relevant to the present essay is Maguire's remark that Krzhizhanovsky's 'Quadraturin'

and Gogol's 'Overcoat' are both '"untimely"', in the sense that they were radically misunderstood by critics of their own time' (182).

11 To compound a rhetorical question with a pedantic answer: O'Brien could have chosen (at least) German, Latin, or Irish for this trick; Krzhizhanovsky could have used (at the very least) Polish, German, French, English, or Latin. The odds that both writers would choose a language different from the base language of his own or the other's text (the effect would have been lost if Krhzizhanovsky had chosen English), but the same as the language of the other's joke, are therefore something on the order of two in fifteen. The odds that they would both choose to make *the exact same joke* in that language remain incalculably small.

12 Thus N. L. Liederman's observation that '[t]o the highest degree characteristic of Krzhizhanovsky's poetics is a tactile perception of phenomena that have been created for the specific purpose of signifying'. See Liederman, 'The Intellectual Worlds of Sigizmund Krzhizhanovsky', *SEEJ*, 56:4 (Winter 2012), 507–35 (p. 513).

13 Pierre Bayard, 'Anticipatory Plagiarism', trans. by Jeffrey Mehlman, *New Literary History*, 44:2 (Spring 2013), 231–50 (p. 233), https://doi.org/10.1353/nlh.2013.0019. The original may be found in Pierre Bayard, *Le Plagiat par anticipation* (Paris: Les Éditions de Minuit, 2009), p. 108.

14 T. S. Eliot, 'Tradition and the Individual Talent', in *Selected Essays of T. S. Eliot*, 2nd edn (New York: Harcourt, 1950), pp. 3–11.

15 In a January 1940 letter to William Saroyan. See Flann O'Brien, *The Third Policeman* (Champaign, IL: Dalkey Archive Press, 1999), p. viii.

16 See Rosenflanz, *Hunter of Themes*, esp. Chapter Two, '*Slova*: Words' (pp. 23–55), and A. V. Sinitskaia, 'Emblematicheskii printsip i prostranstvennye formy v tekste', *Literaturovedenie* [Vestnik SamGU] (2003), 1–10 (p. 3).

17 Nikolay Gogol, *Dead Souls: A Poem*, trans. by Robert Maguire (London: Penguin Classics, 2004), pp. 279–80.

18 On the geometry and ontology of Krzhizhanovsky's imagined worlds, see especially V. N. Toporov, '"Minus"-prostranstvo Sigizmunda Krzhizhanovskogo', in Toporov, *Mif. Ritual. Simvol. Obraz: Issledovaniia v oblasti mifopoeticheskogo: Izbrannoe* (Moscow: Kul'tura, 1995), pp. 476–574; and Karen Link Rosenflanz, 'Overturned Verticals and Extinguished Suns: Facets of Krzhizhanovsky's Fourth Dimension', *SEEJ*, 56:4 (Winter 2012), 536–52.

19 It is too much to suggest, except perhaps in a footnote, that any of our writers were stealing from Christopher Nolan's *Inception* (2010), even if this film does share themes of warped reality and unexpected mind-to-mind contact that we have been discussing, and some economic connections that we will explore later. By 'inception' here I simply mean the initial creation of an imagined space.

20 O'Brien, *Third Policeman*, p. 74.

21 Nikolai Gogol, 'The Overcoat', in *The Collected Tales of Nikolai Gogol*, trans. Richard Pevear and Larissa Volokhonsky, pp. 394–424 (p. 394).

22 Flann O'Brien, *At Swim-Two-Birds* (New York: Signet, 1976), p. 9.

23 Ibid., p. 33.

24 Examples of twentieth-century utopianism are too many and varied to list; they range (at least) from the rise of Taylor's Scientific Management to Scriabin's planned *Mysterium*, an unfinished multi-media piece which was to bring about Armageddon when performed in the Himalayas. For a study of the utopian aspects of the Russian Revolution, see Richard Stites, *Revolutionary Dreams: Utopian Vision and Experimental Life in the Russian Revolution* (New York: Oxford University Press, 1989).

25 Leon Trotsky, *Literature and Revolution*, trans. by Rose Strunsky (Ann Arbor, MI: University of Michigan Press, 1960), p. 256.

26 In an irresistible echo of the de Selby/derselbe quest, the origins of this assertion seem impossible to find. It may have begun in a remark by William James around the turn of the century, or even earlier, in the years just following the American Civil War. In its earliest forms the claim had no percentage; by 1929, readers of the *World Almanac* could read a self-improvement advertisement claiming that 'scientists and psychologists tell us we use only about TEN PERCENT of our brain power'. See Berry L. Beyerstein, 'Whence Cometh the Myth that We Only Use 10% of our Brains?', in *Mind Myths*, ed. by Sergio della Sala (Chichester: Wiley, 1999), pp. 3–24 (p. 11).

27 O'Brien, *Third Policeman*, p. 189.

28 O'Brien, *At Swim-Two-Birds*, p. 250.

29 Ibid., p. 255.

30 O'Brien, *Third Policeman*, p. 70.

31 Ibid., p. 73.

32 The Russian source is N. V. Gogol', 'Portret', in N. V. Gogol', *Polnoe sobranie sochinenii i pisem v dvadtsati trekh tomakh*, ed. by Iu. V. Mann (Moscow: Nauka, 2001-), III (2009), pp. 46–80 (p. 59). The English source is cited from Nikolai Gogol, *Arabesques*, trans. by Alexander Tulloch (Ann Arbor, MI: Ardis, 1982), pp. 56–97 (p. 72).

33 On the demonic aspects of the tailor Petrovich, see Dmitry Chizhevsky, 'About Gogol's "Overcoat"', in *Gogol from the Twentieth Century*, ed. by Robert A. Maguire (Princeton, NJ: Princeton University Press, 1974), pp. 293–322 (pp. 319–20).

34 Gogol, 'Overcoat', p. 416.

35 Ibid., p. 415

36 O'Brien, *At Swim-Two-Birds*, p. 60.

37 Sigizmund Krzhizhanovsky, 'The Unbitten Elbow', in Krzhizhanovsky, *Autobiography of a Corpse*, trans. by Joanne Turnbull with Nikolai Formozov (New York: New York Review Books, 2013), pp. 125–35 (p. 125).

38 Ibid., p. 133.

39 Ibid., pp. 133–34.

40 The theme is familiar, for example, from a scene in Chapter Nine of Mikhail Bulgakov's *Master and Margarita*, where speculation in foreign currency gets Nikanor Ivanovich Bosoy, chairman of a tenants' association, arrested.

41 For a discussion of Pound and monetary theories related to the themes of the present essay, see Richard Sieburth, 'In Pound We Trust: The Economics of Poetry/The Poetry of Economics', *Critical Inquiry*, 14:1 (1987), 142–72, https:// doi.org/10.1086/448432. For a sympathetic explication of Pound's economic thinking, and the underlying theories of Clifford Hugh Douglass, see Hugh Kenner, *The Pound Era* (Berkeley, CA: University of California Press, 1971), pp. 301–17, https://doi.org/10.1525/9780520341104. For an extended treatment of these theories in the context of Pound's anti-semitism, see Leon Surette, *Pound in Purgatory: From Economic Radicalism to Anti-Semitism* (Urbana, IL: University of Illinois Press, 1999).

42 John Lanchester, 'How Money Went Postmodern', *The New Yorker*, 10 November 2008, 80–84 (p. 83).

2. Seeing Backwards: Raphael's Portrait of Nikolai Vasil'evich Gogol[1]

Ilya Vinitsky

> What we need be sensitive to are those traces of the future, learning how to listen to texts differently, while recalling that they are not inscribed in a single linear temporality, moving in a straight line from the past to the future, but rather within the movement of a dual chronology whose different temporal strata encounter and traverse each other.
>
> Pierre Bayard, 'Anticipatory Plagiarism'[2]

> 'When we look back, all we see is ruins.'
> A barbarian perspective, though a true one.
>
> Joseph Brodsky, 'Letters to a Roman Friend'[3]

Sherlock Holmes was right to note a striking similarity between the appearance of the naturalist Stapleton and the portrait of Hugo Baskerville which hung in Baskerville Hall. Stapleton, as Sherlock determined, was actually a Baskerville, 'and hence has the motive for murder: the naturalist wants to eliminate everyone who stands between him and the succession to title and estate'.[4] Although Pierre Bayard wittily debunks this solution in his provocative book on *The Hound of the Baskervilles* (in his interpretation, the real criminal in the story is Stapleton's wife), Holmes' "gallery revelation" may serve as a fascinating metaphor for the deductive method exemplified by the famous detective. It is also helpful for the interpretative experiment conducted in the present essay.

This chapter considers a paradoxical connection between the literary word (text) and the visual image (a painting) presented not by means

 https://doi.org/10.11647/OBP.0241.02

of ekphrasis (the verbal description of an artwork), but rather by spontaneous 'translation' of the written text into the visual image, which serves as a key to the text's enigma. In other words, I will examine a case of a certain old artwork which, like Baskerville's portrait, reveals the mystery of a (bizarre) literary work written by a very unusual author who lived many years after the artwork had been created.

In what follows, I will focus on the striking final request made in Gogol's (in)famous 'Testament' ('Zaveshchanie', 1845) , which opens his *Selected Passages from Correspondence with Friends* (*Vybrannye mesta iz perepiski s druz'iami*, 1847), and which concerns the writer's prohibition of the reproduction and distribution of his portrait and expresses his passionate commandment that those who really love him should instead buy an engraving of Raphael's *Transfiguration* (1516–20) made by one of his friends. The request produced a huge scandal. Gogol was accused of blasphemy, enormous arrogance, madness and complete lack of taste. In this paper I offer an alternative, Bayardian, interpretation of his undoubtedly peculiar request, based on inner, counter-chronological relationships between the two testaments—Raphael's last painting, which, according to Giorgio Vasari, foretold the future development of western art, and Gogol's last will, which effectively ruined his reputation as a writer.

Fooling Everyone Around

Nikolai Gogol's controversial *Selected Passages from Correspondence with Friends* opens with his 'Testament'—one of the strangest and most scandalous works ever written in the Russian language. Every aspect of this text challenges the reader: it manifests as a last will published during the writer's lifetime, and as an introduction to this collection of edifying letters and articles conceived as a redemptive replacement of all the author's previous works.[5] This 'Testament' is addressed to 'all Russia' in general and to every single compatriot in particular and it includes some extraordinary, practically unrealizable, immodest, blasphemous, and paranoid requests.

Thus, in the 'Testament' Gogol demands that his body not be buried 'until such time as clear signs of decomposition have appeared'.[6] On the other hand, should his death have been established without doubt, no monument is to be raised to him, either, except indirectly through the reader's transformation into a better person. Nor should anyone weep for him, since to see his death as a loss would be a sin. Gogol also bequeaths to his friends a short work of his own, which he calls 'The Farewell Tale' ('Proshchal'naia povest''), intended to explain the reasons behind his mysteries (characteristically, there is no trace among Gogol's papers of its ever having been written). The final request (which I will expand on below) deals with Gogol's prohibition of the reproduction and distribution of his portrait and his suggestion that instead, one should buy an engraving of Raphael's *Transfiguration*. The final sentence of this 'Testament' is a sombre warning: 'My testament must be published immediately after my death in all the newspapers and reviews, so that no one may, in ignorance, be innocently guilty towards me and bring reproaches down upon his soul'.[7]

The general reaction of the Russian public to Gogol's 'Testament' might be described by one word: shock. Critics of various convictions tried to guess what had led Gogol to write this weird text: a morbid fear of death? Religious mania? Catholic influence (a kind of 'preacher's narcissism')? 'If it was a joke on your part', Sergei Aksakov wrote to Gogol in January 1847, 'its success exceeded the most ambitious expectations: you made fools of everyone (*vse oduracheno*)!'.[8]

Gogol himself provided his readers with two contradictory explanations for the publication of his last will. In a 'Preface' to his *Correspondence*, he points out that the 'Testament' is to be published in order to apprise 'all Russia' of what people should do in case of his sudden death. At the same time, he confesses to his mother, who was frightened by her dear son's 'Testament', that he merely wished to remind his readers of the existence of death, which threatens everyone in our world in every single moment.

On the one hand, the 'Testament' should be considered literally—as Gogol's real last will, the strict execution of which was just postponed for a while: until his demise. On the other hand, the 'Testament' has an allegorical sense ('memento mori'; or, to be sure, 'remember about *my*, Gogol's, not-yet-happened death'). Yet it is noteworthy that in the very same letter to his mother, Gogol hints that he has other *numerous* reasons for announcing his last will to the world during his lifetime.

What are these reasons?

The Secretics

As is well known, contradictory and vague explanations for his own plots and plans constitute one of Gogol's most frequent rhetorical devices.[9] These vague explanations help him to create an aura of impenetrable enigma around his texts and authorial persona. Unfortunately, Gogol's rhetoric of secrecy has not been studied adequately yet.

I would highlight the following as typical Gogolian devices: frequent usage of aposiopesis (the rhetorical figure of omission or silence); intended unreliability of the source of information; sudden, unmotivated mood shifts by a narrator, or shifts in narration from accounts of heroes to lyrical digression and, especially, to reminiscences; mocking or edifying appeals to the reader; profane, false hints and pseudo-resolutions, which replace each other as fast as thoughts in Khlestakov's head in Gogol's play *The Government Inspector* (*Revizor*, 1836); all taken together with obtrusive suggestions by the narrator or implied author of numerous contradictory interpretative 'keys' to his own texts, and so on.

Many years ago I suggested for future (never realized) elaboration the term 'the secretics' of Gogol, which is both analogous and opposite to a traditional poetics and a relatively young 'prosaics'.[10] Thus, from the 'secretics' point of view, Gogol's hermeneutic traps such as *The Government Inspector* (followed by a cycle of short plays and essays which 'reveal' its hidden meaning),[11] the short story 'The Portrait' ('Portret', 1835 and 1842; both versions), and—especially—the story 'The Nose' (*Nos*, 1836) appear to be powerful means of kindling the reader's interest in the author's persona. Gogol does not quite parody the various authoritative hermeneutical systems. Instead he univocally collapses them in such a way that they annihilate each other in order to assert either directly (as in the unfinished 1842 novel *Dead Souls* (*Mertvye dushi*)) or implicitly (as in 'The Nose') his own privileged position in the text as the *absolutely incomprehensible Master of Meaning*. If anything can oppose 'semiotic totalitarianism' (Gary Saul Morson's term)[12] in Gogol's texts, it is his 'totalitarian secretics', which implies a concentrated, eternal, and always unsuccessful readers' search for a solution to the riddle of the text, or intention, or indeed the earthly mission of the person known as 'Nikolai Gogol'. This quest is not a hoax or a fraud, but a special aesthetic system facilitated by the author's post-factum 'revelations' of mutually exclusive keys to his writings.

As a result, there are 'not secrets to be found out here one by one, but Secrecy'.[13]

Characteristically, one of Gogol's trademark devices deals with offering or hinting at a visual key (or 'pictorial metanarrative') to his *a priori* enigmatic writing. Judith Robey observes that 'moments featuring viewers looking at paintings can be found throughout Gogol's fiction and essays, whether or not they are works explicitly about artists or the arts' (she cites 'The Portrait' among other stories and essays). 'Taken as a whole,' the critic argues, 'these moments correspond to the stages in a metanarrative in Gogol's works', which she defines as 'a conversion tale in which reading is portrayed as a process that can lead to redemption and salvation'.[14]

Possibly the most famous and telling example of Gogol's usage of visual mysteries encrypted into his works is the final 'Silent Scene' in his play *The Government Inspector*, in which all the comic and corrupt bureaucrats of the town stand as if frozen in place for more than a minute. At different stages of his literary career, Gogol offered several (sometimes mutually exclusive) keys to this scene, but, as Iurii Mann convincingly showed many years ago, the famous tableau has its pictorial metanarrative. Mann argued that it was designed to make the audience perceive the image of the Last Judgement as portrayed by Karl Briullov's Romantic canvas *The Last Day of Pompeii* (*Poslednii den' Pompei*, 1833), lauded by Gogol elsewhere.[15]

Fig. 1. Karl Briullov, *The Last Day of Pompeii* (1830–33), State Russian Museum, St Petersburg. Photograph by Dcoetzee (2012), Wikimedia, Public domain, https://en.wikipedia.org/wiki/Karl_Bryullov#/media/File:Karl_Brullov_-_The_Last_Day_of_Pompeii_-_Google_Art_Project.jpg

While Mann's assertion is certainly plausible, I would argue that the silent scene, which took its final shape in 1840, contains another visual reference, intentionally concealed by the author in order to keep his lofty and incomprehensible status.

Let me quote the playwright's 'instructions' (a kind of secret ekphrasis of an unnamed image) replacing the names of comic bureaucrats with X, Y, Z, etc.:

> *X stands in the center rigid as a post, with outstretched hands and head thrown backward. On his right are [two women] Y and Z straining toward him with every movement of their whole bodies. Behind them M, turned toward the audience, metamorphosed into a question mark.* [...]. *To the left of* X is N, his head to one side as if listening. Behind him is O with outspread hands almost crouching on the ground and pursing his lips as if to whistle or say: 'A nice pickle we're in!'. Next to him is P, turned toward the audience, with eyes screwed up and making a venomous gesture at X. Next to him, at the edge of the group, are Q and R, gesticulating at each other, open-mouthed and wide-eyed. The other guests remain standing stiff. *The whole group retain the same position of rigidity for almost a minute and a half.* The curtain falls [italics added].[16]

According to Gogol's plan, the Silent Scene, which had originally been introduced as the final part of the play's Easter performance in 1836, was supposed to last for several minutes, giving the audience enough time not only to recognize but also to comprehend the profoundly serious secret message it comically mimicked and camouflaged. Eventually, Gogol shortened the time for the action of this scene. The well-known drawing which usually accompanies Gogol's editions of the comedy (see below), is utterly misleading if compared with the author's detailed description of the scene. According to A. Nekrasov, the drawing was done by the playwright's friend Aleksandr Ivanov.[17]

Fig. 2. Aleksandr Ivanov, *The Final Scene of* Revizor (1836), a drawing wrongly attributed to Gogol. Public domain, http://n-v-gogol.ru/books/item/f00/s00/z0000002/pic/000005.jpg.

The verbal description of the last moment of the play reveals that with their names and ranks silenced, one can easily recognize what the "late" Gogol may have hinted at and who stands behind this comic scene of judgement with outstretched hands. I will refrain from naming this powerful proto-image and invite the readers of this essay to guess and interpret it as a part of Gogol's secretive message by themselves (please focus on the italicized words of the description above).[18] All in all, I would like to stress here that Gogol's visual secretics works as a kind of reading or seeing backwards, as if what we read or see now had been already foretold and foreseen by other artists.

Rhetoric of the Testament

Let us return to Gogol's secretive antemortem publication of his last will (Andrei Siniavskii ironically dubbed this work a 'poster for one's own death').[19] Although Gogol's contemporaries were shocked by its publication, throughout antiquity the composition of a testament was regarded as a solemn act, proclaimed publicly ('Testamenti factio non privati sed publici juris est').[20] Deeply concerned about the fate of his own (and indeed all Russia's) spiritual housekeeping, Gogol demonstratively returns to the testament the character of a public exhortation—its *primordial* form (this device is, of course, Romantic in character: consider the numerous attempts by the Romantics to resurrect those archaic discourses, which represented, in the estimation of Romantic theorists, the collective consciousness of a nation). In short, the form of the public testament turned out to be aesthetically appropriate for an authorial manifesto addressed to 'all Russia'.

In fact, Gogol's 'Testament' is the testament of *a writer*. It expresses his new authorial creed, but it is addressed to his old readers. Its aim is to persuade the latter of the truth of his new views and to prepare the way for their perception of the important and uneasy message of his ground-breaking book. Old ideas concerning the role of literature in society appear unsuitable for his new missionary goal to help people's suffering souls to return to Christ (*Dead Souls'* arch-plot). Here originates his rejection of his previous, 'useless', literary works—the ones which brought him glory—in favour of his new, *useful*, non-literary (and sometimes never written!) writings. In this sense, Gogol's 'Testament' constitutes a deliberate literary action in his struggle with the traditional (here: secular) vision of literature. It is conceived and constructed as a reevaluation and transfiguration of these views in accordance with his new authorial self-conception. Of course, one may find here the influence of a religious, edifying, literature, but we must not forget to be aware of the messianic literature-centrism of his thinking during this period of his life.

First of all, there was nothing unusual in the very form of the author's testament for Gogol's contemporaries. This was a traditional literary genre with its respectable genealogy and canonical examples—both serious and mock ones (Villon, Shakespeare, Donne). Literary testaments in verse and prose were very popular in Russian Romantic literature (Pushkin, Venevitinov, Lermontov, Shevchenko). These poetical testaments usually included sentimental appeals to friends, the indication of the site where a writer wished to be buried, farewell advice, instructions, and, sometimes, threats. Logically, one of the central motifs of a literary testament was that of the responsibility of the testator's friends towards him.

However, these were conventional, allegorical, sometimes playful testaments, which required an aesthetic, rather than a literal response from the readers. It seems that in his *Correspondence*, Gogol strove to oppose a real, unconventional testament to the literary, conventional genre—that is, his own (not a lyrical ego's) will, a legal rather than a literary document.

I say 'it seems' because in reality we see an extremely interesting case of usage of the semantic possibilities of a legal document for aesthetic purposes. Indeed, within *Correspondence*, the 'Testament' introduces the author's 'real' voice and establishes a peculiar relationship between the author and his readers. The form of the last will and testament allows the author to present these relations as judicially and mystically 'fixed'. They are formulated in terms of unilateral will rather than as a traditional treaty (you must not erect, not cry, not buy, etc.) The realization of this juridical metaphor provides the author's word (at least, in Gogol's view) with an unconditional character—this is his legal demand, and the addressees' duty is to fulfill this will strictly. Moreover, this device creates an illusion that the author *himself* will oversee the execution of the will!

In other words, the Testament presents a legalized request of the dead (as it were) Author, addressed to 'all Russia' (remember that the living Gogol wrote the words 'perhaps my posthumous voice will be a general reminder of caution').[21] This is nothing less than a sort of public posthumous speech ('the fiction of the voice-from-beyond-the-grave,' in Paul de Man's terms),[22] which strives to immortalize, to imprint the image (or, to be specific, the voice) of the author in his compatriots' hearts, or, speaking in Gogolian terms, to set an indestructible and eternal link between his soul and Russia, meaning the Russian nation. This might be called a rhetorical attempt to conquer death by means of a printed text: *a simulation of an afterlife being, a realized prosopopeia of the scale of Russia itself.* Paradoxically, with each utterance it announces that its author is neither properly dead nor alive but somewhere between the two. In Pierre Bayard's terms, this strange text might also be called Gogol's attempt to plagiarize his own forthcoming death, such that 'the *after* may be situated *before* the before'.[23]

The Spiritual Monument

Let me now consider how Gogol's 'Testament' is made. It consists of seven items, connected both functionally (the testator's will) and thematically (the individual faced with death). Each item of the testament begins with the words 'I hereby bequeath (*zaveshchaiu*)...' (*not* to bury my body; *not* to erect a memorial; *not* to weep; the best of everything written; *not* to hasten to praise or condemn). This formal structure (motivated by the format of the 'last will and testament') creates a very palpable rhythmical effect, a kind of 'stanzaic' organization.

In an earlier version of this chapter, 'Exegi Testamentum', I suggested that the implicit addressee of Gogol's provocative last will was Pushkin's 1841 poem 'Exegi Monumentum'—the summa summarum of the classical (secular) conception of poetic self-awareness. I argued that Gogol's text was a *polemical translation* of Pushkin's proud poem and the authoritative tradition that stands behind it into the language of humble sentimental pietism that dwells amidst ruins and graveyard memorials.

So, what kind of spiritual monument, capable of further growth, does Gogol feel to be worthy of a Christian writer? We find the answer in the final, most passionate and mysterious, seventh item ('stanza') of his memorial poem in prose, which contains instructions concerning his portrait: 'I bequeath—but I remind myself that I cannot dispose of some things.' The request stems from Gogol's prohibition of the reproduction and distribution of his portrait, which against his will and without his permission was 'published abroad'. Instead, he suggests that another portrait be substituted, and sold for profit, the one engraved by a fellow artist in Rome, Fedor Ivanovich Iordanov (Iordan). Let us quote this request in full:

> I bequeath—but I remind myself that I cannot dispose of some things. Because of my impudence, my proprietary rights have been stolen from me: against my will and without my permission my portrait has been published abroad. For many reasons that I need not declare, I did not want this; I have not sold anyone the right to publish it and I have refused all the bookstores that have assailed me with their offers. I would contemplate permitting it only in the case that God would help me to accomplish that labor with which my thought has been occupied all my life, and besides, accomplish it so that all my compatriots would say with one voice that I have honestly fulfilled my task and would even wish to learn the lineaments of the man who worked in silence for a long time and did not want to profit from underserved fame. Another circumstance is joined to this one: my portrait could be sold immediately in a great number of copies, which would bring considerable profit to the artist who had engraved it. There is an artist who has labored in Rome for some years engraving the immortal picture of Raphael, 'The Transfiguration of the Lord' [sic]. He has sacrificed everything for his

labor—a labor destroying, devouring years and health, and he has accomplished it with a perfection (it is now approaching the end) that no other engraver has attained. But by reason of his high price and the small number of experts, this print cannot be distributed in sufficient quantities to pay him back for everything. My portrait would help him. Now my plans wrecked: once the image of anyone is published abroad, it is anyone's property, taken up by the publishers of engravings and lithographs. But if it should happen that my posthumously published letters are of some general benefit (even if it be only by their sincere effort to furnish it), and if my compatriots should also want to see my portrait, then I ask all those publishers generously to renounce their rights; those of my readers who, by a vain fancy for things that have enjoyed a certain fame, will have acquire some portrait of me, I ask to destroy it forthwith upon reading these lines, especially since it was badly done and bears no resemblance to me, and to buy only the one on which will appear 'Engraved by Yordanov'. This at least will be a just act. And it will be still more just if those persons who have the means buy, instead of my portrait, the engraving of 'The Transfiguration of the Lord', which, even in the opinion of foreigners, is the crown of the engraver's art and constitutes a Russian glory.[24]

Fig. 3. F. I. Iordan, Engraving (1857) of F. A. Moller, *Portrait of Nikolai Gogol* (1841). Public domain, http://gogol-lit.ru/images/pisma-gogolyu-1397/1397-151_0.jpg.

What does this confusing narrative mean? Why Raphael's *Transfiguration*? Why should Gogol's portrait be engraved by Iordan?

In 1997, Vladimir Paperny suggested an interesting interpretation of Gogol's choice for his memorial painting: 'Raphael's *Transfiguration* offered a sort of model, based upon which Gogol sketched his own "painting," in which he tried to depict himself, and Russia, and also "everything that there is upon earth", depicting this, moreover, by means of an "intellectually glimpsed" incorporation of his own portrait within Raphael's painting'.[25]

Fig. 4. F. I. Iordan, Engraving (1835–50) of Raphael, *Transfiguration* (1516–20). Public domain, http://www.artsait.ru/foto.php?art=i/iordan/img/1.

Simply put, where is Gogol in this engraving?

The Transfiguration

Surely we can argue that Gogol's reference to Raphael's *Transfiguration* transposes the theme of artistic and spiritual metamorphosis, central to his *Correspondence* as a whole, onto the Christological plane as we recall in the last scene of this comedy. Indeed, Gogol was very familiar with

Vasari's description of this last *unfinished* painting by Raphael as the latter's supreme achievement and artistic testament. Vasari wrote:

> He finished the course of his life on the day of his birth, Good Friday, aged thirty-seven [Gogol's age at that point! – I. V.]. We may believe that his soul adorns heaven as his talent has embellished the earth. At the head of the dead man, in the room where he worked, they put the *Transfiguration*, which he had done for the Cardinal de Medici. The sight of the dead and of this living work filled all who saw them with poignant sorrow.[26]

Lastly, Iordan, this Pierre Menard of Russian painting, kept working on this engraving for many years (like Gogol on his *Dead Souls*!—a typically Romantic *dolgostroi*, or lengthy project). In Gogol's eyes, as Paperny noted, Iordan's engraving presented a true monument to the artist's self-sacrifice, as well as to the artistic and spiritual maturity of the Russian nation.

Still, one might suspect some sort of *personal* connections between the writer's true monument and the engraving of Raphael's masterpiece. It actually sounds like the depiction of Christ at the moment of his Transfiguration should take the place of the deceased writer's portrait. Paperny states that 'Gogol "made himself at home", spiritually, in Raphael's painting, "spiritually" exchanging the head of Christ for his own'.[27] No wonder Gogol's Orthodox readers were outraged. With an ill-concealed feeling of anger Aksakov wrote:

> I could not read without revulsion the published testament of a man still alive and well, in which each word smacks of incredible pride [...] where the engraving of *The Transfiguration of Christ* hangs alongside his own portrait.[28]

But was Gogol so grandiosely overconfident that he identified himself with Christ on the painting? I suspect that he meant something very different, but that he nevertheless became a victim of his own secretics as well as of an odd *anxiety of prophetic plagiarism*. As is well known, Raphael did not paint the standard interpretation of the story of the Transfiguration, as seen in other works from the period. Instead, he created a work of extraordinary complexity and *strangeness*, combining in it two closely related, yet distinct, episodes from the Gospel: the Transfiguration of Christ (as seen in the upper part of the canvas) and the Healing of the Lunatic Child (from the lower part, and as described in Matthew 17.1–20).

In Vasari's description, this 'most famous, most beautiful and most divine' work of the artist

> represents Christ transfigured on Mount Tabor with the eleven disciples at the foot, awaiting their Master. A boy possessed by a devil is brought so that Christ when he has come down from the mount may release him. [...] An old man is embracing and supporting him, his eyes shining, his brows raised, and his forehead knit, showing at once his resolution and fear. He steadily regards the Apostles, as if to derive courage from them.[29]

According to Vasari, Raphael, portraying the transfigured Christ, *is himself transfigured*. When Vasari adds that Raphael gave up his last breath after painting Christ's face, he further invokes Saint Paul's words in Corinthians, since the painter now saw Christ 'face to face'.[30] Moreover, Vasari argues that the painting foretells the future development of sixteenth-century art.

Raphael's *Transfiguration* has always been considered a mysterious piece: 'Combining two distinct narrative subjects with anachronistic witnesses in a single setting, it had few equivalents for sheer complexity among altar-places of its period, being marvelous not only for its diversity of elements but also the harmony of their integration'.[31] A contemporary critic interprets the meaning of Raphael's painting as follows: 'Christ is the savior of man; only he can heal the pains of this life. The father of the possessed boy performs a function similar to that of God'.[32] Those who have faith will be saved. The curing of the boy echoes the words of God: believe in Christ's power.

In the 1970s, Dr Gordon Bendersky offered a provocative interpretation of the painting based on medical observations of the boy's figure:

> instead of depicting the boy in the midst of an actual epileptic attack, he is coming out of his convulsion. This focus on the postictal image is consistent with the interpretation that 'God heals.' It also suggests that Raphael depicted the boy as cured, in which case the open mouth is the organ through which the devil issues rather than the site of the boy's cry during the epileptic seizure. [...] Therefore, contrary to the opinion that Raphael primarily shows the apostles failing in the attempt to heal the boy, my neuroiconographical interpretation supports the contention that

> Raphael intentionally linked the divine revelation directly with the cured boy in a causal relation.

In other words, in *The Transfiguration*,

> Raphael functioned as though he were an angelic intercessor. Empowered by his name [which means in the original Hebrew, 'God heals' – I. V.], he facilitated a conjunction between the healer and the healed. For Raphael, life's final irony lay in his theophoric name. It gave him the power to integrate two disparate Biblical sequences in the painting that would be his last.[33]

What was Gogol's secretive take on this painting?

The Likeness

Let us undertake a visual experiment. Look at the face and pose of the sick child's father in Raphael's painting.

Fig. 5. Raphael, *Transfiguration* (1516–20), fragment (a lunatic boy), Pinacoteca Vaticana, Vatican City. Taken from photograph by Alvesgaspar (2015), CC BY-SA 4.0, https://commons.wikimedia.org/wiki/File:Transfigurazione_(Raffaello)_September_2015-1a.jpg.

And now turn to the famous 'shivering' group of a father and a son in the lower right of Aleksandr Ivanov's painting *The Appearance of Christ to the People* (*Iavlenie Khrista narodu*, 1857)—another important 'pictorial metanarrative' used by Gogol.

Fig. 6. Aleksandr Ivanov, *The Appearance of Christ to the People* (1857), fragment (a father and a shivering boy), Tretyakov Gallery, Moscow. Taken from photo by DCoetzee (2012), Wikimedia, Public Domain, https://commons.wikimedia.org/wiki/File:Александр_Андреевич_Иванов_-_Явление_Христа_народу_(Явление_Мессии)_-_Google_Art_Project.jpg.

I believe that the scene in Raphael served as a symbolic prototype for Ivanov's group. Furthermore, as is known, Gogol persuaded Ivanov to portray in this 'shivering' group himself and his young friend Iosif Vielgorskii (the death of the latter in 1840 deeply affected Gogol and led to his conversion to religious mysticism).

Fig. 7. Left: Aleksandr Ivanov's portrait of Iosif Vielgorskii (1817–1839), *Nashe nasledie*, 1998, No. 46. Photograph by Triumphato (2015), Wikimedia, Public domain, https://upload.wikimedia.org/wikipedia/commons/f/fb/ВиельгорскийИМ.jpg. Right: Close-up detail of Figure 6.

Scholars argue that in this group Gogol wanted to personify his spiritual guidance of, and fraternal friendship with, Vielgorskii.[34] Since Gogol's own position in the foreground as the 'shivering' figure was too prominent and very likely to reveal his identity, Gogol and Ivanov eventually decided to create a 'spiritual portrait' of Gogol in the figure of the 'sinner' closest to the Messiah... in the background of the painting.

In the seventh request made in his Testament, Gogol complains that his secret plans were wrecked when Aleksandr Ivanov published his portrait.

Fig. 8. Aleksandr Ivanov, *Portrait of N. V. Gogol* (1847). Photograph by xennex (2013), WikiArt.org, Public domain, https://www.wikiart.org/en/alexander-ivanov/nikolai-gogol-1847.

However, if my hypothesis is correct, Gogol does not discard his former plan, for he secretly names (at the end of his testament) the precise source of Ivanov's and his own mystical and artistic project. Indeed, with some exaggeration and through the 'visual' intermediacy of Ivanov's sketches, one may recognize typical Gogolian features in the image of the father in the Transfiguration, as if divine Raphael had prefigured (or plagiarized by anticipation) the physical appearance (and religious/artistic ideas) of the great Russian writer.

I suspect that Gogol might have 'read' this 'likeness' as a symbolic (*déjà vu*) confirmation of the legitimacy of his own self-imposed mission of bringing sick souls back to Christ, for only Christ can heal them! In this case, the possessed boy may represent his suffering compatriots (the addressees of his Book), as well as his deceased dear friend (the object of his reminiscences and religious aspirations). With an understanding of himself as a healer performing God's work, Gogol assumed a role greater than that of an artist. It is quite understandable now why Iordan's engraving of Raphael's *Transfiguration* remained among Gogol's very few belongings at the author's *real* death in March of 1852.

Once again, it seems that Gogol was far from identifying himself with Christ. Most likely, he wanted to transform the Horatian tomb of Pushkin's secular interpretation into a spiritual monument to the Lord; and to 'reserve' for himself an honourable place on its pedestal. Through the agency of a Russian artist, he probably hoped to conquer death by being literally *en-graved* into a sacral scene, portrayed by the divine Italian Master. Or, in Pierre Bayard's words, Gogol—as interpreter of art—by recognizing in Raphael's painting 'those traces of [his own] future [image]', makes the case for the construction of a new art and literary history, which reverses 'traditional chronology by restoring to authors their true [cultural] place in time [and ...] acknowledging that some are occasionally posterior to writers whom they appear to precede', while 'modifying their biographies' by turning them into 'participants in another temporality, that of literature or art, which obeys its own rhythms'.[35]

Alas, Gogol was misunderstood and condemned by his contemporaries as an arrogant impostor. How could this have happened? I think he fell into his own rhetorical trap. Indeed, the writer's real behest could be considered a further demonstration of his humility (as if he were to state that he devoted his life and oeuvre to God), if not for its *Horatian foundation*. Characteristically, at the very end of his testament, Gogol calls Iordan's engraving of Raphael's *Transfiguration* 'the crown (*venets*) of art' which will further Russia's glory. Gogol's words thus transform the well-known motif of the national poet's crown which Pushkin demonstratively refuses by 'not demanding a wreath' ('ne trebuia ventsa') in the concluding stanza of his poem 'Exegi Monumentum', a poem which marks Pushkin's own transposition of Horace.

This led to an unforeseen consequence: the Horatian subject (the proud poet), which Gogol hoped to transform into a Christlike figure, took the place of the humble and righteous father. That is, the Horatian poet-demiurge 'objectively' turned into Christ himself, and Gogol's last will was textually transformed (if we follow this argument to its logical conclusion) into an equivalent of a Holy Testament. Such a monument, of course, rises even higher than Pushkin's unruly head. But it does sound like unspeakable immodesty *no matter what Gogol actually wanted to say or to conceal by it*. Indeed, in his readers' comprehension, his weird request did not sound as a manifesto of the Christian continuity of art (moving back and forth in time), but rather as a self-parody of the author.[36]

It is precisely this linguistic pose by Gogol which Dostoevsky, as Tynianov convincingly demonstrated and interpreted in his theory of parody as the vehicle of literary evolution, ridiculed in the 'humble' appeal uttered by the pompous windbag Foma Fomich Opiskin in his 1859 novella *The Village of Stepanchikovo* (*Selo Stepanchikovo i ego obitateli*): '"Oh, don't build me a monument! I don't need a monument! In your hearts erect me a monument, and nothing else is necessary, nothing, nothing!"'.[37]

From the Bayardian perspective, a parody precedes the object of its mockery, making the history of literature flow backwards and leaving, to paraphrase Gogol's description of the bird-troika at the end of *Dead Souls*, everything in front. Scholarly spectators, meanwhile, are 'struck with the portent', observing the 'awe-inspiring' movement of a bizarre chronology whose different temporal strata, according to the French theorist, encounter and traverse each other.

Conclusion

In struggling for the encoded restoration of his true spiritual likeness as if anticipated by Raphael, Gogol erected himself a testament. Having read this text, his compatriots decided that the author of *The Inspector General* and *Dead Souls* had indeed died (obviously, as a writer!). None of them saw in this text a hint that he had already been envisioned and immortalized by the divine sixteenth-century artist. What a spectacular failure for the bizarre experiment of inviting the readers to see backwards in order to resolve the author's impenetrable mystery!

Notes

1 An early version of this essay, now substantially reworked and refocused, was published, under the title of 'Exegi Testamentum: Gogol's Posthumous Ode' in the Columbia University Slavic graduate students' journal *Ulbandus Review*, 6 (2002), 85–112.

2 Pierre Bayard, 'Anticipatory Plagiarism: For an Autonomous Literary History', trans. by Jeffrey Mehlman, *New Literary History*, 44:22 (2013), 231–50 (p. 249), https://doi.org/10.1353/nlh.2013.0019. The original may be found in Pierre Bayard, *Le Plagiat par anticipation* (Paris: Les Éditions de Minuit, 2009), p. 148.

3 Joseph Brodsky, *A Part of Speech* (New York: Farrar, Straus and Giroux, 1980), p. 83.

4 Pierre Bayard, *Sherlock Holmes Was Wrong: Reopening the Case of The Hound of the Baskervilles* (New York: Bloomsbury, 2008), p. 25.

5 For more on the paradoxes and idiosyncrasies of Gogol's 'Testament', see: Ruth Sobel, *Gogol's Forgotten Book: Selected Passages and Its Contemporary Readers* (Washington, DC: University Press of America, 1981); Lina Bernstein, *Gogol's Last Book: The Architectonics of Selected Passages from Correspondence with Friends* (Birmingham: Slavonic Monographs, 1994); Iu. Barabash, '"Sootechestveniki, ia vas liubil...": Gogol': zaveshchanie ili "Zaveshchanie"?', *Voprosy literatury*, 3 (1989), 156–89; Alexander Zholkovsky, 'Rereading Gogol's Miswritten Book: Notes on *Selected Passages from Correspondence with Friends*', in *Essays on Gogol: Logos and the Russian Word* (Evanston, IL: Northwestern University Press, 1992), pp. 172–84.

6 Nikolai Gogol, *Selected Passages from Correspondence with Friends*, trans. by Jesse Zeldin (Nashville, TN: Vanderbilt University Press, 1969), p. 7. Hereafter referred to as *Correspondence*.

7 Ibid., p. 13.

8 Cited in N. V. Gogol, *Perepiska N. V. Gogolia v dvukh tomakh*, 2 vols (Moscow: Khudozhestvennaia literatura, 1988), II, p. 30.

9 For more on Gogol's rhetoric, see D. Chizhevskii, 'Neizvestnyi Gogol', *Novyi zhurnal*, 27 (1951), 126–58; Gary Saul Morson, 'Gogol's Parable of Explanation: Nonsense and Prosaics', in *Essays on Gogol: Logos and the Russian Word*, ed. by Susanne Fusso and Priscilla Meyer (Evanston, IL: Northwestern University Press, 1992); Mikhail Vaiskopf, *Siuzhet Gogolia:*

Morfologiia, ideologiia, kontekst (Moscow: Radiks, 1993); and Robert A. Maguire, *Exploring Gogol* (Stanford: Stanford University Press, 1994).

10 Vinitsky, 'Exegi Testamentum', pp. 86–87. On prosaics, see Gary Saul Morson and Caryl Emerson, *Mikhail Bakhtin: Creation of a Prosaics* (Stanford, CA: Stanford University Press, 1990), pp. 15–62.

11 These include the following texts by Gogol: 'Excerpt from a Letter Written by the Author Shortly after the First Performance of The Inspector General' (1836), 'Advice to Those Who Would Perform The Inspector General Correctly' (1842), 'Leaving the Theater' (1842), and 'The Denouement of The Inspector General' (1846).

12 Gary Saul Morson, *Hidden in Plain View: Narrative and Creative Potentials in* War and Peace (Stanford, CA: Stanford University Press, 1987), p. 195.

13 Frank Kermode, *The Genesis of Secrecy: On the Interpretation of Narrative* (Cambridge, MA: Harvard University Prses, 1979), p. 143.

14 Judith Robey, 'Modeling the Reading Act: Gogol's Mute Scene and Its Intertexts', *Slavic Review*, 56:2 (1997), 233–50 (p. 233), https://doi.org/10.2307/2500784.

15 Iurii Mann, '"Uzhas okoval vsekh..." (o nemoi stsene v "Revizore" Gogolia)', *Voprosy literatury*, 8 (1989), 223–35; Robert A. Maguire, *Exploring Gogol*, pp. 97–134.

16 N. V. Gogol, *The Inspector-General: A Comedy in Five Acts*, trans. by Thomas Seltzer (New York: Alfred A. Knopf, 1916), p. 119.

17 A. Nekrasov, 'Pripisyvaemye Gogoliu risunki k "Revizoru"', *Literaturnoe nasledstvo*, 19–21 (Moscow, 1935), pp. 533–35.

18 Il'ia Vinitskii, 'Nikolai Gogol' i Ugroz Svetovostokov: k istokam idei revizora', *Voprosy literatury*, 5 (1996), pp. 167–95.

19 A. D. Siniavskii, *V teni Gogolia* (London: Overseas Publications Interchange, 1975), p. 8.

20 Cited in John George Phillimore's *Introduction to the Study and History of the Roman Law* (London: William Benning & Co, 1848), p. 124. In the *Encyclopedic Dictionary* of Brockhaus and Ephron we read: 'Here as well the T[estament] was at first an ordinance, the directives of a dying man regarding who should head the home and take charge of housekeeping, how to live and how to manage property held in common. The character and content of the T[estament] change radically as the earlier communal

life declines and is replaced by a civil society founded on individualism. ...the T[estament] loses its public character, its affirmation by folk assembly is replaced by its attestation in the presence of witnesses'. F. A. Brokgauz and L. A. Efron, *Entsiklopedicheskii slovar'*, 82 vols (St Petersburg, 1894), XII, pp. 111–14. My translation.

21 Gogol, *Correspondence*, p. 7.

22 Paul de Man, 'Autobiography as De-facement', *Modern Language Notes*, 94:5 (1979), pp. 919–30, p. 927, https://doi.org/10.2307/2906560.

23 Bayard, 'Anticipatory Plagiarism', p. 233.

24 Gogol, *Correspondence*, pp. 12–13.

25 V. Paperny, '"Preobrazhenie" Gogolia (k rekonstruktsii osnovnogo mifa pozdnego Gogola)', *Wiener Slawistischer Almanach*, 39 (1997), pp. 155–73, p. 167.

26 Giorgio Vasari, *The Lives of the Painters, Sculptors and Architects*, trans. by A. B. Hinds (London: Everyman's Library, 1963), p. 247.

27 Paperny, '"Preobrazhenie" Gogolia', p. 167.

28 S. T. Aksakov, *Istoriia moego znakomstva s Gogolem* (Moskva: Izdatel'stvo Akademii nauk SSSR, 1960), p. 165. My translation.

29 Vasari, *Lives of the Painters*, p. 243.

30 Paul Barolsky, *Why Mona Lisa Smiles and Other Tales by Vasari* (University Park, PA: Penn State Press, 2010), p. 39.

31 Christian K. Kleinbub, 'Raphael's Transfiguration as Visio-Devotional Program', *The Art Bulletin*, 20:2 (2008), 367–93 (p. 367), https://doi.org/10.1080/00043079.2008.10786399.

32 Vasari, *Lives of the Painters*, p. 243.

33 Gordon Bendersky, 'Remarks on Raphael's "Transfiguration"', *Notes in the History of Art*, 14:4 (1995), 18–25 (p. 24), https://doi.org/10.1086/sou.14.4.23205609.

34 See N. G. Mashkovtsev, 'Istoriia portreta Gogolia', in Gogol, *N. V. Gogol': materialy i issledovaniia*, 2 vols (Moscow; Leningrad: Izdatel'stvo AN SSSR, 1936), II, pp. 407–22; Vahan D. Barooshian, *The Art of Liberation: Alexander A. Ivanov* (New York: University Press of America, 1987), pp. 34–42; Simon

Karlinsky, *The Sexual Labyrinth of Nikolai Gogol* (Chicago, IL: University of Chicago Press, 1992), pp. 197–201.

35 Bayard, 'Anticipatory Plagiarism', p. 233.

36 Thus 'instead of a speaker's position, we get a speaker's pose'. Iu. N. Tynianov, *Poetika. Istoriia literatury. Kino* (Moscow: Nauka, 1977), p. 310.

37 F. M. Dostoevskii, *Polnoe sobranie sochinenii v 30 tomakh* (Moscow: Nauka, 1972), III, p. 146. Tynianov, *Poetika*, pp. 212–26.

II. DOSTOEVSKY

3. The Voice of Ivan: Ethical Plagiarism in Dostoevsky and Coetzee

Michael Bowden

> Rosewater said an interesting thing to Billy one time [...]. He said that everything there was to be known about life was in *The Brothers Karamazov*, by Feodor Dostoevsky. 'But that isn't *enough* any more,' said Rosewater.
>
> Kurt Vonnegut, *Slaughterhouse-Five, or The Children's Crusade*[1]

The lines above, from Kurt Vonnegut Jr's *Slaughterhouse-Five* (1969), illustrate the chronological tension inherent in the concept of anticipatory plagiarism. Rosewater, portrayed in the novel as an enlightened sage and authority on life, establishes Dostoevsky as a progenitor of that portrayal. In doing so, he allows readers to identify Vonnegut as one of the many authors influenced by Dostoevsky; or, in the parlance of the current collection, as one of the innumerable victims of Dostoevsky's considerable literary theft. By mentioning *The Brothers Karamazov* (*Brat'ia Karamazovy*, 1881), Vonnegut reinforces the chronological continuity between his literary forbear and the publication of his own novel in 1969. Anticipatory plagiarism inverts linear chronology without abandoning it: the shock of reading 'backwards' is found in its perversion of the convention of forward reading. Acknowledging Dostoevsky's influence on *Slaughterhouse-Five* allows the reader to interrogate Dostoevsky's anticipation, and subsequent plagiarism, of Vonnegut. It is an allowance likewise offered by J. M. Coetzee's *Diary of a Bad Year* (2007), which the main part of this paper will explore.

 https://doi.org/10.11647/OBP.0241.03

However, I turn first to the temporal convolutions of *Slaughterhouse Five* and their extreme illustration of Bayard's theme. Rosewater's remarks on *The Brothers Karamazov* establish a chronological break between Dostoevsky's and Vonnegut's respective contexts by calling attention to the transformation of axiological frameworks that correspond with the linear chronology that anticipatory plagiarism claims to subvert. Vonnegut's lines are axiological in nature: the implication is that 'everything to be known about life' refers to the values and principles by and through which an individual and/or a society can focalize its existence—values and principles that a society, as a prerequisite for further cultural discourse, accepts as incontestable. That *Slaughterhouse-Five*, underneath the complexity of its plot, is a denunciation of the 1945 firebombing of Dresden thus frames the axiological rupture in terms that are both chronological and ethical. By suggesting that the wisdom of *The Brothers Karamazov* 'isn't enough any more', Rosewater is claiming that the values and principles of 'life' in Dostoevsky's last novel are not only outdated but alien to a world that can destroy a city as a gesture against the threat of evil. Rosewater's words, and the context of their utterance, place Dostoevsky within an ethical tradition and then claim that the tradition has since collapsed. If Dostoevsky, as noted by Daphna Erdinast-Vulcan, wrote at an historical moment coinciding with 'the awakening of the modernist consciousness, the consciousness of an essentially secular world [...] without recourse to some metaphysical foundational premises', then this now-collapsed ethical tradition is readily identifiable as based within religious or philosophical absolutes, premised on either divine providence or the universalist claim of a moral tradition that reached its apotheosis in Kantian deontology.[2]

Anticipatory plagiarism's inherent tension evolves from this contrast between the chronological continuity necessary for its premise and the axiological permutations contained within that chronology. This essay will attempt to work through such tension by contending that Dostoevsky's own historical context stimulated his plagiarism of Coetzee, thereby consolidating Coetzee's invocation of Dostoevsky as an ethical authority with his recognition, in the manner of Rosewater, that the concept of an ethical authority is no longer 'enough' for a twenty-first-century context which has eschewed monologic authority in general. This consolidation thus allows for an interrogation of Dostoevsky's plagiarism of Coetzee, exploring the ways in which Dostoevsky 'answers' the ethical crises portrayed in *Diary of a Bad Year*. Setting the Bayardian notion of anticipatory plagiarism in dynamic tension with the principle of historical specificity, I argue that Dostoevsky foresaw in his own era the dissolution of religious and philosophical absolutes that offered universalizing ethical edicts. His recognition of this trend, and his anticipation of its consequences, prompted his innovation of the 'polyphonic' novel (as later defined by Mikhail Bakhtin), a form which addresses the requirement for an ethics not dependent upon totalizing absolutes. Building upon the correlation between Bakhtin's study of Dostoevsky and his early ethical writings, I will argue that the polyphonic novel epitomizes the practice of 'answerability'. It thus exemplifies the intersubjective ethics called for by Bakhtin in response to the collapse of absolutist values. Dostoevsky anticipated the twenty-first century's demand for a dialogical understanding of ethics and addressed it through the polyphonic structure of his novels. Thus, Dostoevsky's plagiarism of Coetzee is contingent upon Coetzee's own historically immanent reading of Dostoevsky.

Literary Ahistory

Rosewater's brief reference to Dostoevsky serves as a paradigm for *Slaughterhouse-Five*'s treatment of the interchange between chronological history and ethics. The novel abandons any semblance of linear progression, revealing its last line at the end of its first chapter (*Slaughterhouse*, p. 16). Instead, it conducts a dissection of the concept of linear time by using the horrors of Dresden as its axiological anchor. Its protagonist, Billy Pilgrim, is himself a time-traveller: it is suggested he has become 'unstuck in time' (*Slaughterhouse*, p. 17) as a result of psychosis brought about by his participation in the Dresden firebombing. As part of his pilgrimage between history and science fiction, Billy encounters an alien race, the Tralfamadorians, who perceive time as a static entity rather than a sequence of moments: for the Tralfamadorians, 'all moments, past, present, and future, always have existed, always will exist' (*Slaughterhouse*, p. 19).

The effect is to isolate and contrast a sense of temporal development with the stagnation of human development, particularly with regards to the continued permittance and acceptance of atrocity on both an individual and global scale. Smaller moments of human vengeance and violence permeating the book function as microcosms of Dresden, and to each, as to Dresden, Billy offers the same absentminded aphorism: 'So it goes' (*Slaughterhouse*, p. 16). It is a statement shorn of ethical scrutiny, emphasized by the fact that Billy learns it from the Tralfamadorians, whose view of human life as 'bugs in amber' (*Slaughterhouse*, p. 62) means that they cannot mark the axiological shift engendered by an event such as Dresden.

As a counterweight to the Tralfamadorian perspective, *Slaughterhouse-Five* offers the biblical parable of Lot's wife, punished for refusing to obey a divine injunction not to look back on the destruction of Sodom. Yet for the unnamed narrator of the novel's opening chapter, which poses as a kind of author's introduction, it was precisely her need to look back that made her 'so human' (*Slaughterhouse*, p. 16). Vonnegut thus characterizes the ability to contain within oneself the simultaneous commitment to an ideology of progress and the refusal for ethical retrospection as archetypically inhuman. One would have to be an alien, or live in a fiction far removed from reality, to be so unable to look back. Yet *Slaughterhouse-Five* goes further than the condemnation of an incontestable ideal of progress. Its meandering plot, fantastical elements and frequent cartoonish illustrations signify not merely a shift of ethical perspective but the dead end of all axiological judgements in a manner akin to Adorno's infamous dictum on the barbarity of poetry after Auschwitz.[3] *Slaughterhouse-Five*, displaying a typically postmodern 'incredulity towards metanarratives', suggests that traditional, pre-Dresden novel forms and the axiological contexts they consummated are incompatible with a post-Dresden reality.[4] The 'introduction' itself admits that the novel is 'jumbled and jangled' because 'there is nothing intelligent to say about a massacre [...]. Everything is supposed to be very quiet after a massacre' (*Slaughterhouse*, p. 14). The criteria for ethical judgement have not been relocated but abolished.

The cumulative effect of *Slaughterhouse-Five*'s treatment of time is to destabilize the opposition between chronological progression and atemporal values. Typified by Rosewater's authoritative denunciation of axiological authority, the novel works to disorient the applicability of a set of values and principles, ethical or otherwise, divorced from their historical context. And the reference to *The Brothers Karamazov* in particular strips Dostoevsky's final novel of its axiological weight. Whether it be the universally applicable ethical precepts threatened by the relativism of 'everything is permitted', or the faith that the Elder Zosima and Alesha offer as a counterweight to Ivan's Grand Inquisitor, *Slaughterhouse-Five* uses Dostoevsky to query the validity of any ethical standard independent of its history. If the passage of time from pre- to post-Dresden changes Dostoevsky from an emblem of absolute plenitude to an inadequate partiality, the question is raised as to which other values, if any, can resist similar erosion.

In this respect, Rosewater's renunciation of *The Brothers Karamazov* as an absolute ethical measure stands in contrast with Bayard's investigation of the plagiarism of 'aesthetic territories'.[5] Bayard, taking his cue from earlier Oulipo theorists who see literature in terms of its mathematical potential, expands upon their initial analyses of formal and structural plagiarism by proposing that authors can reach forward in time to plagiarize cultural relevance. In doing so, he confronts the temporal aporia of anticipatory plagiarism, the simultaneous reliance on and subversion of linear chronology, more directly that his predecessors. He offers Sophocles' *Oedipus Rex* (429 BC) as an example of the plagiarism of an aesthetic territory: both the investigative structure and the psychoanalytic implications of the plot, rarely found in contemporaneous Greek theatre, serve as Bayard's evidence that Sophocles intuited both Freud and the modern detective novel. The 'twofold modernity' of *Oedipus Rex* can only mean 'that it is also posterior' to psychoanalysis and detective fiction. The creative force of the play suggests that Sophocles 'was already aware of both and knew how to take adroit advantage of each of them'.[6]

To overcome this tension, Bayard proposes two concurrent understandings of history, one chronological and the other literary. Literary history, where writers are based on formal, cultural or thematic similarities, disregards the linearity of chronological history and so allows for anticipatory plagiarism by displacing the 'overly rigid conception of time' that dominates literary studies.[7] This subsequently situates authors 'at the crux of a dual temporality'.[8] Yet Bayard, with the provocativeness characteristic of his Oulipo antecedents, calls for the abandonment of the chronological in favour of the literary. He even alleges that 'situating a writer historically' is 'fundamentally useless' for literary understanding.[9] Literary understanding need touch 'only lightly on historical reality'.[10] The extreme implication of this theory, as Bayard admits, is that an author's true place in literary history can never be comprehensively known because the necessarily uncharted chronological future does not impinge upon the atemporality of literary history.[11]

It is this atemporality which marks Bayard's literary time as distinctly Tralfamadorian and so in conflict with Rosewater's disinheritance of Dostoevsky as an axiological forbear. Literary time rendered (and isolated) thus would be unable to reflect upon the axiological shifts that run concurrent with the overt rigidity of chronological time, and so Rosewater's comments would impede Dostoevsky's capacity to 'respond' to post-Dresden writers such as Vonnegut and, even later, Coetzee. This difficulty plays into the significant flaw in Bayard's proposal: the fact that literary history is necessarily maintained by the chronological history it seeks to replace. This flaw is most evident when reading the influence of one author on another over an historical period in which momentous shifts in socio-cultural values occur. To claim, as Bayard does, that Sophocles plagiarized Freud is to identify implicitly the vast socio-cultural differences between Greece in BCE 400 and Vienna at the turn of the nineteenth century. The theory of anticipatory plagiarism implies the plagiarist has an extraordinary ability to reach across not only time but also over the socio-cultural values of different eras. To define chronological history as fundamentally useless to literary studies, as in the most provocative formulation of anticipatory plagiarism, robs this feat of important context. A fuller appreciation of anticipatory plagiarism takes into account the ways in which an author's place in an era outside of his or her own biographical history depends on its contrast with the era in which they actually lived. This element of contrast is vital to understanding Dostoevsky's plagiarism of Coetzee because it demands that Coetzee's historically immanent reading of Dostoevsky be recognized. Coetzee's explicit acknowledgement of Dostoevsky's influence over *Diary of a Bad Year* must be set against the novel's portrayal of a political and ethical crisis deeply rooted in the particularities of the early twenty-first century.

Learn to Speak Without Authority

Coetzee's most notable homage to Dostoevsky is his 1994 novel *The Master of Petersburg*, which uses a fictional version of the Russian writer as its protagonist to intensify the ideological conflict of *Demons* (*Besy*, 1872) (Coetzee's 'Dostoevsky' encounters and debates with Sergei Nechaev, the real-life prototype for Petr Verkhovenskii), and then uses this conflict as a metaphor for the transgressive role of authors and artists. Though perhaps less known than *The Master of Petersburg*, *Diary of a Bad Year*, published thirteen years later, is an equally nuanced (albeit more subtle) tribute to Dostoevsky. Set in the early twenty-first century, like *Slaughterhouse-Five* it depicts a world suffering from a moral crisis following the collapse of absolute metaphysical/ethical foundations. Yet unlike Rosewater, *Diary*'s protagonist, an elderly writer named 'C' who shares many biographical details with Coetzee, claims that Dostoevsky remains a source of ethical erudition for the present day: reading Dostoevsky, asserts C, makes him 'a better artist; and by better I do not mean more skilful but ethically better'.[12] As such, Coetzee's novella offers a staging ground for the investigation into Dostoevsky's anticipatory response to twenty-first-century ethics.

Diary combines a fictional plotline containing two narrative voices with a series of short essays on a range of topics such as politics, religion, art and language. Each page is split into two or three sections. The top section of the pages contains the essays, while the fictional narratives run underneath. For the first five essays there is only the first underlying narrative; from essay six onwards the pages are (for the most part) split into three. Moreover, the book as a whole is split into two parts: the dated 'Strong Opinions' and the undated 'Second Diary'.

The plot unfolds as an intertwining of the second and third narrative: it is revealed that C is the author of the second narrative, and that the third is voiced by Anya, a Filipina resident of C's building whom he hires as a typist in a covert attempt to seduce her. Anya is *Diary*'s first, indirect allusion to Dostoevsky. Though uncommon in the Philippines, 'Anya' is a common Russian diminutive of 'Anna', the forename of Dostoevsky's second wife, who was originally his stenographer. In this respect, C's depiction as a writer in search of a stenographer suggests the historical

Dostoevsky even as the initial C evokes Coetzee, and this suggestion is reinforced by the final essay of the novella, 'On Dostoevsky', in which C discusses Book V, Chapter IV of *The Brothers Karamazov*.

C's essays offer *Diary*'s most direct depiction of the political/ethical crises that afflict the twenty-first century. His opening essay, 'On the origins of the state', sets their dominant tone, premising that a democratic state, by imposing the necessity of political choice, at the outset undermines the very freedom it champions. Through similar lines of enquiry, C establishes a narrative role as a social diagnostician, lamenting the absence of a 'moral nobility' (*Diary*, p. 131) in the world as he sees it. Yet his inability to remedy societal ignobleness generates a sense of exasperated ire that extends through later essays such as 'On national shame', 'On Guantanamo Bay' and 'On the slaughter of animals'. These essays are direct criticisms of Western politics, principally of the Bush/Cheney administration and its allies in the Afghanistan and Iraq wars, although less overtly political essays still maintain the overarching tirade against twenty-first-century Western civilization. Even the more personal Second Diary maintains the 'pessimistic anarchistic quietism' of C's 'brand of political thought' (*Diary*, p. 203).

While establishing the tone of socio-political disparagement that characterizes the novel, 'On the origins of the state' also introduces another of *Diary*'s significant themes: the recognition that striving for a 'supra-political discourse about politics' is 'futile' (*Diary*, p. 9). C's political despondency is augmented by the unfeasibility of a definitive political condemnation that is not in itself political, to such an extent that an embittered withdrawal from politics, his 'pessimistic quietism', becomes the only viable solution to his incapacity to critique the system without being complicit in its functioning. This discrepancy runs parallel with the political critique of the essays: throughout, C's desire to write on any subject is tempered by a scepticism that his writings can effect change, or that his position can be anything but hypocritical. He fears his '*lofty judgements*' will always be 'spurned as idealistic' and 'unrealistic' [italics in the original] (*Diary*, p. 126) by those whom he judges, and he often expresses doubts in the validity of his own essays, even admitting that he was only seduced to publish by the 'opportunity to grumble in public' (*Diary*, p. 23).

Diary's consistent tension, therefore, is between C's desire, as an author, for his words to effect meaningful socio-political change, and his scepticism about the possibility of such change. This tension is most clearly manifested as suspicion of authoritative narratives. Several critical responses to *Diary* have noted its uncertain stance with regards to an authoritative narrative voice: David Atwell's essay on *Diary* goes as far as to claim that the 'practice of authorship' is the novel's 'overriding subject'.[13] Johan Geertsema highlights the subtle biographical heterogeneity between C and Coetzee to claim that *Diary* deliberately undercuts any political position it attempts to take, forging for itself 'an ironic nonposition' that would allow it to be politically critical without being political.[14] Along similar lines, Peter McDonald characterizes the essays, in particular the more distinctly critical 'Strong Opinions' that form the first half of the novel, as 'semiparodic' and full of 'relentless equivocations'. Like Geertsema, McDonald builds upon the metafictional effect of Coetzee's avatar C to suggest that *Diary* distances itself from its own socio-political perspective, undermining its own narrative authority. McDonald concludes that *Diary* is 'Coetzee's most elaborate working out of his own discomfort with the expectations and anachronistic forms of authority thrust on him as a writer'.[15]

McDonald's use of 'anachronistic' illuminates Coetzee's literary influences because it reiterates the chronological tension of anticipatory plagiarism. The penultimate 'Strong Opinions' essay, 'On authority in fiction', discusses Tolstoy, thus counterpointing the final essay in the Second Diary on Dostoevsky. It contrasts Tolstoy's 'exemplary' skill 'at building authority' with a Barthesian/Foucauldian discussion 'of the death of the author and of authorship' (*Diary*, p. 149). Paraphrasing post-structuralist literary theory as 'the claim that the authority of the author has never amounted to anything more than a bagful of rhetorical tricks' (ibid.), C expresses the specific challenge faced by twenty-first-century writers with a maxim cited from Kierkegaard, '*Learn to speak without authority*' (*Diary*, p. 151). Tolstoy is offered as an example of a 'great author' whose rhetorical ability was powerful enough to engender a sense that he was 'an authority on life, a wise man, a sage'; whereas the post-structural interrogation of rhetorically manufactured authority exposed great authors as 'otherwise ordinary men with ordinary, fallible opinions' (ibid.). In the manner of Rosewater's reading of *The Brothers Karamazov*, the sense of an historical transition between a bygone era and the present day is framed in terms of declining trust in authoritative narratives

C's remarks on Tolstoy echo an interview with Atwell that Coetzee made over fifteen years earlier. Looking back on his 1985 study 'Confession and Double Thoughts', Coetzee said that the essay 'came out of a rereading of Tolstoy and Dostoevsky, two novelists for whom my admiration remains undimmed'.[16] Coetzee's acclaim for both writers in a 1990 interview and C's reverence for 'the master Tolstoy on the one hand and [...] the master Dostoevsky on the other' (*Diary*, p. 227) make a notable parallel, especially when examined in the light of Coetzee's further clarification:

> I read them on what I take to be their own terms, that is, in terms of their power to tell the truth as well as to subvert secular skepticism about truth [...]. If there is a sense in which my reading of them 'on their own terms' is not simply a repeat of the reading they were accorded in the West during their own day [...] it lies in treating them as men who not only *lived through* the philosophical debates of their day [...], but also were heirs of a Christian tradition more vital, in some respects, than Western Christianity.[17]

Coetzee expresses concern that reading Dostoevsky and Tolstoy in order to subvert scepticism about 'truth' is merely to revert to a late nineteenth-century context, one in which such scepticism is a distinct, but not dominant, ideological position. This concern implies that the 'terms' of authors like Tolstoy and Dostoevsky are not necessarily applicable outside of their contextual value system. Contrary to the divorce of text and context implicit in Bayard's 'literary time', Coetzee's concern is centred upon the distinct socio-cultural diversities at play during the period in which Dostoevsky and Tolstoy wrote and were read. If their power to 'tell the truth' were somehow diminished, or alternatively if they were simply unable to subvert cynical attitudes towards 'truth', particularly religious truth, the 'terms' of Dostoevsky or Tolstoy would be drained of semantic value. Coetzee's response thus reiterates Rosewater's claim that Dostoevsky, post-Dresden, is not 'enough any more'.

It is precisely this sense of scepticism towards the 'truth' of a bygone era that drives both C's ire, his so-called 'Strong Opinions' offered from the perspective of 'old people' who recognize that the 'animating principles' of the nineteenth century are 'dead and cannot be revived' (*Diary*, p. 134), and the textual relationship between C, Anya and

Anya's partner, a neoliberal investment consultant named Alan. The most prominent example of this ethical-temporal linkage appears in the essay 'On Machiavelli' (*Diary*, pp. 17–18), which most clearly delineates an historical transition between an 'old, pre-Machiavellian position' and 'the modern state' in moral/ethical terms. C asserts that the pre-Machiavellian position is the supremacy of moral absolutes, something he conflates with 'the absolute claims of the Christian ethic'. The Machiavellian position, whilst not denying moral absolutes, simultaneously upholds moral relativism. It is analogous (both chronologically and ideologically) to the moral dualism of the Grand Inquisitor. When C claims, therefore, that 'the quintessence of the Machiavellian' is now the quintessence of the modern state, he depicts a world in which Dostoevsky's ideological opposition to the Grand Inquisitor's moral casuistry has lost its capacity to influence 'the man on the street'. 'If you wish to counter the man on the street', writes C, 'it cannot be by appeal to moral principles' (*Diary*, p. 18).

Anya and Alan thus come to represent the people 'on the street' at odds with C's outdated worldviews and cynical of his despair for the decline of his authorial authority. The contrast is developed through Anya's role as C's typist and eventual confidante: it is through her persuasion that he reflects upon how 'alien and antiquated' his views appear to 'thoroughly modern' (*Diary*, p. 137) readers and so begins his Second Diary. Yet the more significant antagonism is established between C and Alan. Alan's neoliberal outlook sees the world as consisting of 'two dimensions': an 'individual dimension' and an 'economic dimension' (*Diary*, p. 79) that transcends the individual. He believes in a type of '[n]atural justice', in which the individual must 'balance the pluses against the minuses and decide' (*Diary*, p. 91) on a course of action.[18] Reinforcing the sense of historical distance between C and himself, he ridicules C's world view as a 'morality play', with the battle of 'good versus evil' at the centre. The market, however, 'transcends individual motives, transcends good and evil' (*Diary*, p. 97). C's moral understanding thus 'comes from another world, another era. The modern world is beyond him'. Even if in the individual dimension maliciousness is the primary catalyst for action, individual motives are just 'vectors of the matrix' that are 'evened out in the long run'. The market Alan believes in 'is beyond good and evil, like Nietzsche said' (*Diary*, p. 98).

At the Crux of a Dual Temporality

Alan's allusion to Nietzsche thus reinforces the sense of an historical transition between adherence to the authority of absolute principles and the collapse of such principles that epitomizes the modern world. It effectively establishes a timeline from the 1880s, when both *The Brothers Karamazov* (1881) and *Beyond Good and Evil* (*Jenseits von Gut und Böse*, 1886) were published, to the novel's present day, which includes the disintegration of C's 'old world' (*Diary*, p. 20) and the amoral egoism typified by Alan's neoliberal convictions. Nietzsche's critique of both religion and Kantian deontology in *Beyond Good and Evil* represents for Alan the divorce from, or overcoming of, both the 'absolute claims of a Christian ethic' and the universality of rational moral law.[19] Towards the end of the novel, Alan mockingly compares C with 'sages with white beards' (*Diary*, p. 207), reminding readers of C's earlier description of Tolstoy. It also resembles remarks Coetzee made in an interview just after winning the 2003 Nobel Prize in Literature. Coetzee expressed his unease perceiving writers as people 'who could offer an authoritative word on our times as well as on our moral life'. It was, claimed Coetzee, perhaps appropriate when the Nobel Prize for Literature was first inaugurated to perceive the writer as 'a sage', but the idea is 'pretty much dead today'.[20] In dismissing the authoritative sage as 'pretty much dead today' (just as the animating principles of the nineteenth century are dead), Coetzee aligns himself with Alan even whilst presenting a fictional variant of himself as Alan's ideological opponent.

The interplay between C's literary influences and his condemnation of the amorality of the twenty-first century positions the novel at the crux of a dual temporality, whereby chronological history cannot be abandoned in favour of literary history. On the one hand, C is employed as an authoritative narrative voice, in the manner of the 'great authors' of a prior generation, who upholds 'the argument that the past was better than the present' (*Diary*, p. 77). On the other, the present that C condemns is characterized by a cynicism towards authoritative narrative voices. C both is and is not part of *Diary*'s present day. He denounces the specificities of the twenty-first century, yet the axiological framework upon which his denunciation is built has grown redundant. He tries and fails to apply pre-Nietzschean judgements to a post-Dresden world: his worldview represents everything that used to be known about life. Even as the novel reaches backwards towards the masters Dostoevsky and Tolstoy, even as transhistorical literary time is invoked, the phenomenon of declining or redundant values and principles suggests that a unidirectional temporality is a fundamental aspect of the novel.

An analysis of the ways in which Dostoevsky can be said to respond to Coetzee must be filtered through ways in which chronological time and literary time affect each other. It must, like *Slaughterhouse-Five*, contain within itself both the Tralfamadorian and generational experiences of time, must hold itself at the crux of a dual temporality in which looking back and looking forward are equivalent. A Tralfamadorian perspective on time would see both *The Brothers Karamazov* and *Diary of a Bad Year* as equally capable of responding to the crisis of valuation presented by *Slaughterhouse-Five*, and thus could seek to read the ways in which Dostoevsky and Coetzee react to the denunciation of authority mentioned by Rosewater and embodied by C. And if *Diary* portrays Tolstoy as the epitome of authorial authority, the way that *Diary* works to distinguish Tolstoy and Dostoevsky offers an avenue for reading Dostoevsky's plagiarism of Coetzee.

The Voice of Ivan

Though Dostoevsky and Tolstoy are both hailed by C as 'masters', a term which evokes authoritative sages preaching now-redundant moral absolutes, the phrasing of C's commendation, separating Tolstoy 'on the one hand' from Dostoevsky 'on the other', suggests that C understands them to be diametrically opposite even whilst identifying both as literary authorities. The suggestion is further reinforced by the way the respective essays on them are counterposed: if Tolstoy is the master at building 'authority in fiction', Dostoevsky's mastery implicitly refers to something other than the rhetorical authoritativeness eschewed by the modern world. The biographical overlap between Dostoevsky and C, combined with the prominent positioning of 'On Dostoevsky', puts significant focus on Dostoevsky in relation to *Diary*'s impasse between literary influence and the historically effected axiological irrelevance of the influencers.

'On Dostoevsky' confirms that *Diary*'s juxtaposition of Dostoevsky and Tolstoy is framed in terms of rhetorical authoritativeness. C relates how a rereading of the 'Pro and Contra' book of *The Brothers Karamazov*, specifically Ivan's rejection of theodicy in Chapter IV, leaves him 'sobbing uncontrollably' (*Diary*, p. 223).[21] Although C disagrees with 'Ivan's rather vengeful views', arguing instead that the Sermon on the Mount's entreaty to turn the other cheek is 'the greatest of all contributions to political ethics', he is nevertheless reduced to tears by Ivan's argument 'in spite of myself' (*Diary*, p. 224). The reason, C writes, is 'nothing to do with ethics or politics, everything to do with rhetoric' (*Diary*, p. 225).

Though C's argument echoes his praise for Tolstoy's rhetorical tricks, 'On Dostoevsky' indicates an evolution in *Diary*'s use of the term 'rhetoric'. The authority Tolstoy was so adept at building was embedded in the seemingly 'natural' quality of his prose, in the way it 'concealed its rhetorical artistry so well' (*Diary*, p. 150). Dostoevsky lacks such artistry: C derides Ivan for the way he 'shamelessly uses sentiment (martyred children) and caricature (cruel landowners) to advance his ends' (*Diary*, p. 225). Dostoevsky's literary mastery is not based upon the effectiveness of his rhetorical artistry, the kind of artistry characterized by Tolstoy's authorial authority. Dostoevsky's skill lies in, for example, the effectiveness of Ivan's rhetorical passion. The tendency of Ivan's 'Euclidean mind' (*BK*, p. 235) towards rationalization (prompting his notion of the Grand Inquisitor) is in many ways a chronological precursor to Alan's market-driven amorality.[22] That C focuses his essay on Ivan thus exemplifies how Dostoevsky's mastery is diametrically opposed to the narrative authority of Tolstoy: C's ethical position is antithetical to the specious arguments of the Grand Inquisitor. Indeed, it is not Ivan's 'reasoning' that moves C: the 'substance of his argument [...] is not strong'. It is instead the 'accents of anguish' in Ivan's argument that affect C. It is 'the voice of Ivan, as realized by Dostoevsky [...], that sweeps me along' (*Diary*, p. 225).

'Reasoning' in this respect can be said to represent the authoritativeness of a solitary ideological truth. It is tantamount to the 'absolute claims' of divine providence or Kantian deontology. The juxtaposition of 'reasoning' and 'voice' suggests that Dostoevsky's value to *Diary*'s historically immanent ethical position, the focal point of his ethical influence, is located in his renunciation of absolute narrative authority.

In his interview with Atwell, Coetzee offered a twofold methodology to avoid repeating the reading Dostoevsky was afforded in his own day: to treat him as an author who lived through the philosophical debates of his day, and as an heir to a vital Christian tradition. Both 'lived through' and 'vital' insinuate that the tradition, as Coetzee understands it, is not based upon a rigorous adherence to absolute dictates. It is instead one that engages in debate, that allows itself to influence and be influenced by the context of its practice. C expresses his 'shock' that 'Dostoevsky, a follower of Christ, could allow Ivan such powerful words' (*Diary*, p. 226). The vitality of the Dostoevskian tradition that impresses upon *Diary*'s ethics, then, is one that shows responsibility for its antagonists. It allows for the articulation of antagonistic voices.

The use of the word 'voice' recalls Bakhtin's theorization of the polyphonic (i.e. 'many-voiced') structure of Dostoevsky's novels. C effectively reiterates Bakhtin's seminal explication of Dostoevskian polyphony as *'a plurality of independent and unmerged voices and consciousnesses'* that are *'not only objects of authorial discourse but also subjects of their own directly signifying discourse'*.[23] Ivan's atheism typifies him as one of Dostoevsky's *'free* people, capable of standing *alongside* their creator, capable of not agreeing with him'. Conversely, the 'monologic' novel articulates only 'a single authorial consciousness', wherein characters serve 'as a vehicle for the author's own ideological position'.[24]

The polyphonic novel, then, is neither an exertion nor imposition of an authorial voice, but a renunciation of absolute narrative authority to allow for a multiplicity of co-existing and competing discourses. It exists as an event through the co-existence of heterogenous voices. Narrative authority can be equated with monologism: *Diary* lends weight to this equation by contrasting Dostoevsky with Tolstoy, the novelist most frequently offered by Bakhtin as the epitome of monologism.[25] And Bakhtin likewise perceives the most precise expression of monologism to be 'idealistic philosophy', specifically the absolutism of German idealism directly influenced by Kantian deontology. Referencing the 'absolute *I*' or 'normative consciousness' of Hegelian philosophy, Bakhtin critiques the 'monistic principle' of idealism that, by converting the 'monism of existence into the monologism of consciousness', inevitably transforms existence 'into the unity of a single consciousness'.[26]

Russia's Crisis of Modernization

In Bakhtin's view, philosophical or religious edicts based in universal absolutes are isolated by the 'ethical solipsism' of monologic authority.[27] The polyphony of Dostoevsky's later novels overcomes monologic solipsism by basing its ethics in the event of being that can only ever be an event of co-being (Bakhtin's *sobytie*).[28] This is what makes C an 'ethically better' artist by reading Dostoevsky: the polyphonic novel offers a prototype for overcoming the incompatibility of universally applicable ethical absolutes in a twenty-first-century context. Moreover, the disposition to understand polyphony in ethical terms is a consequence of Dostoevsky's own particular historical era, something Coetzee elaborates on in a 1995 review of Joseph Frank's *Dostoevsky: The Miraculous Years*. This review offers evidence for the conflation of a dual temporality when reading for ways in which Dostoevsky responds to Coetzee, in that it identifies how Dostoevskian ethics were formed in reaction to his historical context. In it, Coetzee diagnoses a common theme of Dostoevsky's late novels: they conduct 'a searching interrogation of Reason – the Reason of the Enlightenment – as the basis for a good society'. Coetzee claims the reason for the intensity of this interrogation was Dostoevsky's unique position 'at the very center of an historical crisis, Russia's crisis of modernization', and the consequence of this crisis was the emergence of the 'amoral egoism and proto-Nietzschean self-deification' of Russian nihilism.[29]

Although Coetzee borrows 'proto-Nietzschean' from Frank's biography, the association he makes between the historical crisis of Dostoevsky's era and, through Alan, the amoral egoism of the 'modern state' (*Diary*, p. 99) seems too methodical to be mere coincidence.[30] Coetzee's accusation is that Alan's renunciation of individual morality (tantamount to 'self-deification', the belief that one may with impunity benefit one's own interests to the detriment of others) has its roots in the axiological shift typified by Nietzsche's critique of Enlightenment Reason: it was this shift, coterminous with Dostoevsky's later writing, that allowed for the amalgamation of Machiavellian and modern quintessence.

Dostoevsky's anticipation of the post-Nietzschean amorality of the modern world, as Coetzee relates it, came from his engagement with the ideological conflicts of his own era. He perceived traditional ethical absolutes as constraints on moral egoism, and his 'eschatological imagination' foresaw that declining belief in both divine providence and Enlightenment Reason would lead to Nietzschean self-aggrandizement (and its correlate forsaking of others) that 'would culminate in the Bolshevik takeover of 1917'.[31] A section of Coetzee's review laments Frank's sparse discussion of Bakhtin because it 'loses an opportunity' to compare the polyphonic structure with Dostoevsky's 'most radical intellectual and even spiritual courage'.[32] It is precisely such courage that shocks C: the courage to give *'fully valid voices'* to his ideological antagonists.[33] 'Dostoevskian dialogism', writes Coetzee, 'grows out of Dostoevsky's own moral character'.[34] Dostoevsky's development of the polyphonic novel structure can therefore be seen as an ethical response to the amoral egoism emerging from the decline of monistic ethical principles.[35] Coetzee's subsequent claim that Bakhtin 'leaves out' the ethical implications of the polyphonic structure must accordingly be modified through a comparison of *Problems of Dostoevsky's Poetics* (*Problemi poetiki Dostoevskogo*, 1963) with Bakhtin's ethical writings, in particular, the notion of 'answerability' proposed in the early fragments known collectively as *Towards a Philosophy of the Act*.[36] The compatibility of Bakhtinian answerability and the multivocality of Dostoevsky's novels elucidates the ethical dynamic of the polyphonic narrative structure.[37]

Bakhtin's ethics in *Philosophy of the Act*, like his theorization of narrative polyphony, was established in opposition to 'formal ethics of Kant and the Kantians': as such, it proposes the kind of ethical response to the historical crisis of modernization that is missing from proto-Nietzschean amorality.[38] Stating that Kantian formal ethical principles offered 'no approach to a living act performed in the real world', his aim was to reconcile an ethical 'ought' with what he termed the 'once occurrent-moment in Being-as-event', the actuality of a subject in an isolated moment of space and time.[39] The ethical ought of Kantian deontology abstracts individuals into 'autonomous laws', thus negating them 'as individually and answerably active human beings'.[40]

Answerability is, then, a fundamental component of co-being. It is inherent in the 'central emotional-volitional moments' that constitute the subject's once-occurrent moment of Being: 'I, the other, and I-for-the-other'.[41] In the event of co-being, answerability arises as a faculty of the subject's capacity to answer. The cognitive function of language thus presupposes its discursive function. Subjectivity originates from discursive interaction with others. As a consequence, therefore, of their directly signifying subjectivity, characters in a polyphonic novel are imbued with an answerability to others.

Bakhtin's theorization of deontological ethics as an abstraction of the individual's once-occurrent moment of Being, and his resultant venture to source such ethics in the once-occurrent moment of Being (which can only ever be an event of co-being), has its parallel in the ethics of Dostoevsky's late novels, if such ethics can be divorced from their affiliation with a metaphysical presence. In *The Brothers Karamazov*, for example, the distinction between Madame Khokhlakov's theoretical love for 'mankind in general' (*BK*, p. 57) and the 'active love' (*BK*, p. 56) of intersubjective relations advocated by Zosima testifies precisely to the capacity of a speaking subject to breach ethical abstraction. Khokhlakov's fantasy of renouncing her possessions and becoming a sister of mercy is sustained only by the promise of 'a return of love for my love' (*BK*, p. 57). It is sustained only within the confines of her cognition. The possibility of ingratitude on behalf of those she helps would breach the security of a subjective position that constitutes universal, ethical abstractions. The active answerability of 'people in particular' maintains the capacity to breach formal ethical principles applicable to 'mankind in general' (*BK*, p. 57). The speaking subject, as theorized by Bakhtin, is presupposed by the cognition of the words it speaks. It is never final, never complete. Its subjectivity is contingent on the emotional-volitional moments of its once-occurrent moment in Being (reconceiving 'Being' as a process of becoming rather than a cognized state). The character in a polyphonic novel that reveals *'that internally unfinalizable something in man'* thus corresponds with the Bakhtinian theorization of subjectivity.[42]

The ethical dynamic of such subjectivity is contingent on its being subject to the call of the other. Bakhtin found in the very existence of the dialogic relation the ethical transcendence of monologic absolutism. He saw religious/philosophical edicts as impositions on the 'unfinalizability' of a subject in its once-occurrent moment of Being/becoming. Consequently, he theorized an ethical relation consisting of once-occurrent answerability *for* the other, founded on the capacity to answer *to* the other. And this is an ethical theory made manifest by the polyphonic novel structure. Any particular character in a polyphonic novel is presupposed by the event of co-being that comprises the novel form. For a '*genuine polyphony of fully valid voices*' to emerge, an individual voice must always-already be in answer to other voices.[43] Therefore, each individual character is answerable for the existence of the polyphonic novel form (and thus the other characters within it), by virtue of its capacity to answer.

Ethically Better

The polyphonic novel form, in this sense, becomes an archetype for the ethical foundations of subjectivity: as subjects are constituted by and through language, so the polyphonic character transpires by and through dialogic relations with other polyphonic characters. This is the elemental trait of Dostoevskian polyphony. In *The Brothers Karamazov*, for instance, Alesha Karamazov's dialogic interaction with his brother during the 'Rebellion' chapter plays out during a later scene with the cynical seminarian Rakitin, who torments Alesha following Zosima's death and bodily corruption. Rakitin tells Alesha he has rebelled against God in his anger at his master's death. Alesha responds, 'I do not rebel against my God, I simply "do not accept his world"' (*BK*, p. 341).

His repetition of words previously said by Ivan (*BK*, p. 253) disrupts any attempt to monologize his character as the finalized articulation of an idea-consciousness. Rakitin himself cannot comprehend Ivan's words in Alesha's mouth. He claims them to be 'gibberish' (*BK*, p. 341) because his cognition of the world, with its resultant understanding of Alesha as a distinct and finalized being, is at this moment breached. Alesha here is in a period of transition, and that transition is wrought through dialogic encounters with others. Alesha's words are on the threshold between his consciousness and Ivan's. Each encounters the other in a once-occurrent event of Being, and so neither character's thought is finalized, nor is their relationship reduced to one of dialectical opposition.

The dialogic interaction between *Diary*'s characters mirrors this type of relationship. It is through C's dialogic interactions with Anya that he comes to write the Second Diary, and his underlying narrative even ends with a letter from her. Likewise, Anya is constituted by and through her interactions with C. As the novel progresses, she passes from feeling 'crushed between [Alan] and Señor C, between hard certainties [...] and hard opinions' (*Diary*, p. 109) to a rejection of Alan's egoism and a sense of responsibility for C's wellbeing. Though Anya initially rejects dialogic engagement with either C or Alan, preferring instead to 'withdraw and go off by myself' (ibid.), by the end of the novel she has decidedly parted from Alan and plans to care for C during his final days. Her sense of responsibility for him grows from her initial commitment to respond to him.

Furthermore, the fragmented structure of *Diary of a Bad Year* can be understood both as a challenge to a unifying, authorial authority, and, from a perspective based in chronological history, as a structural identification with (perhaps even homage to) the polyphonic novel form. C, who recognizes the death of the animating principles of monologic authority, also recognizes Dostoevsky as an 'ethically better' author because polyphony renounces such authority, precisely because the author of the polyphonic novel speaks as one voice amongst a plurality of independent and unmerged voices. The way *Diary* works to undercut C's own narrative authority becomes testament to the way that the polyphonic structure befits the ethics of the modern age. This is further evidenced by the fact that the final essay of the 'Strong Opinions' series, following that on Tolstoy's rhetorical mastery, is the sole essay in the entire novel unmatched by a counter-narrative. It is titled 'On the afterlife'. While not announcing the 'death of the author', *Diary* does pronounce here the death of monologic authority, at least as an interrelationship of ideas that gravitate towards a single consciousness. Dostoevsky masters his ethical 'authority' only by renouncing his monologic authority, only by allowing Ivan such powerful words.

This renunciation of authorial authority in Dostoevskian polyphony forms the basis for an analysis of the interaction between Dostoevsky and Coetzee that occurs in literary time, and consequently offers evidence of Dostoevsky's anticipatory plagiarism. Yet it is contingent upon Dostoevsky's anticipation of an axiological deviation from stable metaphysical/ethical foundations that very much takes place in chronological history: both Dostoevsky and Coetzee are responding to the historical circumstances that led Rosewater to proclaim Dostoevsky not enough anymore. To make that claim is to invalidate Dostoevsky's putative plagiarism: if Dostoevskian ethics are incompatible with the world after Dresden, post-Dresden ethics are necessarily incompatible with a Dostoevskian context. One possible extension of the Oulipo theory of potential literature, on which Bayard's anticipatory plagiarism is based, is that every text has already been written, and this potential would ultimately nullify the lament of chronological rupture made by Vonnegut's Rosewater. It would be nonsensical to claim that *The Brothers Karamazov* is not enough anymore. It either will always be 'enough', or else it never has been.

Any theory of anticipatory plagiarism, in order to allow for axiological variations, must hold itself at the crux of Bayard's dual temporality, accounting for both the chronological time of Lot's wife and the simultaneity of the Tralfamadorians. Anticipating a future where universalizing moral edicts would no longer be enough, Dostoevsky plagiarized Vonnegut, Coetzee, and Bakthin in prose that foreshadowed the significance of ethical dialogism to the early twenty-first century. That act of plagiarism was dependent on Dostoevsky's historical position: in the white heat of Russia's crisis of modernization, he chose to relinquish monistic narrative authority for the ethical dynamic of narrative polyphony. He relinquished 'reasoning' for 'voice'. Coetzee's reception of Dostoevsky is likewise contingent on Coetzee's own historical position. The ethical dynamic of the polyphonic narrative structure anticipates the specific moral issues of Western society at the beginning of the twenty-first century, as they are presented and addressed by Coetzee. It is the distinctiveness in chronological history between Dostoevsky and Coetzee that allows for each one's plagiarism of the other in literary history.

Notes

1 Kurt Vonnegut, *Slaughterhouse-Five, or The Children's Crusade* (London: Vintage, 2000), p. 73. Hereafter cited parenthetically in-text.

2 Daphna Erdinast-Vulcan, *Between Philosophy and Literature: Bakhtin and the Question of the Subject* (Stanford, CA: Stanford University Press, 2013), p. 36, https://doi.org/10.1515/9780804788397. For more on Dostoevsky's relation to the historical moment of modernism, see Joseph Frank's abridged biography, *Dostoevsky: A Writer in His Time* (Oxford: Princeton University Press, 2010), particularly chapter 25, 'Portrait of a Nihilist' (pp. 341–57), https://doi.org/10.1515/9781400833412. For a comparative essay on Dostoevsky's novels and Kantian deontology, see R. Maurice Barineau, 'The Triumph of Ethics over Doubt: Dostoevsky's *The Brothers Karamazov*', *Christianity and Literature*, 43:3–4 (1994), 375–92, https://doi.org/10.1177/014833319404300311. For an overview of the modernist turn from religious/ethical absolutes, see Zygmunt Bauman's 'Introduction', in his *Postmodern Ethics* (Oxford: Blackwell, 2000), pp. 1–15.

3 Theodore Adorno, 'Cultural Criticism and Society', in *Prisms*, trans. by Samuel and Shierry Weber (Cambridge, MA: MIT Press, 1983), pp. 17–34 (p. 34), https://doi.org/10.7551/mitpress/5570.003.0004.

4 Jean-Francois Lyotard, *The Postmodern Condition: A Report on Knowledge*, trans. by Geoff Bennington and Brian Massumi (Manchester: Manchester University Press, 1984), p. xxiv.

5 I have cited Jeffrey Mehlman's translation of excerpts from Pierre Bayard's *Le Plagiat par anticipation*, as 'Anticipatory Plagiarism' in *New Literary History*, 44:2 (2013), 231–50 (p. 249). The original may be found in Pierre Bayard, *Le Plagiat par anticipation* (Paris: Les Éditions de Minuit, 2009), p. 148.

6 Bayard, 'Anticipatory Plagiarism', p. 233; *Le Plagiat*, p. 108. Other examples offered by Bayard include the characteristically postmodern formal playfulness of Sterne's *Tristram Shandy* (1767) and the bureaucratic depersonalization, common to genocide literature, that pervades Kakfa's writings.

7 Bayard, 'Anticipatory Plagiarism', p. 231; *Le Plagiat*, p. 105.

8 Bayard, 'Anticipatory Plagiarism', p. 244; *Le Plagiat*, p. 136.

9 Bayard, 'Anticipatory Plagiarism', p. 233; *Le Plagiat*, p. 109.

10 Bayard, 'Anticipatory Plagiarism', p. 241; *Le Plagiat*, p. 122.

11 For example, Bayard writes 'it is never possible to be absolutely certain in identifying future writers'. See 'Anticipatory Plagiarism', p. 248; *Le Plagiat*, p. 148.

12 J. M. Coetzee, *Diary of a Bad Year* (London: Vintage, 2008), p. 227. Hereafter cited parenthetically in-text. Though this essay will focus primarily on *Diary*'s relation to *The Brothers Karamazov*, it is worth noting that interplay between political critique and fictional narrative features in both *Diary of a Writer* and *Notes from Underground*.

13 David Atwell, 'Mastering authority: J. M. Coetzee's *Diary of a Bad Year*', *Social Dynamics*, 36:1 (2010), 214–21 (p. 217), https://doi.org/10.1080/02533950903562575.

14 Johan Geertsema, 'Coetzee's *Diary of a Bad Year*, Politics, and the Problem of Position', *Twentieth Century Literature*, 57:1 (2011), 70–85 (p. 80), https://doi.org/10.1215/0041462x-2011-2006.

15 Peter D. McDonald, 'The Ethics of Reading and the Question of the Novel: The Challenge of J. M. Coetzee's *Diary of a Bad Year*', *NOVEL: A Forum of Fiction*, 43:3 (2010), 483–99 (p. 496), https://doi.org/10.1215/00295132-2010-026.

16 J. M. Coetzee, *Doubling the Point: Essays and Interviews*, ed. by David Atwell (London: Harvard University Press, 1992), p. 243.

17 Ibid., pp. 243–44.

18 The ideological antagonism between C and Alan, in this regard, is reminiscent of that between the Underground Man and the Chernyshevskian ideals he decries. Alan is almost a paradigm of the formulaic 'two times two is four' principles that the Underground Man fears are 'no longer life [...] but the beginning of death.' See Fyodor Dostoevsky, *Notes from Underground*, trans. by Richard Pevear and Larissa Volokhonsky (London: Everyman, 2004), p. 32.

19 Erdinast-Vulcan indeed correlates the awakening of a modernist consciousness with a 'post-Nietzschean world'. *Between Philosophy and Literature*, p. 36.

20 Coetzee's words are quoted in McDonald's 'The Ethics of Reading', p. 496.

21 Dostoevsky, *The Brothers Karamazov*, trans. by Richard Pevear and Larissa Volokhonsky (London: Vintage, 2004). Hereafter cited parenthetically in-text (as *BK*). Pevear and Volokhonsky translate the title of this chapter 'Rebellion'.

22 The theoretical overlap between Ivan and Nietzsche, especially between their respective iterations of 'everything is permitted', is reviewed and commented upon by Paolo Stellino in his *Nietzsche and Dostoevsky: On the Verge of Nihilism* (Bern: Peter Lang, 2015), pp. 143–230, https://doi.org/10.3726/978-3-0351-0860-6.

23 Mikhail Bakhtin, *Problems of Dostoevsky's Poetics*, ed. and trans. by Caryl Emerson (Minneapolis, MN: University of Minnesota Press, 1984), pp. 6–7 [Italics in the original], https://doi.org/10.5749/j.ctt22727z1.

24 Ibid., p. 6 and p. 7.

25 Bakhtin writes: 'A second, autonomous voice (alongside the author's voice) does not appear in Tolstoy's world.' Ibid., p. 56.

26 Ibid., pp. 80–81.

27 Ibid., p. 10.

28 See Caryl Emerson's discussion of this term in a footnote to ibid., p. 7.

29 Coetzee, 'The Artist at High Tide: Review of Joseph Frank's *Dostoevsky: The Miraculous Years, 1865–1871*', *New York Review of Books*, 2 March 1995, p. 14.

30 See Joseph Frank, *Dostoevsky: The Miraculous Years, 1865–1871* (Princeton, NJ: Princeton University Press, 1995), p. 101, https://doi.org/10.1515/9780691209371.

31 Coetzee, 'The Artist at High Tide', p. 14. Again, 'eschatological imagination' seems to have been borrowed from Frank.

32 Ibid., p. 15.

33 Bakhtin, *Dostoevsky's Poetics*, p. 6.

34 Coetzee, 'The Artist at High Tide', p. 16.

35 Though Bakhtin calls Dostoevsky 'the creator of the polyphonic novel' (*Dostoevsky's Poetics*, p. 6), he acknowledges polyphony's debt to the carnival elements of Menippean satire.

36 Coetzee, 'The Artist at High Tide', p. 16.

37 Sarah Young has explored the possibility of narrative ethics in Dostoevsky in her study of *The Idiot*. However, Young's focus on how Dostoevskian characters 'script' their own plots differs from my approach. My concern is with the ethical dynamic of the polyphonic narrative structure itself,

rather than the scripting impulse of characters within a polyphonic novel. See Young, *Dostoevsky's* The Idiot *and the Ethical Foundations of Narrative* (London: Anthem Press, 2004), https://doi.org/10.7135/UPO9781843313748.

38 Bakhtin, *Toward a Philosophy of the Act*, trans. by Vadim Liapunov (Austin, TX: University of Texas Press, 1999), p. 27. In his translator's notes, Liapunov even claims that Dostoevsky's novels were 'not only an object, but also a source' for Bakhtin's ethics, especially for his theories on a perceived silence on the problem of 'responsibility' in Husserlian phenomenology. Cf. p. 83 (fn. 16).

39 Ibid., pp. 27, 18.

40 Ibid., p. 7.

41 Ibid., p. 54.

42 Bakhtin, *Dostoevsky's Poetics*, p. 58.

43 Ibid., p. 6.

4. Foretelling the Past: Fyodor Dostoevsky Follows Guzel' Yakhina into the Heart of Darkness

David Gillespie and Marina Korneeva

Questions of crime and its punishment have exercised the minds and pens of Russian writers since the nineteenth century, and, indeed, some, such as Aleksandr Pushkin and Mikhail Lermontov, felt the wrath of Tsars Aleksandr I and Nikolai I and spent several years in exile (Pushkin in the south of Russia from 1820 to 1824, and at his mother's estate in Mikhailovskoe from 1824 to 1826, and Lermontov twice in the Caucasus, from 1837 to 1838 and, fatefully, from 1840 to 1841). Both Anton Chekhov in *Sakhalin Island* (*Ostrov Sakhalin*, 1893) and Lev Tolstoy in his final novel *Resurrection* (*Voskresenie*, 1899), expressed outrage at prisoners' living conditions in penal colonies, while also questioning the legal and moral bases of the concept of 'justice'. In the twentieth century, the harrowing personal testimonies of the Gulag by Aleksandr Solzhenitsyn and Varlam Shalamov have become celebrated works documenting the war waged by the Soviet state against its own citizens.

It is Fyodor Dostoevsky, however, who most consistently explored crime and its aftermath, not only the fact and practice of its punishment, but also its effects on the individual's psyche and society's collective conscience. The purpose of this paper is to explore the relationship between two novels by Guzel' Yakhina from 2015 and 2018, and their 'reimagining' by Fyodor Dostoevsky, especially *Notes from the House of*

 https://doi.org/10.11647/OBP.0241.04

the Dead (*Zapiski iz mertvogo doma*, 1862). We posit the idea that Yakhina's fiction forces us to vividly and directly confront the psychological and philosophical realities of Dostoevsky's world. Looking through the lens of anticipatory plagiarism, we suggest that Dostoevsky's works are, indeed, his response to the horror of twentieth-century totalitarianism.

On first reading, Fyodor Dostoevsky's *Notes from the House of the Dead*, published between 1860 and 1862, and Guzel' Yakhina's multi-prize-winning debut novel about the Stalinist terror, *Zuleikha Opens Her Eyes* (*Zuleikha otkryvaet glaza*),[1] first published in full in 2015, offer striking similarities, despite being written and set more than 150 years apart. Both concern the loss of freedom and the struggle to survive in the extremely harsh physical conditions of political exile in Siberia, and both are based on personal experience. Dostoevsky's own exile near Omsk between 1849 and 1854 served as the basis for his novel, while Yakhina asserts that her story is based on the experiences of her own grandmother, who was exiled from Kazan' to Siberia for sixteen years between 1930 and 1946.[2]

By retrospectively reading *Zuleikha otkryvaet glaza* we get a 'new' view of Dostoevsky's work, whereby the modern reader can reinterpret Dostoevsky's world of brutality and pain as a nineteenth-century analogue of Yakhina's source text. Also relevant here is Yakhina's second novel, *Children of Mine* (*Deti moi*, 2018), which extends the dialogue with Dostoevsky into metafiction and the postmodernist literary space. By juxtaposing these two writers we can integrate past and present literary and historical narratives, yielding significant insights into the key concepts of 'survival' in the narrative's present, and its 'progression' into a literary and lived-in past. The representation of childhood, in particular the suffering of children, is germane to this argument, as it is a feature of both Dostoevsky's other writings and those of Yakhina herself. Indeed, reference will be made to some of Yakhina's published shorter fiction, some instances of which feature children as protagonists.[3]

Dostoevsky's novel is now commonly considered to be a seminal influence on modern Russian interpretations of incarceration, especially in works by Aleksandr Solzhenitsyn, Evgeniia Ginzburg and Varlam Shalamov, for instance. Like these authors, Dostoevsky was punished for his political opinions: in 1848, for the crime of belonging to a secret student society and reading proscribed literature, he was sentenced to five years' penal servitude in a Siberian prison camp, or *katorga*.[4] *Notes from the House of the Dead* adapts Dostoevsky's harrowing experiences in what his twentieth-century biographer Joseph Frank would call 'a world of moral horror' through a fictional protagonist, Aleksandr Petrovich Gorianchikov.[5] Like Dostoevsky, Gorianchikov was a nobleman; unlike his creator, he was a convicted wife-murderer. Both Dostoevsky and Gorianchikov suffer (often brutal) resentment from their fellow prisoners, most of whom are hardened criminals; both endure hard labour, constant dread of corporal punishment, and exposure to the worst side of human nature before ultimately finding legal and (more importantly) spiritual redemption through renewed faith in God and humanity. Dostoevsky was already drafting what would become *Notes* in his so-called 'Siberian notebook' even before leaving the *katorga*; in 1854, he wrote to his brother: 'How many folk personalities and characters have I taken with me from *katorga*! I grew to know them, and therefore, I would seem to understand them pretty well. So many tales of tramps and robbers and generally dark and wretched lives. What a miraculous people'.[6]

Moral Horror and Living Hell: The Prison Camp Experience in Dostoevsky and Yakhina

Guzel' Shamilevna Yakhina was born in 1977 in Kazan', and since 1999 has lived in Moscow. She was born into a middle-class family where her mother was a doctor and her father an engineer. She studied foreign languages (English and German) at the University of Kazan', and subsequently completed a course in screenwriting at the Moscow Film School (*Zuleikha* was filmed by state television as an eight-part series, first broadcast in April 2020).[7] Her first novel, *Zuleikha*, was published, rather surprisingly for a little-known writer, by AST, one of the major and most prestigious publishing outlets in Russia.[8] It has since been reprinted several times, and translated into over thirty languages. She is the recipient of several international literary prizes (for instance, the 'Iasnaia Poliana' and 'Bol'shaia kniga' awards, both in 2015, and the French journal *Transfuge*'s literary award, 2017).

Zuleikha is set between 1930 and 1946, a period that coincides with the exile of Yakhina's grandmother, which began when the latter was only seven years old.[9] The novel's front matter announces that the book is dedicated to all those who were 'dekulakized and deported' (though this acknowledgement is not included in the 2019 English-language translation). It is based on the published memoirs of exiled victims of dekulakization whom Yakhina consulted online, as well as the personal testimony of her grandmother, Raisa Shakirovna Shakirova. The village of Semruk which the deportees build with their own hands in the novel is modelled on the actual village of Pit-Gorodok, which existed until 1994. Some of the characters were inspired by real people, most significantly the German doctor Vol'f Karlovich Leibe (based on the first Rector of Kazan' University, Professor Karl Fuchs).

Zuleikha's central character is Zuleikha Valieva, the devout and obedient wife of the much older peasant farmer Murtaza. They live in a village in Kazan' district, following a pattern of everyday life that has existed for centuries. Their lifestyle is in no way glamorized or idealized. The reader forms the impression that Zuleikha's existence is characterized by endless, physically excruciating drudgery, oppression and hopelessness, although borne with resilience by a woman who knows no other reality. Compared to her later circumstances, however, this life is a veritable haven of stability. She and Murtaza are childless, their four daughters all having died in infancy. Zuleikha regularly and devoutly visits their graves in the neighbouring forest. Her life is one of constant verbal and physical abuse, exacerbated by brutal, soulless sex with her husband and incessant psychological battering from her mother-in-law (whom Zuleikha privately nicknames 'Upyrikha', meaning 'vampire' or 'bloodsucker'), with whom she and Murtaza live.

All this ends suddenly and violently with the arrival of a party of OGPU soldiers, precipitating the murder of her husband and her own arrest, deportation and exile to Siberia (Upyrikha is left behind, presumably to die alone). What follows is an unflinching and detailed account of the horrors of the transit prison in Kazan', and of the even more harrowing six-month train journey from Kazan' to Krasnoiarsk, including the death of hundreds of deportees, especially the young: 'the first to begin dying were the children. One after the other, as if playing tag, the children of the large family of the unhappy peasant left this world: to begin with the two infants (both on the same day) and then the older ones'.[10]

After this hellish train journey marked by physical privation, constant hunger and multiple deaths, the deportees are sent up the Angara river to their 'colony' on barges. Zuleikha's barge capsizes, resulting in the drowning of hundreds of men, women and children. Only a few survive, including Zuleikha (this incident is modelled on an event Yakhina states that her grandmother witnessed).[11] Zuleikha's survival is purely down to sheer good fortune. The role of such good luck in physical survival is a repeated theme in Yakhina's writing. In her 2015 short story 'The Rifle' ('Vintovka'), Maia is a wartime medical orderly who hides from German soldiers in a bombed-out building. The parallel here with Dostoevsky's prose lies in the desperate fate of children, for Maia shoots a German soldier who turns out to be a boy of fourteen, and who takes a long and agonizing time to die. Maia's own survival is ensured by a Red Army officer who lies over her and covers her body to protect her from the blasts and the shrapnel during an aerial bombardment.[12]

Besides Zuleikha, a few survivors eventually reach their destination on the banks of the Angara, where they must manually construct their own 'colony' of robust and safe accommodation while foraging for food, both in the forest and the river, as winter approaches. This is another circle of hell, where death can come from the cold as well as bears and wolves in the forest, and where the odds in favour of survival, especially in the unforgiving cold of the Siberian winter, are very small. Yet the small band of deportees, including their supervising officer Ignatov, do survive, and, as the days, weeks, months and then years go by, they build a community, eventually including a school, hospital, canteen and suitable living accommodation. Indeed, their village of Semruk becomes a haven that is actually safer than the external world of arbitrary arrest and sudden disappearance. Moreover, relationships develop, especially between Zuleikha and her erstwhile captor Ignatov, the man who had killed her husband at the start of her journey.

Surviving extremity is not the plot's main focus, however. People manage to survive physically in the face of the most debilitating and dehumanizing circumstances, but then they ultimately realize and articulate a still more vital need: hope for the future. This theme is conveyed not only through Zuleikha's own experiences, but also through the perspective of various representatives of the intelligentsia, peasantry, and ordinary workers making up the population of the settlement, as well as those who replenish its numbers with each new wave of deportee arrivals. A major theme of the novel is affirmation that a kernel of hope can survive and grow even in the worst time of sorrow. The seed of hope for Zuleikha is her son, Iuzuf, conceived just before her husband's murder, whom she carries inside her throughout the debilitating journeys to Kazan' and then to Krasnoiarsk, and who is born just after the deportees arrive at their destination on the desolate banks of the Angara river. Zuleikha's early years in the exiles' community are single-mindedly devoted to her son's survival: when her milk dwindles, she feeds him on her own blood. The boy survives and grows, learning skills from the other exiles (such as painting), and even learning French from a former Petersburg bourgeoise.

Zuleikha is the female *alter ego* of Dostoevsky's Gorianchikov. He is a land-owning nobleman and a murderer, whereas Zuleikha is an uneducated, devout and at the same time superstitious peasant woman guilty simply of belonging to a land-owning social class outlawed by the state. The shift between female and male narration between these novels throws into relief the origins of Yakhina's novel in her grandmother's experiences, while intensifying reader empathy with an apparently more vulnerable heroine. Male perspectives are not lost in *Zuleikha,* however: Yakhina, unlike Dostoevsky, switches between different narrative viewpoints, including those of Dr Leibe and the OGPU officer Ignatov. The novel ends with the teenage Iuzuf's departure from Semruk, hoping to make a future for himself as an artist in Leningrad. (Such an optimistic if unlikely outcome is foreshadowed in Yakhina's short story 'The Butterfly' ('Motylek', 2014), whose eight-year-old homodiegetic narrator improbably escapes to Kazan' from an island used to forcibly incarcerate those deemed mentally ill, and their relatives.) [13]

We can thus read Yakhina's *Zuleikha* as a modern antecedent to Dostoevsky's *Notes from the House of the Dead,* anticipating the former's depiction of unimaginable living conditions and the daily struggle to survive. In both novels the leading characters are socially stigmatized: Dostoevsky's protagonist Gorianchikov is outnumbered by peasants who resent his noble background, and Zuleikha is a Tartar woman (and a devout Moslem, at least at the start of the novel) surrounded almost exclusively by Orthodox Russians.[14] Both novels' main characters are united by their eventual successful adaptation to difficult circumstances:

despite their initial social (and in Zuleikha's case, also ethnic) otherness, both become accepted by their fellow inmates after undergoing a moral evolution.

Equally, both novels are imbued with the narrator's desire to retain humanity and moral values by forging individual identity through struggle and hardship. Thus, Dostoevsky's narrative may be said to elaborate the idea, put forward in *Zuleikha*, that the place of confinement is a microcosm of society, where various social ranks and diverse nationalities are represented from across the entire expanse of the country. Significant passages from both works highlight this essential affinity. Yakhina describes the community of exiles who survive the journey up the Angara thus:

> Looking into their faces, Ignatov remembers everyone who works in the camp. He finds them in the list, circles them with charcoal, counts them. Together with the Leningraders there are twenty-nine people. Russians, Tartars, a couple of Chuvash, three Mordovians, a Mari woman, a Ukrainian, a Georgian woman and a German who has taken leave of his senses with the high-sounding and affected name of Vol'f Karlovich Leibe. In a word, an entire international community.[15]

The social composition of Dostoevsky's prison is remarkably similar:

> In our prison there were about two hundred and fifty people, a figure that was more or less constant. Some arrived, others finished their sentences and left, while others died. And what a variety of men there was here! I think that each province and each zone of Russia had its representatives here. There were non-Russians as well, and there were even some exiles from among the mountain tribesmen of the Caucasus. They were all divided according to the degree of their crime and consequently according to the number of years determined by their sentence. It must be assumed that there was no crime that did not have its representative here.[16]

Dostoevsky's prison offers a representative cross-section of trades and skills, providing the basis of a working community: 'Here there were also boot-makers, shoe-makers, tailors, carpenters, metal-workers, engravers and goldsmiths. There was a Jew, Isai Bumshtein, a jeweller who was also a money-lender. All of them worked and earned their corn.'[17] The colony of Semruk also contains an abundance of trades that enables it to survive and then develop: Leibe the doctor, Lukka the fisherman, Bogar the builder, Ashkenazi the cook, and Ikonnikov the painter.

There is one major difference between Dostoevsky's and Yakhina's prisons, of course. Most if not all of the inmates of Dostoevsky's prison are actual criminals, whereas the inhabitants of Yakhina's colony are simply individuals unfortunate enough to be socially declassed. Dostoevsky's characters have fallen foul of the criminal justice system, whereas Yakhina's are the blameless victims of ideological rationalization.

Moreover, the casual, animal-like cruelty of Dostoevsky's imperial-era prison guards is a feeble imitation of the ideology-driven malice of the twentieth-century OGPU guards. In his later novels, notably *Demons* (*Besy*, 1872), Dostoevsky shows how political radicals no longer see people as humans, but rather as raw material to be used in pursuance of political goals.

The authorities in Yakhina's work take sadistic pleasure in exploiting this inner cruelty. The suffering, repression and deaths of 'enemies of the people' are of no concern to the OGPU, who regard the loss of human life merely in terms of cold statistics. From the comfort of his own train compartment Ignatov occasionally thinks of the exiles in the overcrowded wagons: 'They are not people, he corrects himself. They are enemies'.[18] The huge number of deaths in the six-month transit from Kazan to Krasnoiarsk (nearly 400, of whom 150 perish from typhus) is considered simply inevitable '*estestvennaia ubyl''* ('natural wastage').[19] The deportees are stripped of their humanity and identity; those who survive the transit are then forced to pay for their 'crimes' through back-breaking labour, and those who do not or cannot work are punished by receiving fewer food rations.

There are subtleties in Yakhina's presentation of the OGPU mentality, all of them insidious. Ignatov is betrayed by his superior Kuznets, left to die on the banks of the Angara together with his charges; the perfidious Kuznets expresses astonishment that Ignatov is still alive when he finally brings supplies several months later in the spring. Kuznets also visits the settlement in the expectation of receiving sexual favours from the female inhabitants. Early in the novel Ignatov is quick to distance himself from his former comrade and friend Bakiev when he learns that the latter has fallen out of political favour (he denies ever having known him). The camp informer Gorelov is keen to intimidate the other exiles not through class or ideological solidarity with his OGPU captors, but simply to exercise power over them. Zuleikha Valieva has no hope of freedom or happiness for herself; she feels destined to end her days in Semruk, and her only ray of hope is the possibility of escape for her son (in reality, Yakhina's grandmother was allowed to return home in 1946). In *Notes*, Dostoevsky's insights into the dark areas of the human soul and the capacity for evil deeds among Gorianchikov's fellow prisoners also echo the inherent evil of those representing the authorities in Yakhina's work.

In *Notes from the House of the Dead*, too, some figures in authority revel in the cruelty they are able to inflict on their charges. Dostoevsky describes one particularly sadistic Major:

> He was a terrible person exactly because he was a commandant with almost unlimited power over two hundred souls. As an individual he was merely ill-disposed and malicious, nothing more. He looked on the convicts as his own natural enemies, and that was his first and main error. He did actually possess some capabilities, but everything, even the good qualities, appeared in him in some twisted form. Unrestrained and malicious, he would burst into the jail even at night-times, and if he noticed a convict lying on his left side or on his back then the following morning he would have him punished. 'Sleep on your right side, he would say, as I ordered.' Inside the jail he was hated and feared like the plague.[20]

Dostoevsky's Major represents the evil in a man's heart that can manifest itself when that man has the ultimate power of life and death over others. Gorianchikov's account of this man's sadism may be said to "echo" Zuleikha's personal insight that the ideology fuelling so much cruelty is inherent in human nature. The seductiveness of rationalist ideas in Dostoevsky's subsequent works paves the way for dehumanization and for a political credo where the end justifies the means.

Yet, over time, the settlement of Semruk becomes a refuge where a semblance of normal life is created by the inhabitants themselves. It is, additionally, relatively secure from the political repression continuing in the rest of the country; under such circumstances, the lack of any prospect of release is both welcome and reassuring. Moreover, the inhabitants of Semruk are isolated from the ravages of war in the European part of the country. Dostoevsky's 'house of the dead' is more "humane" in a progressive sense because it does contain the possibility of freedom through eventual release, a metaphorical resurrection; externally imposed rules ensure that prison conditions are never inhumane, an apparent positive development in penal conditions.

Nevertheless, the relationship between incarceration and wider society in the two novels is existentially inverted. *Zuleikha*'s prison is virtually unregulated, every confinement is potentially a life sentence, and yet it is freer (for its surviving inmates) than the outside world. Semruk is, for its permanent residents, a strange kind of Paradise. On the other hand, whereas Dostoevsky's *katorga* is governed by external regulations and the inmates serve fixed, finite terms, it remains uncompromisingly a place of punishment.

Yakhina does not flinch from describing relentless and harrowing physical details of human suffering and endurance, including Zuleikha's near-drowning under the capsized convict barge, or the deportees' shared struggle when forced to forage for food in the *taiga* and the Angara river and construct accommodation fit to last the winter in the most challenging circumstances. The lot of Dostoevsky's prisoners is comparatively lighter, as most of them will be released when they have completed their sentence, and there is still some compassion and tolerance by the criminal justice establishment; they are still regarded as human beings, although classified among the worst and most base individuals in their society. The exiles in Stalin's Russia have no human worth, nobody cares if they live or die. Ignatov is the human face of this uncaring system, and he does not lack some redeeming human qualities. Though he fears retribution from his superiors when some prisoners escape from the train (rather than when they die), he does ensure that the exiles are sufficiently fed during their journey, even rejecting his own superior food.

In other words, if we (re-)read Dostoevsky's *Notes from the House of the Dead* as a successor text to Yakhina's twenty-first-century narrative, our "new" treatise can reveal themes which transcend Dostoevsky's 1862 narrative, although they are characteristic of most of his work. We have already discussed the contrasting symbolism of the penal colonies in each book, the differing potential for redemption in each, and the ironic polarization of political radicalism—the radical politics persecuted by the authorities in Zuleikha's case have become the orthodoxy of Dostoevsky's era. In a sense, the chronological reversal imposed by backwards reading makes sense of Dostoevsky's own sentencing as well as the fates of the few political prisoners in Gorianchikov's *katorga*: they are being punished for the sins of their figurative twentieth-century children, their political heirs.

Teardrops Unavenged: The Treatment of Children[21]

We turn now to another theme common to Yakhina's and Dostoevsky's fiction: the suffering of children. The Soviet state terrorizes not only its adult 'enemies' but also their children. Yakhina's child characters are deliberately targeted and subject to oppression and physical violence by adults who represent the state in its various forms. Nature can be equally cruel: Zuleikha loses her four daughters in infancy, and we learn that her mother-in-law, the 'Upyrikha', allowed her three older children to die of hunger so that only the fourth, Murtaza, would survive on her milk. The full horror of these times she conveys in a whisper to Murtaza:

> 'Do you hear, my son? We didn't eat them. We buried them. Ourselves, without a mullah, at night. You were just young, you've forgotten it all. They don't have any graves, I've told you this till I'm blue in the face, that in the summer of that year everyone was buried, but without graves. Cannibals were roaming the graveyards in hordes, and as soon as they saw a fresh grave they'd dig it up and eat the corpse'.[22]

In the same breath Upyrikha goes on to deny neighbours' rumours that she and Murtaza did in fact eat the other three children; her insistent refutation is a clear, if implicit, acknowledgement that she and her youngest son did commit cannibalism.

In Yakhina's short story 'The Butterfly' the eight-year-old Mitia (known as Motylek, the titular butterfly) has to endure a relentless barrage of physical beatings by various authorities on the island where he is incarcerated, most savagely inflicted by his own sadistic and alcoholic grandfather, before escaping to Kazan'. This island has its own child population, regimented and repressed by both teachers and hospital personnel, who take a perverse and sadistic pleasure in hunting down children who try to escape. The gradations and intensity of torture and pain inflicted on the young boy are grisly and disturbing, as are the physical tribulations he faces in order to leave the island.

Moreover, if we take Yakhina's text as primary and read Dostoevsky's works as if refracted through it, we can put historical flesh on to the bones of an abstract philosophical thesis. The physicality of Yakhina's evocation of violence gives human meaning to Dostoevsky's more metaphysical musings on suffering and redemption. Yakhina's understanding of materialist reductionism removes any idealism, and thus any realistic hope for a happy end, in a society governed and enforced by an intolerant and murderous ideology. The individual survives only by chance. Solzhenitsyn insisted in his chronicles of the Gulag, both fictional and non-fictional, that physical survival is dependent on spiritual transformation (perhaps significantly, the first chapter of *Zuleikha* is called 'One Day'). Zuleikha survives by physically withstanding and then spiritually transcending her brutal environment, focussing on her duty to bring up her son and help him to survive, and thus she can also be seen to symbolize a 'feminization' of the prison and exile experience that is absent in Solzhenitsyn (or Dostoevsky).

Yakhina's novel shows that exile is mitigated by humanity, manifested as simple kindness and love between those abandoned by an uncaring state, with little hope for survival, never mind spiritual rebirth. They create their own community which is more or less unsupervised externally, and over the years all the deportees originally exiled to Semruk die there, as, the reader knows, eventually will Zuleikha. Yakhina's child characters Iuzuf and Motylek also escape hell on earth, at great risk to their own lives, though there is no suggestion that their physical survival will guarantee a better quality of life: Iuzuf hopes to become an artist, Motylek in adult life is a casual labourer.

Children in Dostoevsky's works also suffer as innocent victims of adult weakness and/or cruelty. In *Crime and Punishment'* (*Prestuplenie i nakazanie*, 1866) the younger children in Semen Marmeladov's household go hungry because he drinks away the family income; his teenage daughter Sonia has to earn money as a prostitute to feed the family. In the same novel Arkadii Svidrigailov preys on young girls, sexually exploiting and abusing them, and only his dreams speak of an awakening consciousness. Stavrogin in *Demons* takes delight in humiliating and abusing eleven-year-old Matresha, who hangs herself in shame after he has raped her (Stavrogin willingly fails to prevent her suicide). In *The Brothers Karamazov* (*Brat'ia Karamazovy*, 1881) the schoolboy Il'iusha Snegirev dies, and at his funeral the novice monk Alesha Karamazov delivers a moving eulogy to the grieving schoolboys on the need for Christian love:

> My fine Sirs, all of you henceforth are dear to me, I shall enclose you all in my heart, and I ask you all to enclose me in yours! And who has brought us together in this fine and good feeling, of whom we shall now always, for our entire life, remember, and we intend to remember, it is Il'iushechka, of course, a kind boy, a nice boy, a boy who will be dear to us for ever and ever! We will never ever forget him, may his memory in our hearts be eternal and good, henceforth and for ever and ever![23]

There is no more abhorrent example in Dostoevsky's work of the suffering of innocent children than the tale told by Ivan Karamazov to his brother Alesha of the murder of an eight-year-old serf boy by a retired army general, who sets his hunting dogs on him. The hounds tear the boy apart in front of his mother. It is in the face of such cruelty that Ivan rejects 'supreme harmony' and God's world:

> it is not worth the teardrop of even one tortured child who beat his chest with his tiny fist in his stinking dog kennel weeping his unexpiated tears and prayed to his Lordy-Lordy. It is not worth it because his tears remained unexpiated. They must be expiated, otherwise there can be no harmony.[24]

Yakhina's children suffer because of the state's ideology and its policy towards 'enemies'. Dostoevsky mitigates official corporate responsibility through the suffering of his children simply as a result of human agency. However, Dostoevsky's fears for the future replicate the fate of children in Yakhina's second novel *Deti moi*, published in 2018.

This novel again begins in a non-Russian community, this time among Volga Germans in the early 1920s. The village is Gnadental' ('Fertile Valley', renamed 'Gennad'ev' after the mass deportation to Kazakhstan of the German population during the Great Patriotic War), and its inhabitants bear names from German and Austrian culture over years and genres: Bach, Grimm, Hoffman, Wagner, Handel, Dürer, Dietrich, Böll, Fromm, Brecht, Mann, Wenders, Grass, Lang.[25] As with Dostoevsky's characters Devushkin, Raskol'nikov, Razumikhin and Myshkin, names here have a symbolic function. If in Dostoevsky names suggest their owners' psychological characteristics, in *Children of Mine* they possess an allegorical significance: the novel is not just about physical survival, but the fate of culture in a militant age.

This novel is fundamentally about an adult's efforts to save and protect the life of a child. The hero is Iakov Ivanovich Bakh (Bach), a teacher in the German colony of Gnadental', who has to raise Anna alone as her mother, his wife Klara, dies in childbirth (the child is not his: Klara became pregnant after she was gang-raped by three itinerant brigands). He begins by stealing milk from the local farms, then, after he is discovered, "earns" milk rations for the baby by writing stories and later fairy tales (*skazki*) for a local newspaper, under the direction of the hunchbacked Party official Hoffman (Gofman):

> He read through the text. Did he write this himself, or was someone moving his pen, suggesting *les mots justes* and weaving them into elegant and exact expressions? He couldn't add anything to what had been written. It seemed in these last lines that he had poured out on to the paper all the remnants of what had built up inside him over these years of isolation and silence. Three months of constant feverish writing—hundreds and hundreds of pages covered in writing: everything that Bach knew and remembered of his native colony and its inhabitants, what he surmised, doubted and managed to rethink—all of this was now cast in words and passed on to the voraciously reading hunchback. Gnadental' appeared in these jottings as a motley, noisy place full of merry and brightly dressed people, the pealing of bells, the singing of women, the cries of children, the lowing of cows and the clucking of fowl, the splashing of oars on the Volga, the fluttering of sails and murmuring of waves, the smell of fresh wafers and watermelon honey—Gnadental' as it used to be. Gnadental' as it is.[26]

Hoffman is unable to contain his enthusiasm: 'You have dug down to the truth, my bearded comrade! You have opened up the soul of this unsociable entity, the Volga German. You have opened it up like a tin of vegetables'.[27] The role of literature, Hoffman tells him, is to 'turn the soul inside out' through tales and legends, as in children's stories, the 'foundation of the soul'.[28] Hoffman is delighted that Bach has turned real life into a fairy tale. For Bach the fairy tale is his only way to feed his adopted family.

Hoffman reveals the true function of art in this society, just as Bach had expressed it in his tales:

> You're a Shakespeare, a Schiller! What is created in that unkempt German head of yours, eh? What demons are lurking in there? [...] Some spirited turns of phrase, however, I admit that. Here we have a fairy tale with the workers' morality, and instructions on how to look after an apple-tree orchard: both the cultural revolution and the agrarian question, all in this

> tiny text. And how beautifully you've phrased it: this shouldn't just be read, it should be recited, as a poem. To be sung like a hymn![29]

The novel is structured according to a timetable that does not follow calendar time, but major events, as in folklore. Thus, for example, the year 1918 is 'the Year of Ransacked Houses', 1921 is 'the Year of the Hungry', 1931 is 'the Year of the Great Lie' and 1933 'the Year of the Great Hunger'. Moreover, Bach knows perfectly well how the laying of the 'foundation of the soul' fits the new world order:

> Bach had long since understood exactly what kind of fairy tales Hoffman expected of him. Stories of a religious nature—about the Virgin Mary, the apostles and the saints—were strictly forbidden; subjects with a mystical quality—about magicians, magical objects, unicorns and dead knights—were also not particularly welcome; but stories about simple people—weavers, cobblers, fishermen, peasants, old and young soldiers—were always needed. Surprisingly, witches and devils were also required, and wood demons with little devils, giants of all breeds and sizes, cannibals with robbers: sublime magic Hoffman did not favour, but 'representatives of the people's beliefs' he certainly did. 'All your magicians with their crystal balls and sorcerers with their staffs—all of them are *former* heroes, believe me,' he would explain to Bach. 'Let *former* people read about them: young grammar-school girls with their grubby army officers and ladies with an intellectual bent. But the people will understand about itself and about those it fears to meet in the granary or neighbouring forest.' The involvement in fairy tales of representatives of the ruling class—of kings, barons and earls—was also welcomed as it ensured that each story had an ideologically correct ending. Also welcome were stories about animals: cowardly sheep, diligent bees, carefree larks, but Bach tackled similar subjects reluctantly as he couldn't imagine himself as a hare or a seal.[30]

The degradation of literature for the purposes of political education and ideological propaganda is a far cry from Dostoevsky's well-known 1880 speech at the unveiling of Moscow's Pushkin monument calling for writers to act as prophets for their people.[31] Moreover, both in this address and in the journalism collected as *Dnevnik pisatelia* (*Diary of a Writer,* 1873–1881), Dostoevsky practised direct communication with his readers, openly engaging in polemics with fellow writers and intellectuals such as Nikolai Leskov, and not only on literary matters: he was also happy to discuss philosophy, history and politics. Though this was not necessarily an 'equal' correspondence (there is ample evidence that Dostoevsky was not interested in argument or discussion, but simply in making points as forcefully as he could), it was a dialogue that assumed another's participation and at least implied a response: Dostoevsky's response to the call for the creation of the 'engineer of human souls' was to depict the offspring of such engineers. In terms of reading 'backwards', we can see Dostoevsky denouncing with increasing vehemence exactly the utilitarian use of literature postulated by Hoffman 150 years later in *Children of Mine*.[32]

Bach's tales are not intended as explicit moral guides, but as parables, exercises in indirectly assimilating the 'correct' values. Yakhina's Soviet-era writers view production and reception as a top-down vertical process, negating the horizontal line of cultural communication envisaged by Dostoevsky, which would be both subverted and inverted by the radical characters Dostoevsky termed 'devils'. The socialist fairy tales created by Yakhina's character Bach were transformed by Dostoevsky into nightmares.

Bach's lifelong mission is to provide and care for Anna, whom he cherishes as his personal responsibility although she is not his biological daughter. She serves as a constant reminder of her mother, the woman he came to love and revere. Bach takes a vow of silence for the rest of his life with Anna (whom he calls 'Antje'), unwilling to communicate with the outside world after his literary 'career' and the debasement of his craft. Bach's unwillingness to speak, and his success as a writer, provide an ironic commentary on the use (and abuse) of thought and communication by those who try to control them.[33] They are joined by the homeless itinerant boy, Vasilii Volgin, known as Vas'ka. Anna and Vas'ka become Bach's 'children', whom he guides through childhood until they leave together to join school in the neighbouring town of Pokrovsk. The novel's epilogue confirms that we cannot expect a happy ending: Bach is arrested in 1938, sentenced to fifteen years' imprisonment and in 1946 is killed in a mining accident in his place of internment in Kazakhstan. In 1948 the entire German population of the Volga region (438,000 people in all) is sent into exile in Kazakhstan. Anna Iakobovna Bach graduates from the Clara Zetkin school in the town of Engel'sk (formerly Pokrovsk); in 1941, as a person of German descent, she is deported to Kazakhstan where five years later she loses a leg as the result of an industrial accident. Vas'ka survives the war and on 8 May 1945 is in the German village of Gnadenthal on the river Elbe (there is an actual German village called Gnadenthal, but it is not on the Elbe). He travels to Kazakhstan to find and marry Anna Bach, then settles down to become a schoolteacher of German. The novel ends with the announcement that Bach's anthology *Fairy Tales of Soviet Germans* (*Skazki sovetskikh nemtsev*) appeared in 1933 and ran to six editions with over three hundred thousand copies, in addition to several successful theatrical adaptations. This collection, of course, is as fictional as its author.

Children of Mine, unlike *Zuleikha,* is occasionally enlivened by touches of humour, though with a dark edge. Several digressions feature Stalin; in the most notable of these, Stalin stops his personal motorcade to get out of his car and observe at close hand a wild dog. Soon an entire pack of dogs appears, and they begin moving threateningly towards him. As he moves away from his escort the dogs attack; in panic, Stalin rushes back to the safety of his car. The guard who kills the lead dog is later investigated for having waited too long before shooting, thereby possibly putting the Leader's life in danger. Clearly, the author's sympathies lie with the dogs. Ivan Karamazov's story of the serf boy set upon by his master's dogs provides an ironic retrospective comment on the worth of human life, with Stalin in the role of victim. Far from having the power of life and death over others, Stalin is reduced to potential dog-meat.[34]

Conclusion

Zuleikha and *Notes from the House of the Dead* share a common premise: the helplessness of the individual confronted by the implacable coercion of the state. Both novels use lived, historical experience to explore and decry the state's callousness and its assault on individuality. Yakhina's novels express greater concern with the physical process of how an entire way of life can be eradicated, whereas in *Demons* and still later in *The Brothers Karamazov*, Dostoevsky would present his fear of the logical (and possible future) outcome of nihilism. In *Children of Mine* the destruction of the 'fertile valley' and an entire way of life in Gnadental' can be seen as a microcosm of the larger Soviet reality, just as the rural communities of Skvoreshniki and Skotoprigon'evsk in *Demons* and *The Brothers Karamazov* respectively serve as fictional backdrops to the formulation and enactment of momentous political ideas.

If we 'read backwards', the real, physical pain and loss depicted by Yakhina is converted into the existential sufferings of the archetypical Dostoevskian hero whose personal philosophy has gone awry. The idea often ascribed to Ivan Karamazov that 'everything is permitted' is the revenge of the nineteenth century on modernity: in Dostoevsky's novels, horrendous lived experiences become abstract ideas, such as the reported atrocities which inform a friendly discussion between two educated brothers, Ivan and Alesha Karamazov. Through the trope of inhumane cruelty, the nineteenth-century literary 'canon' reconfigures twentieth-century reality. This is a postmodern irony that recalls, analogously, Vladimir Sorokin's symbolic dismemberment of the Russian classical canon in works such as *A Novel* (*Roman*, 1985–89), and his semiotic reimagining of it in *The Blizzard* (*Metel'*, 2010).

Dostoevsky's oft-quoted faith as articulated in *The Brothers Karamazov* that 'beauty will save the world' is the final comment on a nihilism lacking any moral restraint or literary prettification. In *Zuleikha*, 'beauty' is reduced to the mutual respect forged by Zuleikha and Ignatov, a relationship born largely of expediency rather than sincere feeling.

The fate of the children particularly foreshadows a world without moral signposts to the future. Bach's 'children' survive in a hostile environment through chance not design, as do the children in other works by Yakhina. Hoffman's praise for Bach's 'fairy tales' in *Children of Mine* makes a child's universe more 'real' than life itself, thereby anticipating Dostoevsky's fears of a utilitarian literature. Dostoevsky's response to the twentieth century's horror is to denounce its reductive simplification, though the wild dogs threatening Stalin remind us that not everything in the 'fairy tale' ends happily ever after, even for dictators.

Notes

1 *Zuleikha Opens Her Eyes* was first translated into English as *Zuleikha* in 2019 by Lisa C. Hayden (London: OneWorld). For simplicity's sake, we will henceforth refer to this novel as *Zuleikha*, even when discussing the Russian edition and/or our own translation of relevant passages.

2 Yakhina has several times indicated that *Zuleikha* in many ways reflects her grandmother's experience: see, for instance, her interview '"Mne nravitsia skladyvat' istorii"', *Voprosy literatury*, 3 (2016), 151–59, especially p. 154.

3 For discussion of the image of the child in Dostoevsky, see the classic study by William Woodin Rowe, *Dostoevsky: Man and Child in his Works* (New York: New York University Press, 1968).

4 See Joseph Frank, *Dostoevsky: The Years of Ordeal 1850–1859* (Princeton, NJ: Princeton University Press, 1983), pp. 49–162, for a full account of Dostoevsky's crime, trial and sentencing, and his subsequent experience in the Omsk prison stockade.

5 Ibid., p. 87 and *passim*.

6 'Skol'ko ia vynes iz katorgi narodnykh tipov, kharakhterov! Ia szhilsia s nimi, i potomu, kazhetsia, znaiu ikh poriadochno. Skol'ko istorii brodiag i razboinikov i voobshche vsego chernogo, goremychnogo byta. Chto za chudnyi narod'. Fedor Dostoevskii, cited in 'Primechaniia' [Editors' 'Notes'], in F. M. Dostoesvkii, *Polnoe sobranie sochinenii v tridtsati tomakh*, ed. by V. G. Bazanov and others, 30 vols (Leningrad: Nauka, 1970–1995), IV (1972), 271–325 (p. 275). I thank the editors for directing me to this source and providing the translation.

7 See Iakhina, '"Mne nravitsia skladyvat' istorii"', p. 152.

8 The novel was initially received rather condescendingly by critics in the 'thick' journals. Valeriia Pustovaia accused Yakhina of writing nothing more than 'belles lettres' (*belletristika*) and avoiding 'great literature' (*bol'shaia literatura*), though she did not define either genre: see Valeriia Pustovaia, 'Bol'shoi roman s vishenkoi', *Voprosy literatury*, 3 (2016), 125–38. In the same issue, Elena Pogorelaia considered the novel primarily in ethnographic terms, as an account of the litany of evils visited on the Tartar community in the Stalin years, in her article 'Chelovecheskoe, slishkom chelovecheskoe', *Voprosy literatury*, 3 (2016), 139–50. This was also the main thrust of the argument put by Mariia Savel'eva in 'Utverzhdenie cherez otritsanie', *Oktiabr'*, 12 (2015), 132–36. Sergei Beliakov discussed the novel in detail as a dissection of Stalinist crimes within a 'fairy tale' narrative,

though his argument is contrived and over-reliant on plot recapitulation: 'Sovetskaia skazka na fone GULAGa', *Ural*, 8 (2015:8), pp. 226–30. On the other hand, reviews by non-professional readers on blogs and websites were overwhelmingly more enthusiastic, which undoubtedly accounts for much of the book's commercial success; see, for instance, www.livelib.ru/book/1001173596 and www.litres.ru/guzel-yahina/zuleyha-otkryvaet-glaza-9527389/otzivi/ [accessed 8 May 2020].

9 See Iakhina, '"Mne nravitsia skladyvat' istorii"', pp. 154–56; also her interview '"U menia est' chetkoe otnoshenie k figure Stalina i periodu ego pravleniia"', *Biznes-online*, 1 November 2015, www.business-gazeta.ru/article/144322 [accessed 29 November 2019].

10 Guzel' Iakhina, *Zuleikha otkryvaet glaza* (Moscow: AST, 2019), p. 173. All translations of texts from *Zuleikha otkryvaet glaza* and *Deti moi* are our own.

11 In *The Gulag Archipelago*, Aleksandr Solzhenitsyn describes the deliberate sinking of barges carrying exiles in the White Sea and Caspian Sea. See Solzhenitsyn, *Arkhipelag Gulag* (St Petersburg: Azbuka, 2019), p. 39. On the terrible conditions of the train journeys of Solzhenitsyn's fellow exiles and prisoners to their various destinations, see *Arkhipelag Gulag*, pp. 409–16.

12 Guzel' Iakhina, 'Vintovka', *Oktiabr'*, 5 (2015), 73–86.

13 Guzel' Iakhina, 'Motylek', *Neva*, 2 (2014), 126–46. This story can also be read as a nightmare experienced by its main character Mitia, where in the course of his dangerous escape he eavesdrops on Ivan the Terrible planning his siege of Kazan' in 1552. 'Motylek' is also the Russian title for the 1973 film *Papillon*, set on the Devil's Island prison colony administered by the French in the early twentieth century.

14 E. F. Tugusheva comments on Zuleikha's character development: 'In a world turned upside down, where violence becomes the demonstration of power, national identity does not manifest itself, and as a whole cultural memory becomes displaced into the sphere of individual consciousness, and in the first instance is the instinct for survival, inner strengths and even super-strengths, considering exile itself for the deportees at the limit of all human possibilities.' See E. F. Tugusheva, 'Etnokul'turnoe svoeobrazie khronotopa v romanakh G. Iakhinoi "Zuleikha otkryvaet glaza" i A. Ganievoi "Zhenikh i nevesta"', *Izvestiia Saratovskogo universiteta. Novaia seriia. Seriia Filologiia. Zhurnalistika*, 18 (2018:3), 351–55 (p. 354).

15 Iakhina, *Zuleikha*, p. 243.

16 Fedor Dostoevskii, *Zapiski iz mertvogo doma* (St Petersburg: Azbuka, 2013), p. 14. By way of establishing a larger trope, in *Ledi Makbet Mtsenskogo uezda* (*Lady Macbeth of Mtsensk*) from 1864 Nikolai Leskov describes the prison

train heading to Siberia from Kazan' as similarly diverse, containing a Russian schismatic, a Jew, a Pole and a Tartar, representatives of various nationalities being punished by secular authority.

17 Ibid., p. 24.

18 Iakhina, *Zuleikha*, p. 178.

19 Ibid.

20 Dostoevskii, *Zapiski*, p. 42.

21 'Teardrops unavenged' is a phrase taken from the conversation between Ivan and Alesha Karamazov on the sufferings of children at the hands of cruel and sadistic adults. See Fedor Dostoevskii, *Brat'ia Karamazovy* (Moscow: AST, 2018), p. 249. Yakhina's third novel, *Convoy to Samarkand* (*Eshelon na Samarkand*, 2021), again focuses on the unhappy fate of children. It is based on the resettling of hundreds of orphaned and homeless children in the 1920s, in this case transported by train from Kazan' to Samarkand in Central Asia. See Guzel' Iakhina, *Eshelon na Samarkand* (Moscow: AST, 2021).

22 Iakhina, *Zuleikha*, p. 57. Upyrikha is roughly aged one hundred, and her son Murtaza is in his sixties, so he would have been an infant in the 1860s. There is no historical evidence of a famine in the Volga region at that time, though the famine of 1891–92 in the Volga basin resulted in up to half a million deaths.

23 Dostoevskii, *Brat'ia Karamazovy*, p. 777.

24 Ibid., p. 248.

25 In actual fact there have been Soviet writers whose surnames resonate with Germanic culture: Franz Bakh (Bach) (1885–1942), Franz Shiller (Schiller) (1898–1955), David Vagner (Wagner) (1914–1977).

26 Guzel' Iakhina, *Deti moi* (Moscow: AST, 2018), p. 191.

27 Ibid., p. 193.

28 Ibid., p. 195.

29 Ibid., p. 211.

30 Ibid., p. 240.

31 For detailed analysis of this landmark speech, see Marcus C. Levitt, *Russian Literary Politics and the Pushkin Celebration of 1880* (Ithaca, NY: Cornell University Press, 1989).

32 Yakhina has also published a short story on the 'power' of literature, though with a darkly ironic twist. In 'Shvaipol't' the down-at-heel former book trader Seregin steals from an old woman what he believes to be an original copy of the first book printed in Cyrillic by the German printer Schweipolt Fiol dating back to 1491, but then, as he flees other robbers, he drowns in a river. The volume vanishes with him. See 'Shvaipol't', *Esquire,* 125 (July 2016), 25–42.

33 For more discussion of this theme see N. I. Pavlova, 'Poetika vizual'nosti v romane G. Iakhinoi "Deti moi": k voprosu o fenomene literaturnogo uspekha', *Kul'tura i tekst*, 34 (2018:3), 52–66, especially pp. 62–64.

34 Stalin is an unambiguously negative character for Yakhina. In her short story 'The Celebration' ('Iubilei', 2018) the Great Leader quickly becomes bored with the celebrations surrounding his seventieth birthday in the Kremlin and is driven to his dacha outside Moscow. In the otherwise dark and deserted streets of Moscow he notices a lone passer-by, and instructs his chauffeur to drive him down and kill him, for no reason other than the sadistic pleasure of taking someone's life. See 'Iubilei', *Oktiabr'*, 1 (2018), 97–104.

5. Notes from the Other Side of the Chronotope: Dostoevsky Anticipating Petrushevskaia

Inna Tigountsova

The *contraintes*, or formal rules for literary games, invented by the Oulipo group are nothing new in literature, as the group's historian Pierre Bayard has noted.[1] Russian literature offers many other examples of invented rules. Amongst these are the militant manifestos of the Cubo-Futurists; for instance, Aleksei Kruchenykh and Velimir Khlebnikov's *Word as Such* (*Slovo kak takovoe*, 1913).[2] A parallel from the 1980s, the Transfurist or Neofuturist grouping, included Sergei Sigei who invented a technique of writing poetry in *so-bukvy* (ligatures).[3] Yet another form of innovation is attained by Fyodor Dostoevsky (1821–1881) with his 'realism in the higher sense' and his experimental *récit Notes from Underground* (*Zapiski iz podpol'ia*, 1864).[4] Dostoevsky's life spans only sixty years. Despite the fact that he is often considered to be, with Tolstoy, one of the two canonical Russian Realist writers, I will show how Dostoevsky's experimental use of narrative in *Notes from Undergound* anticipates and plagiarizes *Time: Night* (*Vremia noch'*, 1992) by the contemporary writer Liudmila Petrushevskaia. While Dostoevsky's well-known novella needs very little introduction, Petrushevskaia's family tale told by a Soviet-era matriarch still has a limited readership in foreign translation.[5]

In this chapter, I shall approach Dostoevsky's *Notes from Underground* and Petrushevskaia's *Time: Night* in light of the ideas of anticipatory plagiarism and polyvalent hybrid authorship proposed by Pierre Bayard. I suggest that in view of the similarities between *Notes from Underground*

 https://doi.org/10.11647/OBP.0241.05

and *Time: Night*, Dostoevsky's *Notes* can indeed be considered a case of anticipatory plagiarism. I also argue that Bayard's model biography of a writer called 'Tolstoevsky' (blending Dostoevsky with Tolstoy) is especially fruitful for analysing the peculiarities of the *Notes* and *Time: Night*. By analogy with the 'Homeric hymns', a term that attributes poems written over several centuries to a single author,[6] I propose to explore both texts as if they had been written by one hybrid author: 'Petroevsky' (or 'Dostoshevskaia'). The collected works of Petroevsky also include Dostoevsky's *Poor Folk* (*Bednye liudi*, 1846), *Crime and Punishment* (*Prestuplenie i nakazanie*, 1866) and Petrushevskaia's novella 'Our Crowd' ('Svoi krug', 1990).

Authorial Merging: The Chronotope of Petroevsky

Bayard's notion of anticipatory plagiarism ('the act of being inspired, whilst concealing the fact, by the works of a later writer'[7]) may at first strike us in the same way as Gary Saul Morson's suggestion that Dostoevsky's *Diary of a Writer* (*Dnevnik pisatelia*, 1873–81) is 'an integral (if idiosyncratic) literary work'— that is, as something quite improbable.[8] If we take a closer look, however, Dostoevsky's *intention* (as both author and editor) to present the *Diary* as a unified work becomes essential for our exploration of its structure and content. Another notion that might initially seem improbable is Bayard's idea of a literary history capable of mobility (a history which is subject to temporal recombination and rearrangement), which I suggest develops Bakhtin's concept of *chronotope* (a literary unity of time and space where time has the more significant role) in a non-linear, "rhizomatic" way.[9] In *A Thousand Plateaus: Capitalism and Schizophrenia* (1980), Gilles Deleuze and Felix Guattari describe two modes of social organization and reality, including literary reality: 'One is arboresque and favors order and hierarchy. The other is rhizomatic and favors an undoing of all such orders and hierarchies.'[10] If we accept their second mode as a viable literary reality, then the borrowing of ideas from future texts begins to appear sensible. Such a multi-directional, non-hierarchical chronotope informs what Bayard calls 'the mobility of the new literary history', with its chronologies that

> cannot be fixed insofar as any new work—and moreover, any work of importance—displaces the whole of the constituted chronology and makes the existing literary panorama appear in a new light.[11]

Who are we, after all, in the post-Stephen Hawking universe, to claim we know exactly which way time flows? Hawking postulates that if the universe was meant to 'finish up in a state of high order...disorder would *decrease* with time'; he argues that in that case human beings 'would have a psychological arrow of time that was backward'.[12] The concept of an a-chronological literary history with its inevitable updates is also mentioned by T. S. Eliot, for whom it takes into account complex networks of interconnected textual dialogue among culturally significant artefacts from different historical periods:

> Whoever has approved this idea of order, of the form of European, of English literature will not find it preposterous that the past should be altered by the present as much as the present is directed by the past.[13]

In his book on anticipatory plagiarism Bayard highlights its usefulness as a pedagogical tool:

> When this notion of anticipatory plagiarism is accepted, it is conceivable that our whole conception of literary history—as taught in educational establishments or universities and presented in textbooks—will have to be altered.[14]

Bayard's theory of anticipatory plagiarism, supported by his idea of the polyvalent personalities of both writers and their characters, allows us to take a fresh look at older texts and to re-position contemporary ones, re-contextualizing both.[15] When I was an undergraduate student of English, my Foreign Literature professor said that although James Joyce's *Ulysses* was mentioned on the reading list, we should wait to read it since we would be not able to understand all the allusions involved. Naturally, I read it right away. Perhaps I did not grasp the intertextual connections, but the *idea of their presence* in the work has been imprinted on my mind ever since that rather unorthodox request from my professor. If we consider the possibility of the digital mapping of an eternally changing network of past and contemporary texts as well as texts yet to come as components of one data map with mobile links between shimmering literary and 'geographical' (spatial) destinations, we will arrive at a different reading of the classics, and our conceptual understanding of them may change.[16]

How does our perception change if we see the New Testament as an older version of *The Idiot* (*Idiot*, 1869)? Or *Crime and Punishment* as borrowing a *topos* from Petrushevskaia's *Number One, or In The Gardens of Other Opportunities* (*Nomer Odin*, 2004) in its entrance-way and attic scenes? What if we imagine that Dostoevsky and Petrushevskaia are indeed one and the same writer, whom we might call 'Petroevsky' and whom we have mistakenly considered separate people, as Bayard does with Tolstoy and Dostoevsky in his recent book on 'Tolstoevsky'?[17] Based on the greater number of similarities and overlapping themes in their writing, would it not make even more sense than Bayard's investigation of Tolstoevsky? After all, Tolstoy and Dostoevsky, even though they merged in a national mytheme well before Bayard, do exhibit significant differences in their writing styles and ideologies.[18]

Or what if we imagined that Fyodor Dostoevsky and his brother Mikhail were the same person, since Fyodor Dostoevsky assumed Mikhail's financial responsibilities after his death and continued writing his multi-narrated texts throughout his life, as is especially evident in *Diary of a Writer*? In the spirit of Eric Naiman's counterfactual question, 'What if Nabokov had written "Dvoinik"?',[19] let us consider how we would read the *Notes from Underground* if Petrushevskaia had written it. Would we demand more from the character of Liza the prostitute, and expect her counter-narrative to be incorporated in the text? Would we expect the Underground Man to be a closeted bisexual or homosexual? Would we anticipate more societal disapproval of Liza, or argue that the relative lack of such disapproval—societal indifference—is more telling than condemnation? I suggest that *Notes from Underground* and *Time: Night* are the quintessential works of 'Petroevsky', who has benefited from the Russian nineteenth-century canon but also from the postmodern tradition, still populated by representatives of the Underground Man type, involving the ideal of Sodom and fragmented narratives. The further asymmetrical development of one element of Petroevsky's polyvalent personality—that of Petrushevskaia—supports Bayard's idea of anticipatory (or reciprocal) plagiarism in a different way.

Bayard argues in favour of Tolstoevsky and his characters having polyvalent personalities: 'Tolstoevsky is multiple, because he is composed of several personalities who are not necessarily in communication with one another, and whose person consists of the conflictual merger of these personalities'.[20] Once again, a Bakhtinian concept relates to Bayard's psychoanalytical literary theory (the Russian translation of Bayard's French original gives 'réunion conflictuelle'[21] as 'raznogolosoe ob″edinenie',[22] recalling Bakhtin's *raznogolosost'*, or vari-voicedness). Bakhtin considers the multi-voicedness and vari-voicedness (*mnogogolosost' i raznogolosost'*) of Dostoevsky's discourse to be its principal features, enabling the exploration of different aspects of a theme from multiple points of view, as well as serving as a pivotal compositional device.[23]

Le Plagiat par anticipation discusses *Oedipus Rex* (429 BC) and *Hamlet* (1609) as examples of literary works that are key to re-writing literary history if we accept the idea of anticipatory plagiarism. Following Bayard, I designate Petroevsky's *Notes from Underground* as another of those key texts that requires us to re-assemble the system of literary works, since this text was treated as an outsider in the literary compendium of nineteenth-century literature and arguably received the most criticism during that era of all of Dostoevsky's *oeuvre*. The *Notes* would be much better placed in the context of the twentieth century, as they are in close dialogue with works by Robert Walser (*The Child* (*Das Kind*, 1924, in *Die Rose*)), Ralph Ellison (*The Invisible Man*, 1952), Evgenii Zamiatin (*We* (*My*, 1924)), Jean-Paul Sartre (*Erostratus*, 1939), Vladimir Makanin (*Underground, or A Hero of Our Time* (*Andegraund, ili geroi nashego vremeni*, 1998)), and possibly Woody Allen (*Notes from the Overfed*, 1968), amongst others. Liudmila Petrushevskaia's prose has a special place in this literary web, as Dostoevsky's *Notes* are much closer to her work than to that of any other twentieth- or twenty-first-century writer. In spite of Dostoevsky-the-editor's footnote to *Notes* to the effect that the Underground Man is a necessary feature of Russian society of his time, the latter lacks companions from his own generation, even if one could argue that the Underground Man is a variation on two nineteenth-century types: the 'superfluous man' and the 'little man'.[24] It is, after all, the latter two types as such that populate nineteenth-century Russian novels and verse. The Underground Man type is distinctly out of place, dissonant with his own time. He is probably the Dostoevsky character least appreciated by nineteenth-century readers; yet we in the twenty-first century easily accept him as a popular type.

Petroevsky's Narrators

A particularly Dostoevskian Russian writer, Liudmila Petrushevskaia, was born at the height of the Stalinist purges in 1938 and survived family traumas, extreme poverty, near-starvation, and displacement, including a period in a children's home where she was placed by her mother in order to avoid desperate circumstances. Her family was ruined by the purges; Petrushevskaia's father left before she was born. Perhaps in part thanks to her family history, Petrushevskaia can be said to '[chart] the daily psychic monstrosities of a spiritual wasteland populated by victims and victimizers bound by an endless chain of universal suffering and abuse' in *The Time: Night* and other works.[25]

Thus in many ways Dostoevsky and Petrushevskaia share a single outlook on the human condition; they are precisely the sort of writers about whom one can easily imagine, with Bayard, 'that they have found a means of traversing the interval of time separating them so as to work together'.[26] What reader of contemporary Russian literature can peruse Dostoevsky's famously provocative *Notes from Underground* and not think of the protagonist of Liudmila Petrushevskaia's novella *The Time: Night*? The image of the notoriously unattractive, manipulative narrator who twists and turns the textual fabric of Dostoevsky's 1864 novella to suit his own needs is refreshed in the reader's mind by Petrushevskaia's 1992 publication. The narrator of *Notes from Underground*, a nameless antisocial paradoxalist intellectual, philosophizes in the plotless first part of his text ('The Underground'), using the second part ('Apropos the Wet Snow') to recall a series of events from his past. 'Apropos the Wet Snow' introduces his so-called friends; a prostitute, Liza, who takes pity on him; and his parodically named servant, Apollon, with whom the narrator squabbles over petty matters. Though not a mouthpiece for the nineteenth-century classic writer, the Underground Man still anticipates posterity on his creator's behalf by claiming superior intelligence. As Dostoevsky-the-editor writes in his footnote to the *Notes from Underground*: '...such persons as the creator of such notes not only can but even should exist in our society…'.[27] By leaving the Underground Man's notes ostensibly unfinished, Dostoevsky invites his fellow woman writer and her female narrator to complete his tale with a story just like his own, or to borrow a phrase from the Soviet-era author Natalia Baranskaia, 'a story like any other'.[28]

What if Petrushevskaia, or indeed one of her heroines, were to finish the *Notes*—which Dostoevsky never provided with a satisfactory conclusion? In his tortured discourse, which Bakhtin called 'the word with a loophole'('*slovo s lazeikoi*'), the Underground Man, as a marginalized intellectual, takes a position analogous to that of Petrushevskaia's Anna Andrianovna writing her notes 'at the edge of the table' in *Time: Night*.[29] In this late twentieth-century *Ich-Erzählung*, Anna Andrianovna narrates events from the life of four generations of her family, in which the misfortunes of its predominantly female members (Anna Andrianovna herself, Anna's mother Serafima, Anna's daughter Alena and son Andrei, her feminized grandson Timochka, and Alena's other assorted offspring) appear to be almost congenital. Parallels with Dostoevsky's nineteenth-century text include narrative structure, type of protagonist, the prevailing poetics of ugliness and disorder, a shared chronotope depicting the family home as dystopic, and the excessive use of colloquial language with diminutives.

The *Notes* are the most popular of Dostoevsky's texts in North American university curricula (thanks to their reputation as a 'short novel', their status as a quintessential Dostoevsky text, and because their author prefigures—or, in Bayardian terms, draws upon—so many twentieth- and twenty-first-century writers in his narrative). This makes me wonder if the idea of the Underground Man as the man of the majority has been somewhat artificially realized among our contemporaries, or—taking into account Bayard's concept of a mobile literary history[30]—if Dostoevsky in fact anticipates posterity in this particular text to a greater degree than anywhere else in his writings. Ironically, Dostoevsky occupies a far more significant literary-historical place (especially in Western scholarship) than Russia's national poet Aleksandr Pushkin, who was Dostoevsky's own ideal of what a writer should be. This is in part because of the difficulty of doing justice to poetry in translation, but mainly because of Dostoevsky's affinities with those late-twentieth and twenty-first-century writers who belong to the postmodern (and post-postmodern) period. As I have argued elsewhere, it is the very concept of the ugly (*bezobraznoe*), depicted so well in Dostoevsky's literary universe, that allows him to take his rightful place in the world of our contemporaries.[31] A literary tradition, in this case that of Dostoevsky (continuing the Gogolian line) and Petrushevskaia, leads us from the proto-modern, protean Dostoevsky to the omnivorous postmodern end of the twentieth century, with Petrushevskaia's dark realism. [32]

Bearing in mind the near-ubiquity of Dostoevsky's novella in post-nineteenth-century cultural discourse (literary and beyond), it would be perverse to discount the significance of influence in what Bayard would call the 'classical' direction. In discussing the status of *Tristan and Iseult* (12th Century) as an outlier in the Middle Ages with regard to its treatment of the themes of love and death, he contends that the authors of the legend must have been inspired by the Romantics. At the same time, Bayard concedes that they have 'exerted considerable influence upon a whole swathe of Western literature, including the Romantic writers':

> Thus it may be appropriate to admit that in certain cases there can occur *simultaneously* plagiarism and anticipatory plagiarism – or, if you like, *reciprocal plagiarism*. There is little doubt that the *Tristan* authors drew upon the Romantic imagination; but it is also likely that the latter were for their part equally inspired by *Tristan*, as if in some way, these authors, surmounting the barriers of time, had been influenced by each other.[33]

Discussing the anticipatory side of this special category of 'reciprocal plagiarism', Bayard focusses on the element of dissonance: 'But here again the feeling of dissonance—Kafka stands alone whilst Volodine is part of a generation marked by totalitarianism and genocides—incites us to see him [Kafka] as plagiarist rather than plagiarized.'[34] Indeed, dissonance seems to be the most important feature in Bayard's classification of the elements of anticipatory plagiarism. The Underground Man, too, is out of place in his historical epoch, contrary to Dostoevsky's provocative note about such men being typical of contemporary society.[35] Only after Hesse, French existentialism and Petrushevskaia's postmodern black realism in *Time: Night* (along with the magic realism/horror hybrid of her novel *Number One, or In The Gardens of Other Opportunities*), can we truly see the significance of this type for literature of the twentieth century and beyond.

Narrative Space in Petroevsky

In the chronotope of the metafiction of the Petroevskian world, the squalid dwelling of the Underground Man is borrowed from the *topos* of *Time: Night*. The deviations from linear *chronos* that we see in *Notes from Underground* appear even more pronounced in Petrushevskaia's *Time: Night*, with its own cyclical time where family history repeats itself through generations of (mainly) female characters.

A typical Petroevskian *topos* is found in the ugly interior of the brothel visited by the Underground Man, in its messiness and disorder. The description of the room where he sees Liza echoes his psychological landscape: 'In the narrow, cramped, low-ceilinged room, cluttered with a huge wardrobe and with cardboard boxes strewn about and all sorts of rags and clothing rubbish, it was almost completely dark.'[36] The space is claustrophobic and chaotic, with a low ceiling alluding to the low motives of the protagonist.[37]

Crime and Punishment offers more details of St Petersburg flats than *Notes from Underground*. This narrative space is just as distorted as in the shorter work: '...a large room, but very low... Sonia's room resembled a shed; it had the look of an irregular rectangle, and this made it seem deformed... monstrously obtuse.'[38] This description of Sonia's room (like Liza, she is a prostitute; her relationship with Raskolnikov resembles Liza's with the Underground Man) includes a striking number of corners and angles, acute and obtuse, ugly and irregular.[39] Like Raskol'nikov's own coffin-like room, Sonia's has a low ceiling; and though it is large, it is sparsely furnished and misshapen. Poverty is everywhere, and two different words for 'ugly' feature in the passage above: *urodlivyi* and *bezobrazno*. There are doors leading directly to another rented room, eliminating any feeling of privacy. Sonia's room is like the marketplace on Sennaia Square, a place of chaos and *bezobrazie*.

Women, including characters like Sonia, make up the majority of the protagonists in Liudmila Petrushevskaia's texts, which mainly deal with specifically female problems and thus fit Monika Katz's definition of 'women's literature'.[40] In the nineteenth century, the image of the strong woman (Turgenev's heroines, for example) was created as a complement to that of the superfluous man, self-focused and looking for his place in society. In Petroevsky's prose, in the particular case of Liza and the Underground Man (a sub-type of the superfluous man), the paragon of a strong woman proves to be a prostitute—traditionally a weak and degraded member of society. However, despite filling the lowest social role imaginable, she proves to have more common sense and compassion than the Underground Man.

Russian literature of the Soviet period depicted women as superheroes, or, indeed, supermen. The true Soviet woman, such as Baranskaia's heroine in the story 'A Week Like Any Other' ('Nedelia kak nedelia', 1969) mentioned above, has to be productive for society both in the private and public sphere, that is, she bears a double burden of responsibility.[41] In post-Soviet literature, the 'strong woman' motif still exists, although it is treated differently. In Petroevsky's prose public life is given little emphasis; the daily life of the female characters is emphasized. Petroevsky's heroines have to struggle to survive, overcoming numerous obstacles in order to feed their children: 'Everything was hanging in the air like a sword, all our life, ready to crash [...]. Are there powers in the world that can stop a woman who has to feed a child?'[42] For these women, life is a battlefield: 'No, you can't move in here, again faces distorted with hatred, seen in our mirror in the hall; we always have rows in the hall, the bridgehead of military actions.'[43] And it is not clear who is winning the battle with the 'loved ones'. In this permanent struggle, family members cannot help but be affected by their dehumanized environment. They lose their capacity for compassion and consideration; violation of human dignity becomes normal for them. In Petroevsky's depiction of the human face, natural features appear beautiful and artificial ones ugly; Liza's artificial smile in the *Notes* is a distorted, ugly facial expression provoked by the Underground Man, whose own face is repulsive and distorted: 'My disturbed face seemed to me repulsive in the extreme: pale, malicious, vile, with unkempt hair. "Let it be, I'm glad of it," I thought, "I'm glad precisely that I'll seem repulsive to her; that pleases me..."'[44]

Space in *Time: Night* is restricted to a two-room flat, which for the members of this family is an object of residential claims. This flat cannot house eight people (including a mentally-ill elderly woman, a disabled alcoholic with a criminal past, two small children and a newborn). The adults in the group fight for shelter. Anna Andrianovna is unable to make the people closest to her secure; she loses everybody in the end.[45] In Bayard's reverse chronology, her ugly and distorted dreams inspire those of the Underground Man. Both characters exaggerate the effect which they think they have on people around them. Both have a high opinion of themselves and are ugly in the celebration of their righteousness: the Underground Man in his speech to the prostitute Liza, and Anna Andrianovna in her real or imaginary conversations with her children—particularly her daughter Alena, who inherits some of the underground features. Alena is consistently described as being in a pit; both her psychological state and real-life accommodation belong to the underground: 'From what terrible dungeons (*podzemelii*) has she surfaced if a room of eighteen square metres for four people seems a refuge to her!'[46]

Petroevsky obliquely addresses the utopian notion of the Crystal Palace in most of his fictional works, through depictions of his characters' Petersburg dwellings. Morson calls *Notes from Underground* and *The Possessed* (*Besy*, 1872) 'two of the most influential *anti-utopias* in European literature.'[47] The dwellings in Petroevsky's texts are the exact opposite of the Crystal Palace in the architectural sense: windows in the cramped rooms of the Petroevskian world are small and the walls are misshapen; galleries (mentioned, for example, in *Crime and Punishment*) are narrow, dark, labyrinthine passages. Consider the following extract from this novel:

> Having found the entrance onto the narrow and dark staircase in the corner of the courtyard, he ascended, finally, to the second storey and came out into a gallery, framing the storey from the side of the yard. For the moment he was wandering in darkness and confusion...[48]

Woll writes that 'all of Petrushevskaia's characters inhabit spaces that steadily shrink'. In this connection, she draws a parallel between Petrushevskaia's texts and 'Dostoevsky's abrasive Underground Man, trapped in his miserable cellar flat, and Raskol'nikov, entombed in his coffinlike room in the Petersburg slums'. As she also notes, twentieth-century Russian writers, in depicting urban dwellings, reflect the actual material constraints of their time. Cramped Soviet flats are a reality of Russia of the twentieth century and beyond, yet they 'resonate within the Russian [nineteenth-century] literary tradition'.[49] The way space is portrayed in *Notes from Underground* and *Time: Night* clearly marks these texts as belonging to the same two authors, fused into one as Petroevsky.

Petroevsky's Poetics of Time

Morson has discussed the structure of Dostoevsky's 'generically problematic and formally anomalous works', writing that

> As Dostoevsky was well aware, his novels were likely to appear shapeless to most readers—'loose and baggy monsters'—as Henry James was to call them—and he therefore outlined a theory of realistic art to justify, and to aid in the development of, his aesthetic practice. Like the novels themselves, which have had such great influence on twentieth-century European literature, this theory seems remarkably modern [...] by the mid-1870s Dostoevsky had come to believe that social 'disintegration', 'fragmentation', and 'dissociation'[...] were, in all probability, literally apocalyptic in extent [...].[50]

Petroevsky also finds ways to write about ugly themes; their (I use this pronoun as a polyvalent hybrid of *his* and *her*) narratives reflect fragmented social situations. Fragmentation is related to the problem of memory: we write the way we remember things and we remember them differently every time, bringing the truth into question; and the chronotope of Petroevsky's narratives, in aiming to represent this truth mimetically, thus appears even more rhizomatic. In my previous work, I have argued that Dostoevsky's treatment of time belongs outside of his historical epoch, suggesting that he offers a *proto-modern* understanding of narrative time.[51] However, we can equally well argue that Dostoevsky offers a postmodern treatment of memory and time, as in the multiply-deviated narrative time we see in works such as *The Possessed*.[52] Time deviates in similar ways in *Time: Night*, when the narrator attempts to record her past.

In terms of narrative structure, Petroevsky's works often feature digressions, dialogic monologues, beginnings *in medias res*, editorial comments, and diaries. *Time: Night*, for example, features an apologue and at least three diaries. Its narrative structure is messy in a Petroevskian way: Alena's diary, one of its constituents, is an example of Petroevskian confessional-type *Ich-Erzählung*, woven into a quilted narrative consisting of the 'ten little sheets' of Alena's diary, the inclusions of Anna Andrianovna's comments on the diary contents, Anna Andrianovna's own textual shreds in verse and prose, the diary entries that she writes on behalf of her daughter, and her own distorted narrative of the story of *Time: Night*, dating from various points in time. The presence of Alena's diary, Alena's voice, and the comments of the editor make this novella fundamentally polyphonic. The text also contains short, apparently randomly inserted narratives unconnected to the story of Anna Andrianovna's family, such as a tale about a 'late abortion'. Structurally, such inclusions are found elsewhere in the works of Petroevsky, for example in their 'Winter Notes on Summer Impressions' ('Zimnie zametki o letnikh vpechatleniiakh', 1863): 'And by the way, can you possibly think that I am getting into Russian literature instead of writing about Paris? That I am writing a critical article? No, I am only doing this from having nothing better to do'.[53]

Alena finds Anna Andrianovna's diary after her death and mails it to a stranger, presumably an editor, lending her diary, titled 'Notes on the Edge of the Table' ('*Zapiski na kraiu stola*'), a found-manuscript provenance analogous to that of Gorianchikov's notes in Petroevsky's *Notes from the House of the Dead* (*Zapiski iz mertvogo doma*), written by the Dostoevsky part of Petroevsky in 1862. The title of the diary in *Time: Night* thus recalls many other editions of *Notes* written by Petroevsky. There are also parallels between the 'editor' present in the text of *Notes from Underground* and in *Time: Night*. Both texts include a forced interruption of the narrative, which is caused by the death of the author in both *Time: Night* and *Notes from the House of the Dead*, as well as by the decision of the 'editor' in *Notes from Underground* to break off the narrative at an arbitrary point. *Time: Night* also has an introductory editorial comment by way of an epigraph, a typically Petroevskian feature from which the reader learns that the diary was written on disparate sheets of paper, school notebooks, even telegram forms, a combination that makes this physically multi-layered narrative remarkably postmodern.

To differentiate among postmodernism, post-postmodernism, proto-modernism, and various other '-isms' is only useful or, indeed, viable within the wider context provided by all of them taken together, and by the web of literary theory. As a point of literary exercise in the spirit of Oulipo, it may be even more productive to modify the context in order to see how the technical features of the '-isms' work in different epochs, in order to find out more about them and the eras with which they are conventionally associated. Romanticism, for example, appears to be a point of both arrival and departure for Dostoevsky; and the influence of European Romanticism, as well as that of Nikolai Gogol's native combination of Romanticism and Realism, are among the reasons for Donald Fanger's classification of Dostoevsky as a 'Romantic Realist'.[54]

Ugliness and Dialogicity in Petroevsky

In his post-exile *Notes from Underground*, Petroevsky has his protagonist condemn dreams as Romantic and repulsive. The Underground Man attacks Schillerian Romanticism, and labels mirages and fantasies (both typical of Romanticism) as repulsive and ugly. Criticism and ridicule of Schillerian Romanticism is expressed already in the *Insulted and Injured* (*Unizhennye i oskorblennye*, 1861), and continues in *Notes from Underground*, where it combines with the Underground Man's disorderly thoughts of revenge against his successful former classmate Zverkov and the rest of humanity:

> They won't go begging on their knees for my friendship. That's a mirage, a banal mirage, revolting, romantic and fantastic—just the same ball at Lake Como. And that's why I must give Zverkov a slap in the face![55]

This adds to the Underground Man's negative characteristics: the "dreamer" side of his character becomes part of his ugly nature—a significant change in the evolution of the dreamer-type protagonist. Sentimentality, which is in general a synonym for Schillerian Romanticism in *Notes from Underground*, is referred to as ugliness (*poganost'*): '...damned romanticism ...Oh the nastiness, oh the stupidity, oh, the narrowness of all these "ugly [*poganykh*] sentimental souls"!'[56] The '*poshlyi mirazh*' ('banal/low mirage') of the Underground Man links the realm of fantasy with the low and vulgar.

Petroevsky parodies Romanticism in *Notes from Underground* in an anticipation of postmodern irony which plays with Romantic ideas as it does with all the rest. By the end of the twentieth century, literature strives for fragmentation rather than congruency, a tendency that the Dostoevsky element in the Petroevsky polyvalent personality plagiarizes from the Petrushevskaia one, as he does the emphasis on multi-layered narratives. Dostoevskian 'loose and baggy monsters' become the artistic norm; fragments become whole works.

The 1894 edition (but not the later, Russian Academy of Sciences edition of the *Complete Works* of Dostoevsky which I cite in this chapter) erroneously claims that *Notes from Underground* first came out in the journal *Time* (*Vremia*) in 1846 (I, II, IV), that is, at the height of Russian literary Romanticism and eighteen years earlier than its actual publication date.[57] Had this been true, it would have provided grounds for a different reading in itself, since its use of Romantic discourse could then have been read non-ironically.

Speaking of discourse, the language of Petroevsky's *Notes* is more colloquial than modern readers often realize, with vocabulary such as '*ni shisha*' ('zilch'), '*nagadil*' ('messed up') and so on.[58] In the early Petroevsky novel *Poor Folk*, the protagonist Makar Devushkin anticipates the Underground Man's diminutives. These often occur in unexpected contexts: for example, when the Underground Man explains that he is not, in fact, an angry man (and 'not even embittered'), claiming that a mere child's toy or a warming drink would suffice to distract him from his rage: 'I might be foaming at the mouth; but bring me some sort of dolly ('*kukolku*') or give me a little tea with a bit of sugar ('*chaiku s sakhartsem*') and I'll most likely calm down'. He goes on to assert that he would be almost religiously affected ('*dushoi umilius''*').[59] Then, however, he admits: 'I'll probably gnash my teeth at myself and suffer insomnia from the shame for months thereafter. That's how I am'.[60]

Based on the narrative of the *Notes*, the experience of this gnashing of teeth typically occurs at night, which may well be when the Underground Man is telling us his stories. This is when he is embarrassed by his philosophizing and his admission of personal vulnerabilities, his confession of sorts, especially with regard to Liza. The emphasis on night as the time of writing, confession, and helpless teeth grinding is clearly filched from *Time: Night*, where the articulation of temporality is stronger than that of *topos*, in accordance with Bakhtin's classic formulation of the more significant role of *chronos* in chronotope.[61] The Dostoevsky personality in Petroevsky also plagiarizes the *skaz* features of *Time: Night* which include colloquialisms and diminutives, for example, 'vazochki, statuetki, flakonchiki' [little vases, statuettes, small bottles].[62]

In the Petroevsky hybrid, Dostoevsky's discredited narrator who claims to be smart is borrowed from Petrushevskaia's 'Our Crowd', a story whose narrator-protagonist is similar to Anna Andrianovna of *Time: Night*. 'I'm a very clever woman', she states.[63] The Underground Man identifies the paradox of 'double temporality'[64] in claiming that he himself could not have become anything on account of his being clever, as dictated by *his time*:

> Now I'm living out my life in my corner, teasing myself with the malicious and useless consolation that a clever person cannot seriously make anything of himself; it's only a fool who can do this. Yes, a person of the nineteenth century should and is morally obliged to be a creature substantially without character...[65]

Petroevsky's Anna Andrianovna emphasizes her superior intellect in her notes as well; for example, when remarking on how a famous line from the children's poet Agniia Barto is not recognized by other characters.[66]

Another instance of the Underground Man's claim to superior intellectual capacity occurs in the following passage of the *Notes*: 'I am, in the first place, to blame because I am smarter than all those surrounding me. (I've constantly considered myself smarter than all those surrounding me, and, would you believe it, sometimes I've been ashamed of it...)'. This is followed by yet another connection between past, present, and future, when Dostoevsky purloins the Faustian notion of the 'person made in a retort' ('*retortnyi chelovek*'), harking both backward to Goethe and forward to the clones of the twenty-first century.[67]

An entirely new area of anticipated posterity opens up if we consider the twentieth-century political overtones of 'podpol'shchik' (a member of a political resistance group; this word is a cognate of 'podpol'e' (underground)), a word that Iurii Kudriavtsev uses in his study of *Notes from Underground* (the title of which is more accurately rendered in French, for example, as *Les Carnets du sous-sol*).[68] The meaning of political resistance, often through non-resistance, by an intellectual in the English translation—and in the Russian study by Kudriavtsev—recalls the anticipatory posterity of political concepts, as when Kafka is revealed by Bayard to have borrowed from the future of ideas concerning the two totalitarian states of the mid-twentieth century.

Conclusion

The narratives in *Notes from Underground* and *Time: Night* are neither linear nor chronological, and their rhizomatic atemporality contributes to our perception of them as simultaneously similar and postmodern. Thinking along the lines of Bayard's reader-response-based theory of anticipatory plagiarism, we discover three main connections between Dostoevsky's *Notes* and Petrushevskaia's *Time: Night* (and also her novella 'Our Crowd'). These include: the type of the hero/anti-hero (the main point of anticipatory/reciprocal plagiarism here); the poetics, especially the rhizomatic chronotope of the novella (*povest'*), of notes as novella; and the element of dialogicity. The complex of plagiarism here is thus threefold. The innovative quality of Dostoevsky's *Notes* means that since he has already availed himself of the favoured tricks of the postmodern trade he is posterior to it, in the same way that Sterne is posterior to Joyce or Woolf, according to Bayard.[69] In this chronology of literary interconnections, 'the after may be situated *before* the before', which is logical, if anti-Hegelian.[70] Dostoevsky after postmodernism, and especially after Petrushevskaia, is a different Dostoevsky, whether Petrushevskaia is regarded as a true postmodern writer or not. In the new mobile literary history which will focus on the future as well as the past, I would place Dostoevsky in the late-twentieth century; he was born in the nineteenth century, but his Other Self (in Proustian terms) clearly does not belong there. If we follow the traditional linear literary-historical path and explore the closeness of the two texts in question through the prism of literary influence, then the question of why this influence occurs in a particular epoch (in our case—the late-twentieth through twenty-first centuries) remains unanswered. If we approach these texts from the viewpoint of 'posterity by anticipation', then this question is moot, as it then becomes rather 'why was Dostoevsky born in the nineteenth century where he does not belong?' There is also a certain local-only significance, a particular temporal provincialism, if the emphasis is placed on the study of Dostoevsky as a solely nineteenth-century writer. My preference is therefore for a rhizomatic literary history with an ever-changing chronology. Bayard's 'heart of a double temporality'[71] within the oeuvre of each author also comes close to the principle behind the Czech Canadian literary theorist Lubomír Doležel's idea of fictional worlds.[72] As the latter writes, 'A radical alternative to mimesis will be a fictional semantics defined within a multiple-world model frame,'[73] which offers us a blueprint for how multiple fictional worlds and their creators might intersect. Doležel's idea could explain both the appearance of the Petroevsky hybrid within the space of intersecting fictional worlds of Dostoevsky and Petrushevskaia, and Bayard's point about reciprocal plagiarism. This type of plagiarism promises to help us read differently, from the perspective of the future, and to find this future-in-the-past in texts of profound originality. For Dostoevsky and Petrushevskaia, these texts coexist in an imaginary space of *time-night*, an example of the variety of 'curvatures of time' which appear if we are willing to read in 'the other direction'.[74]

With this notion of reading backwards, Bayard offers a fresh, anti-Hegelian approach to literary history (and a relevant one, since literary trends overlap and inform one another significantly). A dual chronology for the writer's persona—his Other Self—may apply when s/he does not fit the contemporary canon and needs to be counted elsewhere, as in the case of Sophocles, Stern, Kafka—and Dostoevsky. Instead of focussing either on what is often called the 'prophetic' vision of Dostoevsky in current scholarship from his native land, or on what Nikolai Mikhailovsky famously called his 'cruel talent',[75] I have attempted to outline a new epistemological approach that, in view of the technical aspects of his work, treats Dostoevsky's *Notes* as part of a literary framework belonging to the future.

Of particular interest in the Russian literature that is to be written in this future is the issue of gender. Discussing the German-language literature of Kafka's era, Bayard asserts that the paucity of contemporary women writers whose influence could account for the 'feminine element' in the works of the author of *The Castle* tempts us to search for traces of such influence 'in the future'.[76] This provokes us to consider the analogous situation of Dostoevsky's Russian nineteenth century. Bayard's analysis of Kafka's treatment of 'feminine subjugation' recalls the rejection of the masculine Bykov type—the man of action—in Dostoevsky's texts, as well as his handling of the prostitute type, of which Liza in the *Notes from Underground* is a significant example. Originating in Dostoevsky's *Poor Folk*, the Bykov type reappears in *Notes from Underground*: 'Such a gentleman simply pushes his way forward to his goal like an enraged bull, horns lowered, perhaps with only a wall to stop him'.[77] To evoke the black hole effect, we could predict more changes in the realm of gender or gender-specific writing, and suppose that the more significant future fields of influence for anticipatory plagiarism will be gender studies and pedagogy.[78]

This theoretical framework, although achronological from the traditional linear point of view, is fruitful for teaching as well as for reconfiguring the literary-theoretical system of links amongst authors so as to arrive at a new understanding of classic texts. The principle of anticipatory plagiarism is based on the hermeneutic or epistemological differences between a history based on events and literary history (or the history of art more generally); and the theory offered by Bayard suggests that chronology is not adequate for an analytical approach to the literary text—only for a historical-philological one. It is a brave attempt to predict the literature that is yet to come by shifting the gears of chronology into reverse. Reciprocal plagiarism rather than influence implies a conversation, an exchange, a multi-directional dialogue amongst authors and their texts; and in the case of Petroevsky (or Dostoshevskaia), we may anticipate more texts in their style by women writers, or texts in which notions of gender are more fluid, in the future Russian prose. Bayard's idea of anticipatory plagiarism may be paradoxical, but as the paradoxalist narrator from *Notes from Underground* insists, 'two times two equals five can be a most lovely little thing'.[79]

Notes

1 Pierre Bayard, *Le Plagiat par anticipation* (Paris: Les Éditions de Minuit, 2009), p. 22. I would like to thank Muireann Maguire and Timothy Langen for their patient and thoughtful reading of numerous drafts of this chapter, and for giving me the possibility of bouncing my most extravagant ideas off them. I would also like to thank my generous anonymous reviewers for their kind words and suggestions, and assure readers that any remaining faults in this text are but my own. I am also grateful to my Russian novel students at Queen Mary University of London, who were a part of an experiment involving the idea of hybrid authorship, to Muireann Maguire for her initial introduction to the fascinating world of Pierre Bayard, and to Rolf Hellebust for continuous intellectual support and firm belief in the success of this text.

2 On Cubo-Futurists, see A. Kruchenykh and others, *Slovo kak takovoe* (Moscow: [n. pub], 1913).

3 On Transfurists, see I. Tigountsova, 'Handmade Books and Visual Poems of Sergei Sigei—a Russian Transfurist', *Canadian-American Slavic Studies*, 36:4 (Winter 2002), 471–83, https://doi.org/10.1163/221023902X00072.

4 The Dostoevsky citation is from F. M. Dostoevskii, *Polnoe sobranie sochinenii v tridtsati tomakh*, ed. by V. G. Bazanov and others, 30 vols (Leningrad: Nauka, 1972–90), XXVII: *Dnevnik pisatel'ia* (1984), p. 65. All translations are mine unless otherwise noted.

5 See, for example, Sally Laird's 1994 translation of Liudmila Petrushevskaya's *Vremia noch'* as *The Time: Night* (Evanston, IL: Northwestern University Press, 2000).

6 I thank one of this volume's anonymous readers for this suggestion.

7 Bayard, *Le Plagiat*, p. 154. I am grateful to Rolf Hellebust for assisting with my translations from French.

8 Gary Saul Morson, *The Boundaries of Genre: Dostoevsky's* Diary of a Writer *and the Traditions of Literary Utopia* (Evanston, IL: Northwestern University Press, 1981), p. xi.

9 Bayard, *Le Plagiat*, p. 118. Mikhail Bakhtin's essay 'Formy vremeni i khronotopa v romane: Ocherki po istoricheskoi poetike', in M. Bakhtin, *Voprosy literatury i estetiki: Issledovaniia raznykh let* (Moscow: Khudozhestvennaia literatura, 1975), pp. 234–407 (p. 256). Although originally a botanical term that refers to a type of a root that sprouts shoots in any direction and at any point along its line, this became a notion

explored by post-structuralist literary theory and criticism, starting with G. Deleuze and F. Guattari's *On the Line*, trans. by John Johnston (Cambridge, MA: MIT Press, 1983). It was re-worked as *A Thousand Plateaus*, to which I refer immediately below.

10 G. Deleuze and F. Guattari, *A Thousand Plateaus* in *Literary Theory: An Anthology*, ed. by Julie Rivkin and Michael Ryan (Maldon; Oxford; Carlton: Blackwell, 2004), pp. 278–86 (p. 378).

11 '...ne sauraient être fixes dans la mesure où toute nouvelle œuvre—et, plus encore, toute œuvre d'importance—déplace l'ensemble de la chronologie constituée et fait apparaître sous un nouveau jour le panorama littéraire existant.' Bayard, *Le Plagiat*, p. 118.

12 Stephen Hawking, *A Brief History of Time: From the Big Bang to Black Holes* (London: Bantam Books, 2011), pp. 165–66.

13 T. S. Eliot, 'Tradition and the Individual Talent', in *The Sacred Wood and Major Early Essays* (Mineola, NY: Dover Publications, 1998), pp. 27–33 (p. 28).

14 'Quand cette notion de plagiat par anticipation sera admise, il est vraisemblable que l'ensemble de notre conception de l'histoire littéraire—telle qu'elle est enseignée dans les établissements scolaires ou les universités et présentée dans les manuels—devra être modifiée.' Bayard, *Le Plagiat*, p. 105.

15 Pierre Bayard, *L'Énigme Tolstoïevski* (Paris: Les Éditions de Minuit, 2017), pp. 13–16.

16 Consider digital art experiments that take text beyond the book, in database, data visualization, and mapping projects, as discussed for example in Christiane Paul, *Digital Art* (London: Thames and Hudson, 2003), pp. 174–96.

17 Bayard, *Tolstoïevski*.

18 The exact origins of the Tolstoievskii witticism are hard to pinpoint, but it was used as a pseudonym by Ilf' and Petrov in the late 1920s, and was also mentioned by Kornei Chukovskii, Abram Terz, and Vladimir Nabokov. I. F. Masanov, *Slovar' psevdonimov russkikh pisatelei, uchenykh i obshchestvennykh deiatelei*, 4 vols (Moscow: Vsesoiuznaia knizhnaia palata, 1958), III, p. 170. See also Liudmila Saraskina, '"Pri diktature proletariata satira opolchaetsia..." F. Tolstoevskii protiv Dostoevskogo na territorii Il'fa i Petrova', in *Dostoevskii v sozvuchiiakh i pritiazheniiakh (ot Pushkina do Solzhenitsyna)* (Moscow: Russkii put', 2006), pp. 483–509.

19 Eric Naiman, 'What If Nabokov Had Written "Dvoinik"? Reading Literature Preposterously', *The Russian Review*, 64:4 (October 2005), 575–89, https://doi.org/10.1111/j.1467-9434.2005.00375.x.

20 '...Tolstoïevski est multiple parce qu'il est composé de plusieurs personnalités qui ne communiquent pas nécessairement entre elles et dont la réunion conflictuelle constitue sa personne.' Bayard, *Tolstoïevski*, p. 87.

21 Ibid.

22 *Zagadka Tolstoevskogo*, trans. by Elena Morozova (Moscow: Tekst, 2019), p. 106.

23 M. Bakhtin, *Problemy poetiki Dostoevskogo* (Moscow: Sovetskii pisatel', 1963), pp. 355–57. For an English translation see Mikhail Bakhtin, *Problems of Dostoevsky's Poetics*, ed. and trans. by Caryl Emerson (Minneapolis, MN; London: University of Minnesota Press, 1984), especially pp. 263–65.

24 F. M. Dostoevskii, *Zapiski iz podpol'ia*, p. 99. On the *literary type* in general, as a social model worthy of imitation and as a key concept in the nineteenth-century European (and Soviet) realist novel, see Rene Wellek, *Concepts of Criticism*, ed. Stephen G. Nichols, Jr. (New Haven, CT: Yale University Press, 1963), pp. 242–46. On the specifically Russian variants of the *superfluous* and *little man*, see Andrew Kahn, et al., *A History of Russian Literature* (Oxford: Oxford University Press, 2018), pp. 461–66 and 471–72, https://doi.org/10.1093/oso/9780199663941.001.0001.

25 Helena Goscilo, *Liudmila Petrushevskaia*, in *Dictionary of Literary Biography: Russian Writers Since 1980*, CCLXXXV, ed. by Marina Balina and Mark Lipovetsky (Detroit: Gale, 2003), pp. 220–29 (p. 221).

26 Bayard, *Le Plagiat*, p. 136.

27 '...takie litsa, kak sochinitel' takikh zapisok, ne tol'ko mogut, no dazhe dolzhny sushchestvovat' v nashem obshchestve...' (F. M. Dostoevskii, *Zapiski iz podpol'ia*, in *Polnoe sobranie sochinenii v tridtsati tomakh*, 30 vols (Leningrad: Nauka, 1972–90), V (1973), p. 99.)

28 N. V. Baranskaia, *Nedelia kak nedelia* (*A Week Like Any Other*) (London: Bristol Classical Press, 1993).

29 For more on the Underground Man's 'word with a loophole', see Mikhail Bakhtin, *Problems of Dostoevsky's Poetics*, ed. and trans. by Caryl Emerson (Minneapolis, MN; London: University of Minnesota Press, 1984), pp. 232–35; M. Bakhtin, *Problemy poetiki Dostoevskogo* (Moscow: Sovetskii pisatel', 1963), pp. 312–16. Here is Bakhtin's explanation of the loophole (p.

313): 'Lazeika – eto ostavlenie za soboi vozmozhnosti izmenit' poslednii, okonchatel'nyi smysl svoego slova...Po svoemu smyslu slovo s lazeikoi dolzhno byt' poslednim slovom i vydaet sebia za takoe, no na samom dele ono iavliaetsia lish' predposlednim slovom i stavit posle sebia lish' uslovnuiu, ne okonchatel'nuiu tochku.' Or as Caryl Emerson translates (p. 233): 'A loophole is the retention for oneself of the possibility for altering the ultimate, final meaning of one's own words... Judged by its meaning alone, the word with a loophole should be an ultimate word and does present itself as such, but in fact it is only the penultimate word and places after itself only a conditional, not a final, period.'

30 '...histoire littéraire mobile', Bayard, *Le Plagiat*, p. 113. Also translated as 'mobile literary history' by Jeffrey Mehlman in his 'Anticipatory Plagiarism: Pierre Bayard: For an Autonomous Literary History', *New Literary History*, 44:2 (Spring 2013), 231–50, https://doi.org/10.1353/nlh.2013.0019.

31 Inna Tigountsova, *The Ugly in Russian Literature: Dostoevsky's Influence on Iurii Mamleev, Liudmila Petrushevskaia, and Tatiana Tolstaia* (Saarbrücken: Lambert Academic Publishing, 2010).

32 Ibid.

33 "Ainsi convient-il d'admettre qu'il puisse, dans certains cas, y avoir à la fois plagiat et plagiat par anticipation, ou, si l'on préfère, plagiat réciproque. Il ne fait guère de doute que les auteurs de Tristan ont puisé dans l'imaginaire des Romantiques, mais il est vraisemblable que ceux-ci, en retour, se sont également inspirés de Tristan, comme si, d'une certaine manière, ces auteurs, surmontant les barrières du temps, s'étaient influencés les uns les autres." Bayard, *Le Plagiat*, pp. 53–54. [Italics in the original].

34 Ibid., p. 137. [Volodine is a contemporary Russian-French novelist — I. T.]

35 F. M. Dostoevskii, *Zapiski iz podpol'ia*, in *Polnoe sobranie sochinenii v tridtsati tomakh*, 30 vols (Leningrad: Nauka, 1972–90), V, p. 99.

36 Ibid., p. 152.

37 The Russian expression *nizmennye pobuzhdeniia* ('vile or base motives') is almost a cliché.

38 '...bol'shaia komnata, no chrezvychaino nizkaia... Sonina komnata pokhodila kak budto na sarai, imela vid ves'ma nepravil'nogo chetyrekhugol'nika, i eto pridavalo ei chto-to urodlivoe... uzhe slishkom bezobrazno tupoi'. F. M. Dostoevskii, *Prestuplenie i nakazanie*, in *Polnoe sobranie sochinenii v tridtsati tomakh*, 30 vols (Leningrad: Nauka, 1972–90), VI (1973), pp. 241–42.

39 Ibid.

40 Monika Katz, 'The Other Woman: Character Portrayal and the Narrative Voice in the Short Stories of Liudmila Petrushevskaia', in *Women and Russian Culture: Projections and Self-Perceptions*, ed. by Rosalind Marsh (Oxford: Berghahn, 1998), pp. 188–97 (p. 189).

41 See N. V. Baranskaia, *Nedelia kak nedelia*.

42 L. S. Petrushevskaia, *Vremia noch'*, in *Sobranie sochinenii v piati tomakh*, 5 vols (Moscow: TKO ACT, 1996), I, pp. 311–98 (pp. 340, 369). (In my translation of Petrushevskaia, I have retained her language irregularities where possible; however, some sacrifices have had to be made to preserve comprehensibility — I. T.)

43 Ibid., p. 366.

44 Dostoevskii, *Zapiski iz podpol'ia*, p. 151.

45 L. Petrushevskaia, *Vremia noch'*, https://libking.ru/books/prose-/prose-contemporary/42569-26-lyudmila-petrushevskaya-vremya-noch.html#book [accessed 27 May 2020].

46 Ibid., p. 385.

47 Morson, *Boundaries of Genre*, pp. 36–37. [Emphasis mine. — I. T.]

48 'Otyskav v uglu na dvore vkhod na uzkuiu i temnuiu lestnitsu, on podnialsia, nakonets, vo vtoroi etazh i vyshel na galereiu, obkhodivshuiu ego so storony dvora. Pokamest on brodil v temnote i nedoumenii...' (Dostoevskii, *Prestuplenie i nakazanie*, p. 241.) For more dark and confused spaces, see p. 188.

49 Josephine Woll, 'The Minotaur in the Maze: Remarks on Liudmila Petrushevskaia', *World Literature Today*, 67 (Winter 1993), pp. 125–30 (p. 125), https://doi.org/10.2307/40148873.

50 Morson, *Boundaries of Genre*, p. 8.

51 Inna Tigountsova, *The Ugly*, p. 154.

52 Arkadii Klioutchanskii, 'On the Chronology of *Besy*', paper delivered at the annual meeting of the Canadian Association of Slavists (5 May, 2001).

53 F. M. Dostoevskii, 'Zimnie zametki o letnikh vpechatleniakh', in *Polnoe sobranie sochinenii v tridtsati tomakh*, 30 vols (Leningrad: Nauka, 1972–90), V (1973), pp. 46–98 (p. 51).

54 Donald Fanger, *Dostoevsky and Romantic Realism: A Study of Dostoevsky in Relation to Balzac, Dickens, and Gogol'* (Cambridge MA: Harvard University Press, 1965), p. 101.

55 'Na koleniakh umoliat' o moei druzhbe—oni ne stanut. Eto mirazh, poshlyi mirazh, otvratitel'nyi, romanticheskii i fantasticheskii; tot zhe bal na ozere Komo. I potomu ia dolzhen dat' Zverkovu poshchechiny!' (Dostoevskii, *Zapiski iz podpol'ia*, p. 149.)

56 Ibid., p. 166. Note that an archaic meaning of '*poganyi*' is 'pagan', 'foreign', or 'non-Christian.' '*Poganyi*' in the sense of 'pagan' fits into Berdiaev's explanation of the changes in Dostoevsky's view—from humanistic to religious. (See Nikolai Berdiaev, *Mirosozertsanie Dostoevskogo* (Prague: YMCA, 1923), p. 20.) The word '*nemets*' ('German,' or, in an archaic sense, a 'foreigner' or 'pagan') is also frequently used in criticism of Schillerian idealism in *Notes from Underground*. (Cf. Nikolai Gogol''s 'Night before Christmas', in which the devil is called '*nemets*'.)

57 F. M. Dostoevskii, *Polnoe sobranie sochinenii* (St Petersburg: A. F. Marks, 1894–1895). Further bibliographic information is unavailable due to libraries' closure during the Covid-19 pandemic. *Notes from Underground* first appeared in *Epokha* in 1864.

58 From a close reading of the 1894 and 1972–1987 editions of Dostoevsky's *Sobraniie sochinenii* (*Complete Works*), the colloquial features of the *skaz* style seem more evident in the older orthography, which visually emphasizes it.

59 Dostoevskii, *Zapiski iz podpol'ia*, p. 100.

60 Ibid.

61 Bakhtin, 'Formy vremeni i khronotopa v romane: ocherki po istoricheskoi poetike', in *Voprosy literatury i estetiki: issledovaniia raznykh let* (Moscow: Khudozhestvennaia literatura, 1975), pp. 234–407 (p. 239).

62 L. Petrushevskaia, *Vremia noch'*, https://libking.ru/books/prose-/prose-contemporary/42569-lyudmila-petrushevskaya-vremya-noch.html [accessed 27 Apr. 2020]

63 '"Ia chelovek zhestkii, zhestokii, vsegda s ulybkoi na polnykh, rumianykh gubakh, vsegda ko vsem s nasmeshkoi... Ne dlia moego, koroche govoria, ponimaniia, a ia ochen' umnaia. To, chto ne ponimaiu, togo ne sushchestvuet voobshche."' ('"I am a coarse person, a cruel person, always with a smile on my full, rosy lips, always with a snigger at all of them... In short, not for my understanding, and I am very smart. What I do not understand does not exist at all."') L. Petrushevskaia, 'Svoi krug',

in *Kolybel'naia ptich'ei rodiny* (St Petersburg: Amfora, 2008), pp. 84–118 (p. 84).

64 Bayard, *Le Plagiat*, p. 136.

65 'Teper' zhe dozhivaiu v svoem uglu, draznia sebia zlobnym i ni k chemu ne sluzhashchim utesheniem, chto umnyi chelovek i ne mozhet ser'ezno chem-nibud' sdelat'sia, a delaetsia chem-nibud' tol'ko durak. Da-s, chelovek deviatnadtsatogo stoletiia dolzhen i nravstvenno obiazan byt' sushchestvom preimushchestvenno bezkharakternym...' Dostoevskii, *Zapiski iz podpol'ia*, p. 100.

66 Petrushevskaia, *Vremia noch'*, p. 315.

67 Dostoevskii, *Zapiski iz podpol'ia*, p. 103–04.

68 Iu. G. Kudriavtsev, *Tri kruga Dostoevskogo* (Moscow: Izdatel'stvo Moskovskogo universiteta, 1979), p. 230.

69 Bayard, *Le Plagiat*, p. 120.

70 Ibid., p. 109. [Italics in the original].

71 Ibid., p. 136.

72 See Lubomír Doležel, *Heterocosmica: Fiction and Possible Worlds* (Baltimore, MD: Johns Hopkins University Press, 1998).

73 Lubomír Doležel, 'Mimesis and Possible Worlds', *Poetics Today*, 9:3 (1988), 475–96 (p. 481).

74 Ibid., p. 147.

75 N. K. Mikhailovskii, 'Zhestokii talant', http://az.lib.ru/m/mihajlowskij_n_k/text_0042.shtml [accessed 27 May 2020].

76 Bayard, *Le Plagiat*, p. 139.

77 Dostoevskii, *Zapiski iz podpol'ia*, p. 103.

78 I refer to Stephen Hawking's discussion of the inference from radiation analysis that black holes must exist. See Hawking, *A Brief History of Time* (pp. 91–112).

79 Dostoevskii, *Zapiski iz podpol'ia*, p. 119.

III. TOLSTOY

6. Master and Manxman: Reciprocal Plagiarism in Tolstoy and Hall Caine[1]

Muireann Maguire

In the winter of 1906, a reception was held in a Westminster flat for Mr and Mrs Maksim Gor'kii on their return from an exhausting and scandalous American tour (the title of "Mrs" was tactfully bestowed on Gor'kii's mistress Maria Andreeva, whose presence had triggered the American scandal). Gor'kii had personally requested each guest; collectively, they represented a 'galaxy of genius', according to journalist Robert Ross.[2] They included H. G. Wells, Bernard Shaw, Henry James, Thomas Hardy, the historical novelist Maurice Hewlett, the radical journalist Henry Nevinson, and A. W. Clarke, whose *Jaspar Tristram* (1899) was a fictionalized memoir of English boarding-school life. Ross himself was present as the editor of his friend Oscar Wilde's *De Profundis* (1905), which would appear in Russian translation in 1909. Every guest was promised fifteen minutes' audience with Gor'kii, described as 'an astonishing shaggy figure in a blue sweater, who seemed a cross between a penwiper and an Eskimo';[3] however, as Bernard Shaw monopolized the great man for a full two hours, it was not until four in the morning that Gor'kii and Andreeva ultimately departed. As their host walked Gor'kii to his cab, the other guests lingered anxiously to hear his verdict on the evening.

> We waited like boys waiting to hear the result of a scholarship examination; it was an awe-inspiring moment. Each man felt that no common evening had closed. 'Gorky wants me to tell you that he has

 https://doi.org/10.11647/OBP.0241.06

> spent an evening he will never forget; that to-night he met almost everyone he admired in England; everyone he wanted to meet.' There was a murmur of gratuitous deprecation. 'There are only *two other* writers he wanted to see,' our host went on. The coats and mufflers were adjusted; there was an awkward pause. I knew what was coming; but we pressed him to be more explicit. 'The only others Gorky hoped to have seen here… were Hall Caine and Marie Corelli!!'[4]

An alternative version of this party describes Gor'kii 'search[ing] the room in vain for a looked-for face. At last, he could keep these feelings to himself no longer. "But the Great Man," he asked, "is he not here? Is he not coming?" ... He could see no sign of Hall Caine.'[5]

Both these writers, whom Gor'kii was so disappointed to miss, have now disappeared into a possibly deserved obscurity. Although Caine and Corelli were best-selling, influential authors in their late-Victorian heyday, we remember them now, if at all, as a footnote to others' work. Corelli is the prototype for the title character in her friend E. F. Benson's *Lucia* novels (1920–1939); Caine, as 'my dear friend Hommy-Beg', is the dedicatee of Bram Stoker's *Dracula* (1897).[6] Caine shares with Corelli an additional, if rather doubtful, honour: both were regarded with contempt by Lev Tolstoy. Tolstoy often excoriated popular icons (famously, Shakespeare) and bestowed praise on obscure or unexpected writers (regular reading of the Tauchnitz collection of British novels introduced him to the romances of Mrs Henry Wood and Mary Elizabeth Braddon).[7] He did admire Dickens, Trollope, and George Eliot, but he could be caustic about other popular authors.[8]

Ironically, Tolstoy's novels often had more in common with the kind of romantic melodrama which he deplored than he chose to acknowledge. The case of Hall Caine (1853–1931) is particularly illuminating. Not only was Caine's immense (if transient) popularity as a fiction writer equal to Tolstoy's, the British novelist strenuously aspired throughout his career to achieve professional and reputational parity with Tolstoy, disregarding the latter's disdain. By exploring the narrative themes and humanitarian concerns shared by Caine and Tolstoy, this essay will reveal considerable common ground between the novel of ideas and the novel of sensation at the turn of the nineteenth century.

The great Russian author's scorn must have stung Caine, who had spent years establishing himself in British circles as an authority on Russia (particularly on Russian Jews) while intermittently courting

Tolstoy's favour. Journalists frequently compared Caine to famous European writers: as early as 1890, following the success of his early novels, the popular weekly *Sunday Words* ran a cover feature on 'Hall Caine, The English Victor Hugo'.[9] Several of Caine's books, including an edition of his collected works in 1915, were translated into Russian; *The Eternal City* (1901) was even translated (as *Vechnyi gorod*, in 1902) by Konstantin Konstantinovich Tolstoy, a doctor and writer, and a distant relation of Lev Nikolaevich.

It was galling for a famous author, hailed by some reviewers as 'the English Tolstoy' and fond of emphasizing his own moral and imaginative sympathy with the Russian author, to be unable to provoke more than the faintest praise from his idol.[10] Caine, or his publishers, swiftly recycled any appearance of encouragement from Tolstoy as a selling point for his own novels. One editor's introduction to Caine's *The Bondman* (1890) assured readers that 'Leo Tolstoy read the book with "deep interest"'.[11] The original phrase was 'great interest', and this formulaic politeness was relayed by Tolstoy's daughter Tatiana in a note acknowledging receipt of a gift copy of *The Bondman*.[12] Despite the flimsiness of this connection, Hall Caine was not above exploiting it again in a preface to a later novel, referring to information received from Tolstoy 'through his daughter'.[13] The jacket of the 1927 reprint of one of Caine's bestsellers avers that '*The Christian* provoked world-wide discussion, in which Tolstoy took part'[14]—which was, as we shall see, a remarkably neutral description of Tolstoy's actual contribution. More subtle tokens of respect can be found in Caine's epigraph to *The Bondman*, 'Vengeance is mine—I will repay', which is of course also the epigraph to Tolstoy's *Anna Karenina* (1878; first English translation, 1886). Even the title of Caine's last major novel, *The Master of Man: The Story of a Sin* (1921), seems to echo the various English translations of Tolstoy's frequently anthologized short story, 'Master and Man' ('Khoziain i rabotnik', 1895).[15]

Thanks to Pierre Bayard's concept of anticipatory plagiarism, we can now regard Caine's unrequited admiration for Tolstoy from a new and illuminating perspective. Bayard cites multiple cases where chronologically precedent writers have borrowed, or plagiarized, specific *contraintes* (sets of literary rules) from their posterity. As an example, he cites Voltaire's novella *Zadig* (1749), which includes an episode of deductive reasoning by the title character which could well have been pilfered from Conan Doyle's Sherlock Holmes series, despite preceding the deerstalker-wearing detective by almost one hundred and forty years.[16] It is extremely doubtful that Conan Doyle plagiarized *Zadig* in the traditional direction, since as Bayard admits, Voltaire's novella in no other way resembles a detective story, nor does its titular hero indulge in other flights of deduction.[17] The existence of two markedly similar passages in otherwise completely unrelated and temporally distant texts is sheer coincidence—or, in Bayardian terms, a vindication of non-chronological literary cross-pollination.

In other cases of anticipatory plagiarism, however, it is impossible to deny a relationship between the texts: the later text has been influenced by, and has even borrowed from, the earlier one, compounding as if condoning the earlier text's theft.[18] Bayard gives the examples of the twelfth-century legend of Tristan and Iseult and nineteenth-century Romanticism, which he claims share the *contrainte* of depicting romantic passion as self-destructive (even when it is reciprocated). In other words, while the core theft (the *contrainte* of self-destructive love) was perpetrated by medieval troubadours against the French Romantic poets and novelists, the latter group subsequently read and admired the medieval lyric poems and thus (however paradoxically) borrowed back their own ideas, which duly informed the Romantic movement. Bayard calls this phenomenon reciprocal plagiarism: an instance 'where two authors, separated by time, inspire each other'.[19] It is my main contention in this essay that Caine and Tolstoy formed just such a pair of chronologically separate, yet mutually influential, reciprocal plagiarists. Their literary careers overlap between Caine's debut as a novelist in 1885 and Tolstoy's death in 1910; Caine was already popular in the late 1880s, when the first English translations of Tolstoy's fiction were appearing. Caine was thus the first of the pair to establish an anglophone reputation, and so, to coin an oxymoron, the original plagiarist.

I argue that Caine's admiration for Tolstoy was so extreme that he plagiarized the latter's novel *Resurrection* (*Voskresenie*, 1899) five years before it was actually published; that Tolstoy returned the favour by plagiarizing, in *Resurrection*, Caine's 1921 novel *The Master of Man*; and that Caine continued to plagiarize Tolstoy in the standard chronological direction until the end of his career. Moreover, Caine plagiarized in advance not only the Russian writer's literary themes, but also Tolstoy's internationally praised statements of protest against the persecution of religious minorities through his own publicity networks. I begin this essay by reviewing Hall Caine's reputation and literary career, including those novels which plagiarize Tolstoy either proleptically or analeptically; secondly, I use new archival research to study Caine's fascination with Russia and Russian Jews, which peaked with his journey to Russia in 1892; and in the last section, I look at the history of Caine's relations with Tolstoy. In conclusion, I suggest that Caine's facility in plagiarizing Tolstoy's last major novel suggests that these two authors had more in common—creatively and ideologically—than the living Lev Tolstoy would ever have conceded.

Caine, *The Manxman*, and Mutual Plagiarism

Fig. 1. Hall Caine, Self-portrait (caricature) (1892), MS 09542, from the papers of Sir Thomas Henry Hall Caine (1853–1931), Manx National Heritage Museum, Douglas, Isle of Man. Used with permission of the Manx National Heritage Museum.

Thomas Henry Hall Caine (known as Tom to his intimates), although born and educated in Liverpool, came of Manx stock on his father's side; in 1870, aged seventeen, after a brief apprenticeship to an architect, he moved to the Isle of Man to assist his uncle as a village schoolteacher.

Two years later, influenced by Ruskin's political and aesthetic writings, he returned to Liverpool where he became known as a journalist. A positive impression upon the ailing Dante Gabriel Rossetti, who later invited him to London as his assistant, secured Caine's entrée into the British literary elite. In 1885 he published his first novel, *The Shadow of a Crime*, a historical melodrama set in rural Cumberland. *The Deemster* (1887), a historical novel set on the Isle of Man, and *The Bondman* (1890), a melodrama set between Man and Iceland, established Caine's archetypal plot: an intrigue affecting humble individuals in remote, primitive communities, portrayed realistically in the manner of Pierre Loti, Knut Hamsun and Gor'kii himself. Caine owed his rapid popularity to the complex love triangles, extramarital sex, and melodramatic cliff-hangers in his fiction. Yet his authorial intentions were invariably modern and humanitarian. He carefully researched the exotic locations of works like *The Bondman*, *The Scapegoat* (1891; set in Morocco), and *The White Prophet* (1909; set in Egypt), while his ambitious treatment of Vatican politics in *The Eternal City* (1901) and of urban poverty and prostitution in his blockbuster romance *The Christian* (1897) were openly morally didactic (even if their appeal derived from the descriptions of immorality which they condemned).

Modern readers may marvel that, at a reception including Wells, James, Shaw and Hardy, Gor'kii was chagrined by the absence of two merely popular novelists. But this view underestimates Hall Caine's colossal fame on both sides of the Atlantic from around 1890, until at least the start of the First World War. His greatest triumph, *The Christian*, appeared serially in *The Windsor Magazine*; when published in book form, it sold 150,000 copies within six months, later becoming the first British novel to sell a print run greater than one million.[20] Like most of Caine's fiction it was successfully adapted for the theatre and toured internationally. It was also widely translated (the first Russian version, *Khristianin*, by Aleksandra Lindegren, appeared in 1901). Caine was talented and prolific; he was, as we shall see, genuinely troubled by humanitarian questions, principally child poverty, the persecution of Jews, and the fate of unmarried mothers; and he was a consummate self-publicist and networker. The combination was unbeatable, though not unmockable. Oscar Wilde said of him: 'Mr. Hall Caine, it is true, aims at the grandiose, but then he writes at the top of his voice. He is so loud that one cannot hear what he says'.[21] The relentlessly noble profile which both Caine and Tolstoy projected to their public was easy to lampoon: since Caine owed his success to the facility rather than the originality of his prose, he made a softer target than Tolstoy for both journalists and unsympathetic peers.

The literary *contrainte* which Caine plagiarized by anticipation from Tolstoy—and which he would later borrow back—was a version of the theme of the ingenuous young woman abandoned by her inconstant lover. This *contrainte* differentiates Tolstoy's and Caine's stories from myriad similar scenarios in contemporary literature (to name just two examples, Hardy's *Tess of the D'Urbervilles* (1891) and Chekhov's *The Seagull* (*Chaika*, 1896)) by stipulating two specific, obligatory narrative steps: (a) the man sits in judgement over his beloved in a court of law, and (b) he subsequently decides to rescue her and redeem himself. Both Caine and Tolstoy's narratives unite legal with moral awakening: after the unexpected courtroom encounter with his former mistress, each male protagonist realizes that even if society is prepared to ignore his previous behaviour, he must undertake public confession, renunciation of wealth and position, and restitution (by marrying or otherwise supporting the wronged woman). To study this *contrainte* and to fully expose the multidirectional plagiarism at work here, I will begin by summarizing the best-known narrative example—Tolstoy's 1899 *Resurrection*—before contrasting the plots of two novels by Caine which respectively anticipate and recapitulate it, *The Manxman* (1894) and *The Master of Man* (1921).

As Tolstoy's final novel, *Resurrection* was perhaps his fullest condemnation of the far-reaching consequences of casual sex. It was based on a real-life melodrama Tolstoy learned of in 1887 from his friend, the reform-minded judge Anatolii Federovich Koni, and which probably took place in the early 1870s. The individuals concerned were a wealthy St Petersburg nobleman, later vice-governor of a Siberian province; and a young Finnish peasant girl, Rozaliia, who became a prostitute after their affair. She was arraigned for theft, and thus the nobleman saw her again in a courtroom. Events resembled the first part of *Resurrection* closely, but in real life, Rozaliia's death from typhus in prison terminated their relationship.[22] This was the story that Tolstoy fictionalized. Rozaliia became Katiusha (Katerina) Maslova, an illegitimate peasant raised 'half servant, half young lady' as the ward of two elderly aunts on a small country estate.[23] At the age of seventeen, she is seduced by their nephew, Prince Dmitrii Nekhliudov, who insensitively pays her off with a hundred roubles. Maslova, although abandoned and pregnant, does not acknowledge the hopelessness of her situation until a chance sighting of Nekhliudov departing on a train convinces her of his indifference.

Losing faith 'in God and in goodness',[24] Maslova gives her newborn to a nurse who sends it to a foundlings' home; after an unsuccessful spell as a servant, she becomes a prostitute in the capital, St Petersburg. There, eight years after their fateful affair, Nekhliudov recognizes Maslova among the defendants on trial for robbery and conspiracy to murder. As a juror, Nekhliudov has no difficulty in steering the sympathetic jury towards a verdict of '"Guilty, but without intent"', which carries a mild sentence; unfortunately, in their ignorance and confusion, they fail to use the necessary formula '"Guilty, but without intent to cause death"'.[25] Because of this technical error, Maslova is condemned to four years' exile in Siberia. Horrified by the baleful effect he has twice had on this woman—first by ruining her, and secondly by unintentionally exacerbating her sentence—Nekhliudov alters his entire way of life. He strives to get her sentence annulled (an appeal to the Senate and a petition to the Tsar both fail); he breaks off an advantageous engagement as well as an affair with a married woman, in order to become engaged to Maslova; he deeds his lands to the peasants who work them; finally, he accompanies Maslova to Siberia, as her fiancé. The theme of private awakening and public confession recurs throughout *Resurrection*.

> I have lived a double life. Beneath the life that you have seen there has been another—God only knows how full of wrongdoing and disgrace and shame. [...] Let it be enough that my career has been built on falsehood and robbery, that I have deceived the woman who loved me with her heart of hearts [...]. The moment came when I had to sit in judgement on my own sin, the moment when she who had lost her honour in trusting to mine stood in the dock before me. I, who had been the first cause of her misfortune, stood on the bench as her judge. She is now in prison and I am here. The same law which has punished her failing with infamy has advanced me to power. [...] When I asked myself what there was left for me to do, I could see but one thing. It was impossible to go on administering justice, being myself unjust [...]. I could not surrender myself to any earthly court, because I was guilty of no crime against earthly law. The law cannot take a man into the court of his own conscience. He must take himself there.[26]

The citation above, however, is not from *Resurrection*. It comes from Caine's *The Manxman*, published in 1894 before *Resurrection* existed even in draft form; it was alluded to in Tolstoy's notes only as 'the Koni story' ('Konevskii rasskaz').[27] From the records of Tolstoy's private library at Iasnaia Poliana, we know that he possessed copies of *The Bondman*, *The Christian* and *The Eternal City*, at least one of which was a gift from the author; there is no evidence that Tolstoy ever read *The Manxman*. Yet it is hard to deny correspondences between the passage cited above and Nekhliudov's private reflections after hearing Maslova's sentence:

> [Nekhliudov had undergone ...] defilement so complete that he despaired of the possibility of getting cleansed. [...] But the free spiritual being, which alone is true, alone powerful, alone eternal, had already awakened in Nekhludoff, and he could not but believe it. Enormous though the distance was between what he wished to be and what he was, nothing appeared insurmountable to the newly-awakened spiritual being. 'At any cost I will break this lie which binds me and confess everything, and will tell everybody the truth, and act the truth,' he said resolutely, aloud. [...] 'I shall dispose of [my] inheritance in such a way as to acknowledge the truth. I shall tell her, Katusha, that I am a scoundrel and have sinned towards her, and will do all I can to ease her lot. Yes, I will see her, and will ask her to forgive me. Yes, I will beg her pardon, as children do.' ... He stopped—'will marry her if necessary.' He stopped again, folded his hands in front of his breast as he used to do when a little child, lifted his eyes, and said, addressing some one: 'Lord, help me, teach me, come enter within me and purify me of all this abomination.' He prayed, asking God to help him, to enter into him and cleanse him; and what he was praying for had happened already: the God within him had awakened his consciousness.[28]

For both Caine and Tolstoy, these fictional travails—and their moral underpinnings—were greeted by controversy. In 1894, the year Heinemann published Caine's *The Manxman*, they also brought out Tolstoy's influential treatise *The Kingdom of God Is Within You* (*Tsarstvo Bozhie vnutri vas*, 1894) in Constance Garnett's English translation. Tolstoy insisted in this work that every human being has 'rational conscience' as his 'sole certain guide' to moral justice. He stirred public outrage by implying that reasoning Christians can choose to ignore the laws of Church and state.[29] These arguments, followed by *Resurrection*'s cruel critique of Orthodox clergy, eventually led to Tolstoy's 1901 excommunication from the Russian Orthodox Church.[30] Caine would have his own brush with religious controversy twenty years later thanks to his novel *The Woman Thou Gavest Me* (1913), when the unhappily married heroine yields her virginity to her childhood sweetheart rather than her husband. But, as a stringent Catholic, she refuses to remarry even after her husband divorces her, since while '[t]he Church may [give] a wrong interpretation' of sexual freedom, the marriage vow itself remains 'divine and irrevocable'.[31] This exercise in Christian self-determination almost ruined both Heinemann's finances and Caine's reputation, when the circulating libraries of the United Kingdom decided to ban the book after a print run of five thousand copies had already been produced. Fortunately, Caine's influential contacts prevailed over trade scruples, and the ban was relaxed.[32] In the year 1894, however, Tolstoy appeared to have plagiarized the appeal for independent ethical thinking made in *The Kingdom of God* from *The Manxman*, where Caine's hero realizes '[t]he law cannot take a man into the court of his own conscience. He must take himself there.'[33] Similarly, the sense of moral and physical suffocation experienced by Caine's characters immediately prior to their spiritual awakening seems to prefigure Tolstoy's claustrophobic evocation of an immature conscience:

> Every man of the present day with the Christian principles assimilated involuntarily in his conscience, finds himself in precisely the position of a man asleep, who dreams that he is obliged to do something which even in his dream he knows he ought not to do. He knows this in the depths of his conscience, and all the same he seems unable to change his position; he cannot stop and cease doing what he ought not to do. And just as in a dream, his position becoming more and more painful, at last reaches such a pitch of intensity that he begins sometimes to doubt the reality of what is passing and makes a moral effort to shake off the nightmare which is oppressing him.
>
> This is just the condition of the average man of our Christian society. He feels that all that he does himself and that is done around him is something absurd, hideous, impossible, and opposed to his conscience; he feels that his position is becoming more and more unendurable and reaching a crisis of intensity.[34]

The plot of *The Manxman* establishes just such a crisis of intensity. Like most Caine novels, it involves a love triangle between childhood friends—Philip Christian, grandson of the Deemster (or chief Judge) of the Isle of Man; his illegitimate cousin, Pete Quilliam; and the local miller's daughter, Kate Cregeen. Pete and Kate become engaged; but while Pete is seeking his fortune abroad, Philip and Kate fall in love and sleep together. Philip breaks off with Kate, ostensibly from belated loyalty to Pete but primarily because he knows that Kate's inferior education and social class would stymie his legal career. When Pete returns as a wealthy man, he persuades Kate to marry him; but shortly after the wedding, Kate realizes she is pregnant with Philip's child. No public scandal materializes, since Pete, who is apparently deficient in either arithmetic or biology, happily accepts the infant as his own. Kate, unable to bear the hypocrisy of living with a husband she cannot love, deserts her family. Philip is appointed Deemster. Kate, now suicidal, is arrested for self-harm. Her unexpected appearance in the Deemster's court triggers Philip's repentance and spiritual awakening. He renounces both the office of Deemster and the newly offered position of Governor of the entire island; he publicly confesses his part in Kate's disgrace; and he embarks on a new life with her. The all-condoning Pete divorces Kate and sails conveniently away.

Vivid characterization and local colour redeem *The Manxman*'s improbably fraught plot. From this outline, we can see that Caine plagiarized from *Resurrection* the following tropes: an unequal, short-lived sexual liaison; a fortuitous pregnancy; the heroine's arrest and court appearance; the hero's repentance and confession. In 1921, having already outlived his heyday, Caine plagiarized *Resurrection*—or perhaps his own *Manxman*—all over again in his new novel, *The Master of Man*. In his 'Author's Note', he thanks two sources for inspiring Chapter Forty-four of the novel (in which the hero commits increasingly illegal manoeuvres to restore justice). The first is his old friend, the Galician Jewish author Karl Emil Franzos (1848–1904), whose novel *The Chief Justice* (*Der Präsident*, 1884) was another Heinemann acquisition admired by Caine for its realistic treatment of the lives of Russian Jews.[35] As for the second source, Caine writes, 'I wish to say that Tolstoy told me, through his daughter, that similar incidents occurring in Russia (although he altered them materially) had suggested the theme of his great novel, "Resurrection"'.[36] While some borrowings are explicit (the use of 'Resurrection' as the title for the final section and one of the final chapters of *Master of Man*), others are more subtle. Caine's narrative features a love rectangle rather than a triangle, set once again on the Isle of Man around the turn of the nineteenth century. The Deemster's son Victor Stowell, and Fenella Stanley, the Governor's daughter, appear destined to marry. He is a rising lawyer; she is a passionate and expensively educated Christian feminist. Inspired by Fenella, Victor persuades juries to acquit abused wives who have murdered their husbands in self-defence. Yet Victor commits two deeply dishonourable acts: he sleeps with a lower-class local girl, Bessie Collister; and he allows his best friend Alick Gell to become engaged to her, without revealing his own prior liaison.

Naturally, as a good Edwardian heroine, Bessie becomes pregnant after sleeping with Victor once. Having concealed her condition, she accidentally suffocates her newborn. Police apprehend her trying to conceal its body. Meanwhile, Victor has been appointed Deemster; Bessie's trial for infant murder takes place in his court. From this point onwards, *The Master of Man* retraces the plot of *The Manxman*, now complicated by Fenella's fervent espousal of Bessie's cause. Victor, caught between public disgrace and the loss of Fenella if he confesses his own involvement, and moral ruin if he allows Bessie to hang, tries to recuse himself from the latter's trial. When Bessie is sentenced to death, he abuses his authority as Deemster to free her from prison, sending her to safety under the protection of Alick Gell. Eventually, Victor confesses and is forgiven by both Fenella and Alick; the former Deemster is sentenced to two years in a Manx gaol for abusing his office; and Fenella, in a neat reversal of Nekhliudov's vow to follow Maslova into Siberian exile, becomes a prison warder in order to be near him. They even get married in prison (in Tolstoy's *Resurrection*, Nekhliudov and Maslova never marry, because Maslova develops an affection for another convict). It falls to Fenella to dramatize Victor's spiritual resurrection in the final paragraph of *The Master of Man*:

> But well she knew that the victory had been won, that the resurrection of his soul had already begun, that he would rise again on that same soil on which he had so sadly fallen, that shining like a star before his brightening eyes was the vision of a far greater and nobler life than the one that lay in ruins behind him, and that she, she herself, would be always by his side to 'ring the morning bell for him'.[37]

The final lines of *Resurrection* read like a more concise and equivocal description of a similar mental state:

> And a perfectly new life dawned that night for Nekhludoff, not because he had entered into new conditions of life, but because everything he did after that night had a new and quite different significance. How this new period of his life will end, time alone will prove.[38]

Who is copying from whom? Was Caine's *Manxman* plagiarizing Tolstoy's *Resurrection* in advance, or did his *The Master of Man* retroactively steal from Tolstoy's novel? Or was Tolstoy copying *The Manxman* while effecting an anterior plagiarism from *The Master of Man*? If we accept *Resurrection* as an intermediate text simultaneously provoking and pillaging the novels Caine wrote at opposite ends of his career, our next question must be the motivation behind Caine's and Tolstoy's shared and enduring fascination with this particular *contrainte* of illicit passion, legal consequence, and repentance.

Unlike Tolstoy, who carefully documented his premarital liaisons with serfs, prostitutes and women of his own class,[39] Caine had no reason to feel personally guilty for the exploitation of women or the neglect of illegitimate offspring. While his own wife, Mary Chandler, was underage at the time of their liaison (she was thirteen when they began living together in 1882), Caine married her in 1886. Their first son, Ralph, was born technically illegitimate, but his father later legally adopted him. Numerous letters home attest that Caine was a loving husband and an attentive father to both his sons (Derwent was born in 1891). Yet neither writer allowed domestic content to blind them to the adverse social consequences of sexual exploitation and social hypocrisy upon the lives of women and children. We know that Tolstoy contemplated the anecdote that would become *Resurrection* for more than a decade preceding the book's 1899 publication; during this period, he wrote other influential and highly melodramatic fictions about the pernicious effects of socially condoned fornication: *The Kreutzer Sonata* (*Kreitserova sonata*, 1889); *The Devil* (*D'iavol*, 1889); and *Father Sergei* (*Otets Sergei*, completed in 1898). In 1888, Tolstoy told W. T. Stead that he was planning *The Kreutzer Sonata* as 'a romance exposing the conventional illusion of romantic love'.[40] In an 1890 interview, Caine claimed:

> I agree very largely with Tolstoi in his 'Kreutzer Sonata', and hold that the love passion, both on its spiritual and its sensual sides, is exalted by modern writers to such undue importance that it seems to consume the best energies of man. If we believe the novels and plays of the time there is next to nothing in life but love, and next to nothing in love but

> lust. Love is a part, not the whole of life. But it so dominates literature now that if it was forbidden to dramatists and novelists to touch upon the illicit side of love early all the theatres would be closed, and not a hundredth part of the novels would be written.[41]

In other words, while rejecting lust as a negative force, both writers were resigned (Caine openly so) to writing about it, if only to draw attention to its deleterious moral effects.

Presumably this was how Caine justified his decision to revisit, between 1885 and 1897, his preferred plotline of illicit lust. The motif of two brothers or close friends competing for one woman appears in his very first novel, *The Shadow of a Crime* (1885); a year later, in *A Son of Hagar* (1886), three brothers are vying for the same inheritance and the same heiress, with the added sub-plot of one brother's cast-off peasant mistress and their illegitimate child. In *The Christian*, the two main characters—the passionate Christian socialist preacher, John Storm, and the aspiring actress, Glory Quayle—lead turbulent but ultimately moral lives, despite exchanging the peaceful Isle of Man for London's fleshpots. But one of Glory's aristocratic admirers has an illegitimate child, whose mother commits suicide at her faithless lover's wedding to an heiress. Unlike *Resurrection*, there is no evidence that these books were inspired by real-life events. Archetypal fallen women, short-lived babies, unnatural mothers, and irresponsible fathers were recycled and recombined in almost all of Caine's works; Tolstoy, by contrast, was unlikely to blatantly re-use a plot motif or duplicate a character, even if some of his characters experience similar traumas and exigencies.[42]

After prostitution and unmarried pregnancy, a third and less well-known consequence of sexual inequality which both writers denounced was the practice of baby farming. In baby farms, usually private homes, unscrupulous nurses accepted payment from unwed mothers to feed and house their infants. In an impassioned 1890 essay on the notorious Skublinskaia baby farm in Warsaw, where over a hundred infants were thought to have died of malnutrition and neglect, Tolstoy rejected the moral hypocrisy of denouncing the matron Skublinskaia and her ilk as 'beasts' ('zveri'), when the Russian government practised comparable acts of murder and imprisonment against its own population.[43] Tolstoy's initial, outspoken horror at the atrocity of murdered and abused children shades into an early version of the call for empathy and rational moral autonomy which he would reassert in *The Kingdom of God Is Within You*.

Baby farms also feature in Caine's novels *The Christian* and *The Woman Thou Gavest Me*; in the first of these, Glory Quayle and John Storm are instrumental in exposing and closing down one such organization.[44] In 1909, Caine wrote to the Lord Mayor of London offering financial support to a charitable organization for 'fallen women', the Sisterhood of the West London Mission. Caine praised the Sisterhood's policy of extending charity and shelter without requiring the women to leave the streets, adding,

> The great problem of the fallen woman is not to be easily solved, but it is the plain and urgent duty of Society to lessen as far as lies within its power the perils under which so many of the frailest of our fellow creatures spend their lives.[45]

Clearly, both Caine and Tolstoy blamed society, rather than individual women, for the degraded and occasionally criminal lives led by unmarried mothers and by prostitutes; and they both used their fiction, their media presence, and their status as household names to bring questions of gender injustice to the forefront of public debate.

Caine, Russia, Jews and Doukhobors

The second *contrainte* shared by Caine and Tolstoy is the mobilization of literary capital (and, to differing degrees, the financial capital gained from one's literary production) to assist a persecuted religious minority. This section will show how Caine's widely publicized support for persecuted Russian Jews, pursued on the back of a new novel with a Jewish protagonist, plagiarized elements from Tolstoy's world-famous advocacy for Russia's threatened Doukhobors. In 1891, Caine published *The Scapegoat*, whose Jewish hero successively overcomes the negative stereotypes associated with his co-religionists—greed, pride, enmity, persecution, poverty—to attain a happy ending. As Anne Connor suggests, *The Scapegoat* was Caine's response to a question he would pose rhetorically in a later speech: how literature could be used to defeat anti-Jewish prejudice in the UK and Europe.[46] In May 1892, Caine's lecture 'The Jew in Literature' (given at a dinner hosted by a Jewish club, the Maccabees) decried Jewish stereotypes in fiction, praised Jews as 'notoriously assimilable and clubbable', and, while drawing attention to 'dark and distressful' developments in some parts of Europe, urged Jews to fight back against cultural misconceptions and political mistreatment by writing more fiction. He concluded:

> The Jew is now a great figure in literature, both as creator and subject of it. No base tyranny can be perpetrated on the Jews in any nation with the old impunity. Let the lowest of nations turn the Jews out of their country, and the pen in effect turns that nation out of Europe and out of the world of civilized man.[47]

This and similar speeches, combined with sales of *The Scapegoat*, gained Caine the reputation of a sincere and unprejudiced advocate for Jewish culture. It led to a friendship with Israel Zangwill, an emerging British-Jewish novelist, and an invitation to join the newly formed Russo-Jewish Committee, which reported on pogroms and other anti-Semitic behaviour in Russia while attempting to manage the heavily politicized issue of the immigration of Jewish refugees from Eastern Europe to the UK and US.[48] In 1891, Caine's emergence as a literary spokesperson for assimilationist Jews led the British Chief Rabbi, Hermann Adler, to suggest he visit Russia to report on the condition of Jews in the western borderlands. The Russo-Jewish Committee would provide an interpreter, and Caine could carry out abundant fieldwork for the Russo-Jewish romance he was contemplating.[49]

Caine's support of the Jewish community in the UK was, of course, anticipatory plagiarism of Tolstoy's celebrated patronage of the Russian Doukhobor sect. In the 1890s, the pacifist Doukhobors' civil disobedience, including abstention from military service, had provoked increasingly punitive measures against them, such as internal exile. Nor were they permitted to emigrate in order to pursue their way of life in a more tolerant milieu. In 1895, Tolstoy published his first public request (in the *London Times*) for the Doukhobors to be allowed to leave Russia, followed by a second appeal a year later and in 1898, a successful petition to Tsar Nicholas II.[50] Meanwhile, the need to raise money for the Doukhobors' travel stimulated Tolstoy to complete *Resurrection* in 1899. Its 'phenomenal and unprecedented' overseas success was orchestrated by Tolstoy's international network of followers, notably Vladimir Chertkov, whose 'Free Age Press' in Essex was founded in 1900 to distribute translations of Tolstoy's writings, particularly those banned or censored in Russia.[51] *Resurrection* was immediately and widely translated; it ran to multiple editions within a year; and the sale of the French and British rights, accompanied by generous gifts from private donors, allowed Chertkov and his network, assisted by Tolstoy's son Sergei, to charter ships for the Dukhobors and ultimately to help over 7,500 of them travel to sanctuary in Canada by mid-1899.

Although the logistics were on a much smaller scale for Caine's trip *to* Russia undertaken seven years earlier in the summer of 1892, both journeys required diplomatic delicacy. Caine was supposed to travel discreetly, in order to avoid provoking the Russian government, who might decide to impede his trip. Unwisely, in 1891 Caine mentioned his forthcoming journey to a journalist, provoking a media flurry about his so-called 'Russian mission',[52] reproaches from the Russo-Jewish Committee, and a clarification from Caine himself:

> My object is a simple and, I trust, a harmless one. It is that of studying on the spot the life of the Russian Jews. I shall go, if I am allowed to do so, with an open mind, easily touched to sympathy with terrible sufferings, but primed with no apocryphal horrors; indignant at injustice, but holding no wild and mischievous notion of the cruelty of the Russian people; resolved to find the truth and equity of the question, as far as my powers of observation and judgement will permit; but determined to say exactly what I feel, even if that should be partly a warning to the Jews themselves to avoid those dangers which are said to have helped bring these evils upon them.[53]

Caine's insistence on his status as an independent author did not fully convince journalists: as demonstrated by this comparatively measured commentary from *The British Weekly* (printed a few days after Caine's statement above), most felt that he must have, at the very least, a literary agenda. Note the facile reference to Tolstoy.

> It hardly needed Mr Caine's letter to the *Times* to dispose of the absurd statement that he was going to Russia with a brief from a Jewish society, pledged to denounce Russia and to be blind to any faults on the other side. [...] The other day, when Count Tolstoi was consulted on the subject of the famine in Russia, he had no very immediate remedy to suggest; but he thought the hearts of the rich might be effectively appealed to were someone to write a book. So did the Russo-Jewish Committee; and they have asked Mr Caine to write one. It is not a very speedy method, but that it can be successful, 'Uncle Tom'—which, however, was not written by suggestion—can testify.[54]

Not every report was as forgiving:

> The popular novelist and the Czar of All the Russias being the only two omnipotent persons left, it is very right and proper that they should try conclusions with one another [...]. We do not know whether it is more immoral for a novelist to hold a brief than for a barrister to do so; but, in accepting this commission from the London Jews, Mr. Hall Caine is at least consenting to hold their brief, is he not? But Holy Russia can look after herself. Let Mr. Hall Caine see to it that, after being duly tried, he is not sent off to Siberia.[55]

When after several postponements, Caine reached the Continent in midsummer 1892, he travelled on to the Russian borderlands via Brussels and Berlin. In Berlin, awaiting his interpreter, Caine spent time with his friend Emil Franzos, who had moved from the territory of modern Ukraine to Germany in the hope of avoiding persecution. Caine had not learned his lesson about unwanted self-publicity: Heinemann warned him again against advertising his whereabouts lest 'the enemy' (presumably Russian government agents) take action against him, while insisting:

> I am strongly of opinion [sic] that you see a great deal more of the persecution of the Jews in Berlin than you will ever see in Russia. What Franzos tells you I consider worth nothing at all. It is not people of his calibre who conquer the world, but the English who go out unafraid, as you did, until you met him.[56]

In keeping with his opinion of English courage, Heinemann recommended an ambitious route into Russia: 'south right through Hungary, and get in from the Black Sea through the Crimea'.[57] Rumours of cholera in the borderlands compelled Caine to abandon his plans to see St Petersburg and Moscow after visiting only a few cities such as Krakow, Warsaw and Breslau; the fact that his Jewish interpreter was not permitted to enter Russian territory was an added complication. On his return to Britain, Caine delivered a detailed, deeply felt report about the poverty and deprivation he had witnessed to the Jewish Working Men's Club, subsequently published in the *Jewish Chronicle*.[58] Caine supported Zionism; and as late as 1921, he was still raising funds to alleviate famine in Russia.[59] While not on the same scale as Tolstoy's support for the Doukhobors, Caine's advocacy of Jewish culture was a lifetime commitment, and certainly not a mere publicity stunt for *The Scapegoat* or for his projected, never-written Russo-Jewish novel.

Given that Caine was unable to refrain from advertising his journey to Russia, he clearly used his status as a goodwill ambassador for Jews to promote his own work. However, even Tolstoy's high-profile advocacy of the Doukhobors was not without a smidgeon of self-publicity. While by the 1890s, Tolstoy was seen as the leader of international pacifism, the various pacifist factions were divided and ineffective. Tolstoy was frustrated by the lack of political reform following his argument, cogently expressed in *The Kingdom of God* and elsewhere, that individual enlightenment prefigures enlightened societies. The Doukhobor Rebellion of 1895, instigated by the sectarians' spiritual leader Petr Vasil'evich Verigin, provided a timely opportunity to re-energize Tolstoy's message. Although the Doukhobors were not Tolstoyans, Verigin's personal philosophy coincided conveniently with Tolstoy's principles.[60] Hence, while neither *Resurrection* nor the Doukhobors' resistance were publicity stunts, they display Tolstoy's and Verigin's ability to adroitly manipulate audiences and harness public sympathy.[61] The fact that both Hall Caine and Tolstoy could be savvy media operators detracts neither from their pacifism, nor from their impartial faith in the power of imaginative literature to unite disparate cultures. As Caine wrote in 1908:

> In the progress of the nations from the barbarity of statecraft I see no force that is so surely making for the peace of the world as the force of education whereby the great national literatures are becoming one literature. I may hate and loathe the Russian government, and in any difference it may have with the government of England I may be a rabid Englishman, but when I open the books of Tolstoy and enter with him into the houses of the moujiks, and live their lives and share their joys and sorrows, I love the Russian people and hate the thought that my country can ever go to war with them.[62]

Caine and Tolstoy

As Dante Gabriel Rossetti's personal secretary in the last year of the artist's life, the young Hall Caine met or corresponded with many luminaries. He notes in a memoir that 'Tourgenieff' [sic], on a visit to London, attempted to call on Rossetti after the latter had recovered from a seizure.[63] Caine's biographer comments that '[t]here were few men Caine would have liked to meet more but he had to put him off along with the rest. Turgenev [...] died in 1883 and Caine never again had a chance to meet him'.[64] It was Tolstoy, however, who quickly became Caine's lodestar among Russian writers and indeed among all authors. On tour in America to promote *The Christian*, Caine praised *Anna Karenina*'s successful combination of realism and idealism: 'I claim for Victor Hugo and Count Tolstoi that, with Walter Scott, they will in the time to come be recognized at [sic] the three greatest novelists of the nineteenth century'.[65] Although Shakespeare had been (with Ruskin) Caine's earliest and most enduring idol, Caine even defended Tolstoy's critique of the bard. Caine wrote to a friend: 'At present the spectacle of utter idolatry, as though every word in Shakespeare were divinely inspired, is, as Tolstoi says, a great evil and a great untruth'.[66]

Fig. 2. Hall Caine looking Tolstoyan. Hall Caine at Tynwald Fair, unknown photographer (1930). PG/0203, from the archive of Sir Thomas Henry Hall Caine (1853–1931), Manx National Heritage Museum, Douglas, Isle of Man. Used with permission of the Manx National Heritage Museum, https://www.imuseum.im/search/collections/archive/mnh-museum-114514.html.

Caine's attempts to meet or correspond with Tolstoy were, as we have seen, frustrated first by the cholera epidemic of 1892 and secondly by the Russian author's refusal even to reply directly. An 1890 note from Tolstoy's daughter Tat'iana, assures Caine blandly that her father 'is much moved by your high opinion of the direction in which he labours and by your sympathy to his aims'.[67] It must have galled Caine that Tolstoy followed up his anodyne response to the gift of *The Bondman* with consistently negative assessments of *The Christian*, whose titular hero, the radical preacher John Storm, was the most consciously Tolstoyan of all Caine's characters. Caine probably read the report by Harold Williams, a *Manchester Guardian* correspondent who visited Tolstoy at his Iasnaia Poliana estate in 1905, that '[Tolstoy's] estimate of Miss Marie Corelli and of Mr. Hall Caine, particularly of the latter, was extremely unfavourable'.[68] It was fortunate, however, that Tolstoy's introductory essay to the Russian translation of *Der Büttnerbauer* (1895) by the German realist novelist Wilhelm von Polenz (1861–1903) has never been translated into English. Ironically enough, the novel's Russian title was *The Peasant* (*Krest'ianin*), not to be confused with its near-homophone *Khristianin* (*The Christian*). In this essay, Tolstoy singled out Caine's *Christian* for unfavourable comparison with von Polenz's 'indubitably beautiful' ('nesomnennoe prekrasnoe') work:

> Books, journals, and especially newspapers have become in our times immense monetary undertakings, requiring the maximum number of customers for their success. The interests and tastes of the majority of customers are always low and crude, and therefore for the success of a printed work it is necessary for that work to respond to the requirements of the greater number of customers, i.e. to touch on low interests and correspond with crude tastes.
>
> [...]
>
> Moreover, thanks to chance or excellent advertising, several bad books, such as Hall Caine's *The Christian*, a novel which is false in content and not literary, which has sold a million copies, receives, like eau-de-cologne or Pears soap, vast fame which is not justified by its virtues.[69]

Still worse than this (but also mercifully unknown to Caine during his lifetime) was the verdict Tolstoy scribbled to his daughter Tat'iana, who had formerly corresponded with Caine. Tatiana's letter to her father has not been preserved, but she must have mentioned *The Christian*. Perhaps she was noting receipt of a gift copy (possibly the volume still in the Iasnaia Poliana library today). Tolstoy responded: 'Hall Caine is a publicist ('reklamist') and his "Christian" is a dreadful book ('preskvernoe sochinenie')'.[70]

It was a poor return for decades of mutual theft.

Conclusion

As Bayard reminds us, the benefit of anticipatory plagiarism as an approach to literary criticism lies in the way it reveals how 'each text enriches the other, and even transforms it'. In the special case of reciprocal plagiarism, 'each text is doubled under the influence of the text [which it has] plagiarized, which plagiarizes certain points from it in its turn'.[71] Taking Hall Caine and Tolstoy's interactions as an example not only of plagiarism, but of reciprocal plagiarism, we have identified two major shared *contraintes*. The first is an unusual twist on the tired convention of the fallen woman: the trial of said woman by her former lover, followed by his sincere repentance. The second common *contrainte* is the metaliterary use of fictional melodrama to benefit a religious group threatened by persecution—for Tolstoy, the Doukhobors; for Caine, the Russian Jews. Our approach reveals that, all Bayardian conceits aside, Hall Caine did actually anticipate one of Tolstoy's major literary themes; and that Caine, from his stronghold 'Greeba Castle' on the Isle of Man, did in fact precede the sage of Iasnaia Poliana's defence of the Doukhobors by effectively combining self-promotion and humanitarian advocacy to help the vulnerable Jewish community. In fact, the criticisms Tolstoy levelled against Caine (indulgence in melodrama; self-advertisement) appear intrinsic to his own aesthetic and professional practice. By studying these two writers as a mutually influential dyad, we realize how much they shared thematically and philosophically—and how, for almost three decades, they enjoyed arguably equal fame.

Moreover, since Caine outlived Tolstoy yet continued to plagiarize him (as both the epigraph and ruling metaphor of *The Master of Man* demonstrate), we can apply the Bayardian term *revenant* to Tolstoy's role in mentoring his fellow author: 'a writer from the past with whom a [later] writer holds a dialogue'.[72] In life, Tolstoy viewed Caine's work with contempt: in death, 'separated by the illusory barrier of time, [authors] found a means of working together'.[73] Bayard envisaged the latter-day reciprocal plagiarist enjoying what he called 'a privileged connection' with his predecessors, 'as with benevolent ghosts from whom he occasionally asks, despite the intervening years and because he knows them to be located beyond time, advice and protection'.[74] In the spirit of Flann O'Brien, who wrote a series of comic vignettes picturing John Keats (born in 1795) and George Chapman (who died in 1634) jovially if anachronistically sharing a bachelor existence,[75] I like to imagine Lev Tolstoy and Hall Caine reconciled as literary chums in the ahistorical space of reciprocal plagiarism, setting the world to rights with a winning combination of spiritual rhetoric and titillating melodrama.

Fig. 3. Hall Caine's tombstone in Maughold Churchyard, Isle of Man, sculpted by Archibald Knox. Photograph by author (2019). Copyright author's own.

Notes

1 The author thanks Dr Richard Storer (Leeds Trinity University), Dr Cathy McAteer (University of Exeter), Professor Jacob Emery (Indiana University Bloomington) and Professor Timothy Langen (University of Missouri) for their invaluable feedback on this chapter. I also greatly appreciate the help and resources generously shared with me by the staff of the Manx National Heritage Museum, especially Ms Wendy Thirkettle, without whose assistance I would never have discovered Hall Caine's views on Tolstoy.

2 Robert Ross, 'The Literary Log', *The Bystander*, 19 October 1910, pp. 144–45 (p. 144). Although Ross never reveals the name of the host on this occasion, his coy description of 'a distinguished man of letters' and 'a fluent Russian scholar' suggests none other than Maurice Baring, whose monograph *Landmarks in Russian Literature* was published by Methuen & Co. in 1910; and who is known to have shared a house in Westminster with his friend Auberon Herbert, the ninth Baron Lucas, before the outbreak of the First World War. See Richard Davenport-Hines, 'Baring's Religious Faith', *Chesterton Review*, 34:1/2 (2008), 311–14 (pp. 312–13), https://doi.org/10.5840/chesterton2008341/2122.

3 Ibid.

4 Ibid.

5 Frederick Whyte, *William Heinemann: A Memoir* (London: Jonathan Cape, 1928), pp. 52–53.

6 On Corelli's reincarnation as Lucia, see Teresa Ransom, *The Mysterious Miss Marie Corelli: Queen of Victorian Bestsellers* (Stroud: Sutton, 1999). On her extreme popularity and its complete eclipse following the First World War, see Richard L Kowalczyk, 'In Vanished Summertime: Marie Corelli and Popular Culture', *Journal of Popular Culture*, 7:4 (Spring 1974), 850–63, https://doi.org/10.1111/j.0022-3840.1974.0704_850.x. On Stoker's dedication, 'Hommy-Beg', literally 'small Tommy', was an affectionate Manx-vernacular nickname for the diminutive Caine. For more on this moniker and on the Stoker-Caine relationship, see Richard Storer, 'Beyond "Hommy-Beg": Hall Caine's Place in *Dracula*', in *Bram Stoker and the Gothic: Formations to Transformations*, ed. by Catherine Wynne (London: Palgrave, 2016), pp. 172–84, https://doi.org/10.1057/9781137465047_12.

7 For more on Tolstoy's Tauchnitz readings and his opinions about Wood and Braddon, see Edwina Cruise, 'Tracking the English Novel in *Anna Karenina*: who wrote the English novel that Anna reads?', in *Anniversary Essays on*

Tolstoy, ed. by Donna Tussing Orwin (Cambridge: Cambridge University Press, 2010), pp. 159–82, https://doi.org/10.1017/CBO9780511676246.009.

8 See Galina Alekseeva, 'Dickens in Leo Tolstoy's Universe', in *The Reception of Charles Dickens in Europe*, ed. by Michael Hollington (London: Bloomsbury Academic, 2013), pp. 86–93.

9 Anon., 'Hall Caine, The English Victor Hugo', *Sunday Words*, 8 June 1890.

10 For example, when Caine's *The Master of Man* (1921) appeared, the *Daily Graphic* critic was confident that it would 'stand as the English "Anna Karenina"'; the *Leeds Mercury* claimed that 'it places him [Caine] to the same rank, as a great world novelist, with Zola, Hugo and Tolstoy'; and the critic J. Cuming Walters, writing in the *Manchester City News*, wrote that 'Sir Hall Caine in "The Master of Man" has shown himself to be the English Tolstoy'.

11 Uncredited introduction to *The Bondman*, in Sir Thomas Henry Hall Caine, *Complete Works of Hall Caine* (Hastings: Delphi Editions, 2016), online edition [n.p.].

12 T. L. Tolstaia, letter to Hall Caine, 3 August 1890. The papers of Sir Thomas Henry Hall Caine (1853–1931), MNH MS 2306, held in the Manx National Heritage Library and Archives. Quoted courtesy of Manx National Heritage.

13 Hall Caine, 'Author's Note', in *The Master of Man: The Story of a Sin* (Philadelphia, PA and London: J. P. Lippincott, 1921), online edition, http://www.gutenberg.org/files/61865/61865-h/61865-h.htm. This later correspondence has not been preserved.

14 Sir Thomas Henry Hall Caine, anonymous blurb for *The Christian* (London: Cassell & Co., 1927).

15 As 'Master and Man' was first translated into English in 1895 by S. Rapapert and J. C. Kenworthy, and subsequently re-translated by Constance Garnett and by Louise and Aylmer Maude, Caine would have had no difficulty in reading a copy.

16 Holmes first appeared in print in *A Study in Scarlet* (1887).

17 Pierre Bayard, *Le Plagiat par anticipation* (Paris: Les Éditions de Minuit, 2009), p. 38. My translation.

18 Ibid., p. 53.

19 Ibid., p. 154.

20 See Whyte, *William Heinemann*, p. 174; and Vivien Allen, entry on Sir Hall Caine, *Oxford Dictionary of National Biography*, https://www.oxforddnb.com.

21 Oscar Wilde, *The Decay of Lying* [1889] (New York: Brentano, 1905), page unknown.

22 See V. A. Zhdanov's detailed reconstruction of Koni's anecdote in *Tvorcheskaia istoriia romana L. N. Tolstogo "Voskresenie"* (Moscow: Sovetskii pisatel', 1959), pp. 3–6.

23 Lyof N. Tolstoi, *Resurrection*, trans. by Louise Maude, in *The Complete Works of Lyof N. Tolstoi* (New York: Thomas Crowell & Co, 1898–1911), XXIII-XXIV (1900), p. 6, http://www.gutenberg.org/files/1938/1938-h/1938-h.htm.

24 Ibid., p. 157.

25 Ibid., pp. 95–99.

26 Hall Caine, *The Manxman* (Part IV, Chapter XXII), in Sir Thomas Henry Hall Caine, *Complete Works of Hall Caine* (Hastings: Delphi Editions, 2016), online edition [n.p.].

27 For a detailed timeline of Tolstoy's composition of *Resurrection*, see Zhdanov, *Tvorcheskaia istoriia romana L. N. Tolstogo "Voskresenie"*, esp. pp. 9–49.

28 Tolstoi, *Resurrection*, pp. 121–22.

29 Count Leo Tolstoy, *The Kingdom of God Is Within You*, trans. by Constance Garnett, 2 vols (London: William Heinemann, 1894), II (1894), p. 265.

30 See Rosamund Bartlett, *Tolstoy: A Russian Life*, pp. 387–94, for the background and aftermath of Tolstoy's excommunication, which was widely perceived at home and abroad as an act of petty political vengeance.

31 Hall Caine, *The Woman Thou Gavest Me*, Chapter 68, online edition, http://www.gutenberg.org/files/14597/14597-h/14597-h.htm.

32 Whyte, *Heinemann*, pp. 284–85.

33 Hall Caine, *The Manxman* (Part IV, Chapter XXII), online edition [n.p.].

34 Count Leo Tolstoy, *The Kingdom of God Is Within You*, II, pp. 237–38.

35 Hall Caine, 'The Jew in Literature', speech to the Maccabeans, printed in *The Literary World*, 20 May 1892, 482–84, p. 482.

36 Hall Caine, 'Author's Note', in *The Master of Man*, https://www.gutenberg.org/files/61865/61865-h/61865-h.htm#chap0102.

37 Hall Caine, *The Master of Man*, online edition.

38 Tolstoi, *Resurrection*, p. 270.

39 For more on Tolstoy's diaries, and how his wife Sofiia Andreevna reacted to reading them, see Bartlett, *Tolstoy*, p. 154 and pp. 157–58.

40 See W. T. Stead, 'Count Tolstoi's New Tale: With a Condensation of the Novel [The Kreutzer Sonata]', *Review of Reviews*, 1 (April, 1890), 330.

41 Interview with Hall Caine, 'Unmanliness in Modern Literature', *Pall Mall Gazette*, 24 June 1890. *British Library* Newspapers, link.gale.com/apps/doc/Y3200423930/BNCN?u=exeter&sid=BNCN&xid=400309fa. Accessed 22 Mar. 2021.

42 For example, in *Resurrection* (pp. 156–57), the pregnant and despairing Maslova almost emulates Anna Karenina by throwing herself under a train, but she changes her mind after feeling her unborn child move.

43 L. N. Tolstoi, 'Po povodu dela Skublinskoi', 18 February 1890, http://tolstoy-lit.ru/tolstoy/chernoviki/po-povodu-dela-skublinskoj.htm. For more on baby farms in late Imperial Russia, see ChaeRan Y. Freeze, 'Lilith's Midwives: Jewish Newborn Child Murder in Nineteenth-Century Vilna', *Jewish Social Studies*, 16:2 (Winter 2010), 1–27, https://doi.org/10.2979/jss.2010.16.2.1.

44 Caine was not alone among authors of his generation in attacking baby farms: George Moore's bestselling *Esther Waters* (1894) excoriates a similar institution.

45 Hall Caine, personal letter to the Lord Mayor of London, 25 October 1909. The papers of Sir Thomas Henry Hall Caine (1853–1931), MNH Box 63, held in the Manx National Heritage Library and Archives. Quoted courtesy of Manx National Heritage.

46 For more substantive discussion of Caine's relationship with the Jewish community and his literary representation of Jewish characters, see Anne Connor, 'The Spiritual Brotherhood of Mankind: Religion in the Novels of Hall Caine' (unpublished doctoral thesis, University of Liverpool, 2017), pp. 154–96, https://search.proquest.com/docview/2500014798.

47 Hall Caine, 'The Jew in Literature', 483–84.

48 On this important transitional period in British Jewish affairs, see Sam Johnson, 'Confronting the East: *Darkest Russia*, British Opinion and Tsarism's "Jewish question," 1890–1914', *East European Jewish Affairs*, 36:2 (2006), 199–211, https://doi.org/10.1080/13501670601026781; and David Cesarani, *The Jewish Chronicle and Anglo-Jewry, 1841–1991* (New York: Cambridge University Press, 1994), esp. pp. 32–102.

49 Anne Connor, 'Spiritual Brotherhood of Mankind', pp. 180–81.

50 On Tolstoy's early advocacy of the Doukhobors, see Nina and James Kolesnikoff, 'Leo Tolstoy and the Doukhobors', *Canadian Slavonic Papers*, 20:1 (1978), 37–44 (pp. 37–38), https://doi.org/10.1080/00085006.1978.11091554; and Josh Sanborn, 'Pacifist Politics and Peasant Politics: Tolstoy and the Doukhobors, 1895–1899', *Canadian Ethic Studies*, 27:3 (1995), 52–71, https://www.proquest.com/scholarly-journals/pacifist-politics-peasant-tolstoy-doukhobors-1895/docview/1293167948/se-2?accountid=10792.

51 Bartlett, *Tolstoy*, p. 378. On the history of the Free Age Press, see Michael J. De K. Holman, 'Translating Tolstoy for the Free Age Press: Vladimir Chertkov and His English Manager Arthur Fifield', *The Slavonic and East European Review*, 66:2 (1988), 184–97, https://www.jstor.org/stable/4209734.

52 Anon., 'Mr. Hall Caine's Russian Mission', *The British Weekly*, 15 October 1891.

53 Hall Caine, 'Mr Hall Caine and the Russian Jews', Letters to the Editor, *The Times*, 12 October 1891.

54 Anon., 'Mr. Hall Caine's Russian Mission', *The British Weekly*, 15 October 1891.

55 Anon., *The Birmingham Daily Gazette*, 6 October 1891.

56 William Heinemann, letter to Hall Caine, n.d. The papers of Sir Thomas Henry Hall Caine (1853–1931), MNH Box 63, held in the Manx National Heritage Library and Archives. Quoted courtesy of Manx National Heritage.

57 Ibid.

58 Hall Caine, 'Scenes on the Russian Frontier', *Jewish Chronicle*, 16 December 1892.

59 Vivien Allen, *Hall Caine: Portrait of a Victorian Romancer* (Sheffield: Sheffield Academic Press, 1997), p. 385.

60 See April Bumgardner, 'The Doukhobors: History, Ideology, and the Tolstoy-Verigin Relationship' (unpublished MPhil thesis, University of Glasgow, 2001), esp. pp. 94–97, http://theses.gla.ac.uk/76168/1/13818981.pdf.

61 See Sanborn, 'Pacifist Politics and Peasant Politics', 52–71.

62 Hall Caine, *My Story* (London: William Heinemann, 1908), p. 387.

63 Ibid., p. 215.

64 Allen, *Hall Caine*, p. 136.

65 Hall Caine, drafts for American speeches; draft address to the Pen and Pencil Club in Philadelphia, n.d., pp. 25–26. The papers of Sir Thomas Henry Hall Caine (1853–1931), MNH MS 09542, held in the Manx National Heritage Library and Archives. Quoted courtesy of Manx National Heritage.

66 Hall Caine, personal letter (addressee unknown), 27 November 1906. The papers of Sir Thomas Henry Hall Caine (1853–1931), MNH MS 09542, held in the Manx National Heritage Library and Archives. Quoted courtesy of Manx National Heritage.

67 T. L. Tolstaia, letter to Hall Caine, 3 August 1890.

68 Harold Williams, 'A Visit to Count Tolstoy', *Manchester Guardian*, 5 February 1905.

69 L. N. Tolstoi, 'Predislovie k romanu V. Fon-Polentsa « Krest'ianin »', in L. N. Tolstoi, *Polnoe sobranie sochinenii i pisem v devianosto tomakh*, ed. by V. G. Chertkov, 90 vols (Moscow: Gosudarstvennoe izdatel'stvo khudozhestvennoi literatury, 1928–58), XXXIV (1952), pp. 270–78 (p. 278).

70 L. N. Tolstoi, letter to T. L. Sukhotina, 8 March 1901, *Polnoe sobranie sochinenii*, LXXIII (1954), pp. 47–48 (p. 48).

71 Bayard, *Le Plagiat*, p. 54.

72 Ibid., p. 154.

73 Ibid., p. 55.

74 Ibid.

75 Myles na Gopaleen (Flann O'Brien), *The Various Lives of Keats and Chapman* (London: Hart-Davis MacGibbon, 1976).

7. The Posteriority of the Anterior: Levinas, Tolstoy, and Responsibility for the Other

Steven Shankman

'The Russian novelists', the French philosopher Emmanuel Levinas (1906–1995) remarked, 'ceaselessly wonder about the philosophical problem understood as the meaning of the human, as the search for the famous "meaning of life".'[1] While literary scholars have written extensively about Dostoevsky and Levinas, relatively little has been said of how powerfully the fiction of Tolstoy anticipates key aspects of Levinas's philosophical thought.[2] The chief preoccupations of *Totality and Infinity* (*Totalité et infini: essai sur l'extériorité*, 1961) and *Otherwise than Being, or Beyond Essence* (*Autrement qu'être ou au-delà de l'essence*, 1974) correspond to the two phases of Tolstoy's literary career as a novelist. In the first phase, *War and Peace* (*Voina i mir*, 1869) anticipates what Levinas means by his pairing of totality with war and of infinity with peace. Indeed, both authors, as young military officers, experienced the horrors of war first-hand, Tolstoy in the Crimean War and Levinas in World War II. In the second phase, beginning with *Anna Karenina* (1878) and culminating in his late novel *Resurrection* (*Voskresenie*, 1899), Tolstoy understands religion, or the word God, as bearing witness, above all, to ethical obligation. Tolstoy's critical portrait of the dogmatic Christian believer Aleksei Aleksandrovich Karenin is a bridge between these two phases of Tolstoy's literary career.

Our volume of essays has been inspired by the concept of 'anticipatory plagiarism', a notion that defies logic. How can an author plagiarize a

 https://doi.org/10.11647/OBP.0241.07

text from a later time period? How, more generally, can the after influence the before, the posterior the anterior? Yet the influence of the posterior on the anterior is precisely Levinas's claim in a key passage from the early pages of *Totality and Infinity* in which he describes the necessary separation of the subject from totality lest that totality swallow up—i.e. assimilate—that subject. 'The posteriority of the anterior', Levinas writes, is 'an inversion' that is 'logically absurd'. In what Levinas calls the interiority of the separated subject, 'the *After* or the *Effect* conditions the *Before* or the *Cause*.'[3]

Let us now try to unpack Levinas's rather dense articulation of anterior posteriority in this passage. I think now, in the present. All thought happens in the present, even the thought that thinks of a before that precedes the present, and that conditions the present. In the famous Cartesian articulation, I think, and therefore I am: *cogito, ergo sum*. Thought proceeds from the *cogito*. As Descartes discovers in his *Third Meditation*, however, in chronological time, in the time of thinking, this very *cogito* discovers that it does not, in fact, proceed from itself. The *cogito* discovers this when it thinks the idea of infinity, an idea which, Descartes posits, cannot originate in the *cogito*, because that *cogito* is finite. The finite cannot contain the infinite. Its source must therefore be infinite; must, in fact, be God, the infinite being, who put this idea into my consciousness, which is finite. 'The being infinitely surpassing its own idea in us—God in the Cartesian terminology', Levinas writes, 'subtends [*sous-tend*]' or underlies 'the evidence of the *cogito*'.[4] What was posterior, what emerged in the chronological time of thinking, is now understood—in the time of thought—to have preceded thought, to be anterior to thought. As William Large explains this phenomenon, '[w]hat comes first in terms of the exposition is second in terms of the condition.'[5] In the course of reading Descartes' *Third Meditation* (*Méditation troisième*, 1641), in the time of our reading, we come to learn that subjectivity, in Large's words, 'is in fact dependent on the existence of God. In the same way', Large continues, 'although Levinas [in *Totality and Infinity*] first of all describes the separate existence of the self, we later discover that without the relation to the other, this existence would not have been possible.'[6]

It is logically absurd that Tolstoy could have plagiarized Levinas, that the later author could have influenced the earlier one, that the posterior could have conditioned the anterior. But what is not logically absurd—and this is my argument—is that Levinas recognized this logical absurdity, as did Tolstoy. Both Tolstoy and Levinas posit a self that is primordially haunted by the other. Tolstoy articulates and embodies this in his fiction, which in turn had a profound effect on Emmanuel Levinas, who expounds the meaning of the 'posteriority of the anterior' in *Totality and Infinity.*

Totality and Infinity as War and Peace

In the first part of this essay, I shall comment on the first of the two phases of the correspondence between the philosophy of Levinas, the poetic philosopher, and the fiction of Tolstoy, the philosophical poet. Levinas's *Totality and Infinity* is a philosophical meditation—evoking Tolstoy's *War and Peace*—on war as totality and peace as infinity. In *War and Peace,* Tolstoy sees war as a grimly anonymous totality that is, stunningly, ruptured by the face of the other. For Levinas, inspired by Tolstoy, peace is produced when I, breaking the 'anonymous utterance of history', see, and address, the face of the other; and when, in seeing and responding to the face, I break 'with the totality of wars and empires in which one does not speak'.[7] Thus for both Tolstoy and Levinas, 'ethics', as Levinas puts it in the preface to *Totality and Infinity,* 'is an optics': or, *'l'éthique est une optique'*.[8]

Levinas makes a number of explicit references to Tolstoy in his writings. He was particularly struck by Prince Andrei's famously transformative vision, after being wounded on the battlefield at Austerlitz, of the infinite height of the sky.[9] In the course of *War and Peace,* Tolstoy transposes the vertical infinity of physical or cosmic space to the horizontal ethical dimension, namely to the infinity of the other in front of me. The infinity of the far, of the distant, becomes the infinity of the near.

Just after he is badly wounded at Austerlitz, Andrei opens his eyes and sees

> nothing but the sky—the lofty sky, not clear yet still immeasurably lofty. [...] How was it I did not see that lofty sky before? And how happy I am to find it at last! Yes! All is vanity! All falsehood, except that infinite sky.[10]

What we see ruptured here is the totality of war understood as the system, the totality in which Andrei had been seeking the meaning of life in glory and fame. The infinity of the sky reveals a beyond of the brutality of war, a beyond of the totalizing system in which Andrei had been immersed.

There had been an absurdity at the very heart of Prince Andrei's commitment to a military career in the Russian army. His hero was Napoleon, and yet it was against Napoleon that he and his fellow Russians were fighting. When the wounded Prince Andrei now encounters Napoleon beneath this 'lofty sky', he sees him as an 'insignificant', mean-spirited 'little' man.[11]

Totality and the Face of Vereshchagin

Napoleon's forces have now invaded Moscow. The Russian General Kutuzov concludes that it is impossible for the Russian army to defend Moscow. Count Rostopchin, governor of Moscow, deeply disagrees with Kutuzov's decision, but Moscow must be emptied. One of the political prisoners to be evacuated is the young Vereshchagin, who becomes the focus of Rostopchin's frustrations. When Rostopchin learns from a subordinate that Vereshchagin is among the political prisoners, he angrily shouts, '"Vereshchagin! Hasn't he been hanged yet? [...] Bring him to me!"'.[12] The face of Vereshchagin makes its appeal to Rostopchin, but in vain. Vereshchagin's 'emaciated young face, disfigured by the half-shaven head, hung down hopelessly. At the Count's first words he [Vereshchagin] raised it slowly and looked up at him as if wishing to say something or at least to meet his eye. But Rostopchin did not look at him'.[13] Rostopchin orders that the pitiful young man be turned over to an unruly mob of incensed Muscovites, who beat him to death.

Rostopchin tries to soothe his guilty conscience by maintaining to himself that he had acted for the public good. In deciding to throw Vereshchagin to the mob, Rostopchin tries to excuse himself by saying that he acted not as the private individual Fyodor Vassilievich Rostopchin but rather as a representative of the ruling authorities, including the tsar. '"If I were merely Fyodor Vassilievich"', Rostopchin comments, '"*ma ligne de conduite aurait été tout autrement tracée* [my line of conduct would have been drawn quite differently], but it was my duty to safeguard my life and dignity as commander in chief."'[14]

Vereshchagin is a prisoner in chains, young, vulnerable. He is thus what Levinas describes as the Stranger, 'l'absolument Autre'.[15] The absolutely Other, Levinas continues,

> is the Other human being in front of me [Autrui]. He and I do not form a number. The collectivity in which I say 'you' or 'we' is not the plural of the 'I.' I, you—these are not individuals of a common concept. Neither possession, nor unity of number nor the unity of concepts link me to the Stranger, the Stranger who disturbs the being at home with oneself. But Stranger also means the free one. Over him I have no *power.* He escapes my grasp by an essential dimension, even if I have him at my disposal. He is not wholly in my site.[16]

If the Other is truly other, he and I do not, in truth, comprise a totality in which 'I' am reduced to a public official and the other to a threat to the public good. The only way to rupture this totality is for the I to see the face of the other and to speak to him. But this is what Rostopchin refuses to do.

The stranger is the one who troubles the being at home with oneself. Over him, Levinas insists, I have no power, even if I have him at my disposal. Just after the mob murders Vereshchagin, Rostopchin, leaving the site of the carnage he had licensed in his carriage, encounters a 'lunatic' who has just been released from an asylum as part of the exodus of the Russian population from Moscow ordered in anticipation of Napoleon's arrival. The 'gaze' of this madman—with his 'solemn, gloomy face [...] with its beard growing in uneven tufts' and his 'black, agate pupils with saffron-yellow whites' moving 'restlessly near the lower eyelids'—was 'fixed' on Rostopchin. Rostopchin orders his driver to fly past the madman. Rostopchin then hears 'the insane despairing screams' of the madman 'growing fainter in the distance'. The screams are those of the madman, but Rostopchin's 'eyes saw nothing but the astonished, frightened, bloodstained face'[17] of Vereshchagin. Rostopchin is haunted by the face of the stranger whom he has betrayed and over whom, in truth, he has no power.

Rostopchin fails to respond to the face. Some pages later, the notoriously cruel French general Davout, in contrast to Rostopchin, does indeed respond to the face of the other. Pierre and several other Russians, charged with being incendiaries in now French-occupied Moscow, are brought before Davout. Davout accuses Pierre of being a Russian spy. Pierre insists he is not. 'Davout looked up and gazed intently at him', Tolstoy writes. 'For some seconds they looked at one another, and that look saved Pierre.'[18] Unaware that Davout has just decided to pardon him, Pierre imagines that he is being escorted to his death by an anonymous totality. Who, precisely, Pierre wonders,

> was executing him, killing him, depriving him of life—him, Pierre, with all his memories, aspirations, hopes, and thoughts? And Pierre felt that it was no one. It was a system—a concurrence of circumstances. A system of some sort was killing him—Pierre—depriving him of life, of everything, annihilating him.[19]

Pierre is spared execution, but he witnesses the execution of other fellow Russians and, as a result, he 'felt it was not in his power to regain faith in the meaning of life'.[20] Pierre is brought back to life by his encounter with the kindly peasant Platon Karataev.

The Rupture of Totality: Enjoyment

The novel's protagonist Pierre Bezukhov had, before his capture by the French, consistently found himself in situations which reduced his role to a part in an anonymous drama: a loveless marriage to a shallow and beautiful socialite—a marriage to which he felt fatally and helplessly drawn despite his better instincts. And now, in Moscow, after being seduced by numerology, he is convinced that he is predestined to kill Napoleon and thus to free Russia of this scourge. Pistol in hand, he goes in search of Napoleon through the streets of Moscow. But rather than acting as a pawn of his imagined fate (killing Napoleon), Pierre finds himself responding to the face of the other in front of him: he saves the French officer Ramballe and then goes on to rescue, at great personal risk, a young girl from the flames of her burning house.

Levinas is known as the philosopher of the ethical relation, of the I who is called into question by the other in front of me. We have just seen how Pierre experiences and exemplifies precisely this transcendence of the I towards the other. What is often not sufficiently appreciated about the work of Levinas, and about *Totality and Infinity* in particular, is that, while Levinas compellingly shows how totality is ruptured by my response to the face, by my responsibility for the other, the I, even before its being called into question by the other, escapes totality through enjoyment. The I, for Levinas, is what in *Totality and Infinity* he calls a *psychism* with its own interiority.[21] The self has an active existence. It lives in enjoyment, already outside of history and of any totality.

Pierre makes this discovery, remarkably, while in captivity in Moscow. Prince Andrei, Pierre reflects while in prison, 'had thought and said that happiness could only be negative [...] as though all desire for positive happiness is implanted in us merely to torment us and never be satisfied.' For Pierre, however, 'the satisfaction of one's needs and consequent freedom in the choice of one's way of life, now seemed to be indubitably man's highest happiness.' Pierre continues:

> Here and now for the first time he fully appreciated the enjoyment of eating when he wanted to eat, drinking when he wanted to drink, sleeping when he wanted to sleep, of warmth when he was cold, of talking to a fellow man when he wished to talk and hear a human voice. The satisfaction of one's needs–good food, cleanliness, and freedom–now [...] seemed to Pierre to constitute perfect happiness [...] and for the rest of his life, he thought and spoke with enthusiasm of that month of captivity, of those irrecoverable, strong, joyful sensations, and chiefly of the [...] inner freedom which he experienced only during those months.[22]

As Levinas writes in *Totality and Infinity,* '[t]he imprisoned being, ignoring its prison, is at home with itself.'[23] Pierre soon finds his separation from totality, his interiority, his enjoyment, his *psychism* threatened by the anonymous totality that is war. Just as Pierre was speaking to a French corporal about what could be done to assist a very sick Russian soldier, Tolstoy writes, 'the sharp rattle of the drums on two sides drowned out the sick man's groans.' Tolstoy continues: '"There it is! ... *It* again!" ['*Vot ono!.. Opiat' ono!*'] said Pierre to himself, and an involuntary shudder ran down his spine.' Having experienced himself in prison as an independent being, Pierre now once again feels 'that fatal force which had crushed him during the executions, but which he had not felt during his imprisonment'. This force was 'terrible,' Pierre remarks, but he now feels that 'there grew and strengthened in his soul a power of life independent of it'.[24]

That evening, Pierre is sitting by the campfire and enjoying conversation with his fellow prisoners. He decides he wants to cross the road to visit with the 'common soldier prisoners'. On the road a French sentinel orders him back to the side of the road which he has just crossed. Before he rejoins his 'companions by the campfire', he stops, thinks, and laughs loudly as he rejoices in the recognition of his separation from the totality that is war, of the joyful independence of his being, what Levinas would call his *psychism*:

> 'Ha-ha-ha!' laughed Pierre. And he said aloud to himself: 'The soldier did not let *me* pass. They took *me* and shut *me* up. They hold *me* captive. What, *me*? *Me*? *My* immortal soul? Ha-ha-ha! Ha-ha-ha!...' and he laughed till tears started to his eyes. [...] Pierre glanced up at the sky and the twinkling stars in its faraway depths. 'And all that is *mine*, all that is *me*, all that is within *me*, and it is all *I*!' thought Pierre.[25]

As Levinas writes in *Totality and Infinity*, the essence of enjoyment is 'the transmutation of the other into the same: [...] an energy that is other, recognized as other, recognized [...] as sustaining the very act that is directed upon it, becomes, in enjoyment, *my* own energy, *my* strength, *me*'.[26]

Infinity and the Face of Karataev

In *Totality and Infinity*, Levinas speaks of how the self, before taking responsibility for the other, enjoys his spontaneous freedom. When confronted with the other, I sense a prior responsibility that this spontaneity had in fact betrayed. The other calls this spontaneity into question. It is not necessarily a pleasant experience! It is, rather, a shameful one. Pierre, after experiencing the happiness of his freedom while imprisoned in the shed, on his march with the other prisoners from that location was loath to see and hear how the French army under whose authority he was travelling 'shot the prisoners who lagged behind, though more than a hundred perished in that way'. Nor did he 'think of Karataev, who grew weaker every day and evidently would soon have to share that fate'.[27] One evening, just after midnight, 'Pierre reached the fire and heard Platon's voice enfeebled by illness, and saw his pathetic face brightly lit up by the blaze'. Pierre feels 'a painful prick at his heart. His feeling of pity for this man frightened him, and he wished to go away, but there was no other fire, and Pierre sat down, trying not to look at Platon'.[28] Similarly, just before Karataev is shot by his captors, the kindly Karataev looks at Pierre, but Pierre 'was too afraid for himself'[29] and, pretending that he did not see Karataev look at him, Pierre 'moved hastily away'.[30]

It was largely his encounter with the kindness of Platon Karataev that brought Pierre back from a state of despair after he had witnessed the pitiful and pointless execution of his fellow Russian prisoners. The narrative proper of *War and Peace* ends with a paean to Karataev and what he meant to Pierre, the novel's protagonist, and what he continues to mean to him after he returns from his war-time experiences, marries Natasha, becomes a parent and begins family life.

Tolstoy's description of Pierre's discovery of faith in this concluding section of the narrative of *War and Peace* consists in Pierre's seeing, in Karataev, the witness of someone who is devoted 'to love life in one's suffering, in innocent sufferings'.[31] The infinity that, earlier in the novel, Tolstoy associates with the height of the sky here finds its locus in the near, which Pierre had previously dismissed as mere commonplace. In his captivity, Tolstoy writes, Pierre had learned that 'in Karataev God was greater, more infinite and unfathomable than in the Architect of the Universe recognized by the Freemasons'. Tolstoy continues:

> He felt like a man who after straining his eyes to see into the far distance finds what he sought at his very feet. All his life he had looked over the heads of the men around him, when he should have merely looked in front of him without straining his eyes.[32]

In what ways is God greater, more infinite and unfathomable in Karataev than in the Architect of the Universe recognized by the Freemasons? As a moral example, surely, of an innocent suffering that bears witness, nonetheless, to the joy of living. But for Pierre the memory of Karataev also brings vividly to mind a responsibility for the other, for the stranger, that Pierre had, to his shame, tried to shirk, to ignore—regardless of the fact that, for his own survival at that point in the narrative of *War and Peace*, it was arguably necessary for Pierre to ignore that crippling sense of shame. Tolstoy, through his portrayal of Prince Nekhliudov, the protagonist of his last novel *Resurrection*, will go on to fully confront this sense of shame that goes ignored or repressed in the perhaps somewhat smug happy ending of *War and Peace*. Pierre, just before that happy ending, recalls his encounter with Karataev as an encounter with what Levinas refers to as 'the Most-High'. '[T]his height is', however, 'no longer' found in 'the sky [*le ciel*]'. It is rather in the infinity I encounter in the face of the other in front of me, an infinite responsibility that is, for Levinas and increasingly for Tolstoy, 'the very elevation of height and its nobility.'[33]

Religion, Faith, and the Resistance to Vulnerability in *Anna Karenina*

In *War and Peace,* Tolstoy anticipates what Levinas means by his pairing of totality with war and of infinity with peace. In *Anna Karenina* and culminating in his late novel *Resurrection*, Tolstoy understands religion as bearing witness, above all, to ethical obligation, as does Levinas in his late work. Tolstoy's critical portrait of the dogmatic Christian believer Aleksei Aleksandrovich Karenin, Anna's husband, whom she leaves for the other Aleksei, the dashing Count Aleksei Kirillich Vronskii, can be seen as a bridge between these two phases of Tolstoy's literary career. In this section, I will show how Karenin sacrifices Anna's otherness to a notion of religious belief that is divorced from ethics, a notion of religion that Emmanuel Levinas labels as 'primitive': 'Everything that cannot be reduced to an interhuman relation', he writes in *Totality and Infinity*, 'represents not the superior, but rather the forever primitive, form of religion.'[34] Karenin's dogmatic understanding of Christianity, his determined resistance to vulnerability, makes it impossible for him to hear Anna's voice, to see her face, to register her otherness, her alterity. Tolstoy's critique of conventional religious belief as a refusal of vulnerability is sounded again and again throughout the remainder of his career as a writer and thinker.

Before we turn to Karenin's refusal of vulnerability, let us look at two passages from Levinas about vulnerability, a term that is central to his late work. The first is from an interview that is included in *Of God Who Comes to Mind* (*De Dieu qui vient à l'idée*, 1982):

> The Bible is the priority of the other [*l'autre*] in relation to me. It is in the other [*l'autrui*] that I always see the widow and the orphan. The other [*autrui*] always comes first. This is what I have called, in Greek language, the dissymmetry of the interpersonal relationship. If there is not this dissymmetry, then no line of what I have written can hold. And this is vulnerability. *Only a vulnerable I can love his neighbor* [italics added].[35]

The second is from Levinas's account of sensibility in *Otherwise than Being*:

> Exposure as a sensibility is [...] like an inversion of the *conatus* of *esse*, a not finding any protection in any consistency or identity of a state. It is a having been offered without any holding back and not the generosity of offering oneself, which would be an act. [...] In the having been offered without any holding back, it is as though sensibility were precisely what all protection and all absence of protection already presuppose: vulnerability itself.[36]

Levinas insists that I can love my neighbour only when I find no protection in identity, when I am vulnerable.

It is not as if the spiritually flat, unimaginative bureaucrat Karenin is incapable of vulnerability. He is in fact deeply vulnerable, but—perhaps because he was brought up as an orphan,[37] adopted by an uncle who was a bureaucrat, and as a young child was deprived of maternal love—he is terrified by his own vulnerability. As Tolstoy informs us,

> None but those closest to Karenin knew that this to all appearances supremely cold and sensible man had one weakness that contradicted his general cast of character. Karenin could not bear to hear or see the tears of a child or a woman. The sight of tears put him in a state of great distress, and he lost the ability to think. His head clerk and secretary knew this and forewarned lady petitioners that they were by no means to cry if they did not want to spoil their case. 'He will get angry and will not listen to you,' they would say. Indeed, in those instances, the emotional distress produced in Alexei Alexandrovich by tears was expressed in impatient fury. 'There is nothing I can do, nothing. Would you kindly get out!' he would shout in those instances.[38]

Karenin considers himself a believer, a religious man. Religion, for him, however, is a mere matter of rules. As Tolstoy comments, Karenin 'was a believer interested in religion primarily in its political sense'.[39] His embrace of religion in a political rather than in an ethical sense is precisely the opposite of how Levinas, in *Totality and Infinity*, understands religion:

> For the relation between the being here below and the transcendent being that results in no community or concept or totality—a relation without relation—we reserve the term religion.[40]

In a remarkable passage early in the novel, Tolstoy shows how Karenin is utterly incapable of encountering his wife Anna from a "religious" perspective, in Levinas's sense of the word "religious", i.e. as absolutely other than himself. Karenin now has good reason to suspect Anna of infidelity. As he prepares to confront Anna in their home in St Petersburg, before she returns from a tryst with Vronskii, he enters her sitting room and looks at her things. He and Anna have been married for eight years, but it is here, for the very first time, that he finally recognizes that Anna has an existence separate from his own. This extraordinary passage is worth quoting at length:

> Here, looking at her desk with the malachite blotter lying on top and a note she had started, his thoughts suddenly changed. He began thinking about her, about what she thought and felt. For the first time he vividly imagined her private life, her thoughts, her desires, and the thought that she might and must have her own separate life seemed to him so terrible that he hastened to drive it away. This was the abyss into which he was afraid to look. Trying to imagine the thoughts and feelings of another being was an emotional exercise alien to Alexei Alexandrovich. He considered this emotional exercise harmful and dangerous fantasizing.
>
> 'What is most horrible of all,' he thought, 'is that now, as my work is drawing to its conclusion'—he was thinking about the project he was overseeing now—'when I need all the tranquility and strength I can muster, now I am being inundated with this senseless worry. What else can I do, though? I'm not one of those people who suffers upset and alarm and lacks the strength to look them in the face.'
>
> 'I must think this through, come to a decision, and set it aside,' he said out loud.
>
> 'Questions of her feelings, of what has and might come to pass in her soul, that is none of my affair, it is the affair of her conscience and falls under religion,' he told himself, feeling relief at the awareness that he had found the established formal category [*punkt uzakonenii*] under which the newly arisen circumstances rightly fell.[41]

Karenin refuses to see his part in his failed marriage. He takes no responsibility for Anna's unhappiness, which drove her towards her liaison with Vronskii, whose aggressive advances she at first staunchly resists. Karenin characterizes Anna as

> 'Without honor, heart, or religion. [...] I made a mistake in linking my life with her; however, there is nothing bad in my mistake, and so I cannot be

> unhappy. It's not I who am to blame [*Vinovat ne ia*],' he told himself, 'it's she. But she's no business of mine. For me, she doesn't exist.'[42]

In Dostoevsky's 1881 novel *The Brothers Karamazov* (*Brat'ia Karamazovy*), the jury renders its guilty verdict against Dmitrii Karamazov with the word *vinovat* ('guilty'). Dmitrii is not technically guilty of his father's murder, but he is certainly responsible (*vinovat*), in no small measure, for his disciple and bastard half-brother Smerdiakov's crime. Karenin, unlike Dmitrii Karamazov, refuses to take responsibility for a crime (for Karenin, adultery rather than parricide) that he did not technically commit, but for which he is nevertheless in large part responsible. Note that, in the quotation cited above, Karenin explicitly says that he is not 'responsible' (*vinovat*) for Anna's adulterous affair.

Karenin comes closer to a embracing a truly religious attitude—to embracing vulnerability—at Anna's bedside when, in attempting to give birth to the child she conceived with Vronskii, she is perilously close to dying. In response to Anna's desperate urging, Karenin forgives Vronskii:

> At his ill wife's bedside, for the first time in his life, he surrendered to the warm compassion which other people's suffering evoked in him and which had previously embarrassed him as a harmful weakness; and his pity for her, and remorse for having wished her death, and, most of all, the very joy of forgiveness made him feel not only relief from his sufferings but also a spiritual peace he had never before experienced. He suddenly felt that the very thing that had been the source of his sufferings had become the source of his spiritual joy; that what had seemed insoluble when he had condemned, reproached, and hated became simple and clear when he forgave and loved.[43]

Forgiving Vronskii is not sufficient, however. In order to truly save Anna, to allow Anna her absolute otherness, Karenin must be willing to agree to a divorce. A divorce can be granted, according to the male-centred laws of the time, only if the husband admits to being at fault, i.e. to being the adulterer. Anna, however, is the adulterous party, so Karenin must take the blame in spite of his (technical) innocence. He agrees to do so, but more as a martyr than as someone who truly takes responsibility for his part in his failed marriage. Karenin at first agrees to permit Anna to divorce him, but even in this consent we can already sense that his transcendence before Anna is not quite transcendent enough, for he finally balks and refuses the divorce. We sense this failure of transcendence in his response to Anna's brother, Stiva Oblonskii, who comes to see Karenin to plead, on Anna's behalf, for the divorce.

> 'Yes, yes!' Karenin exclaimed in a shrill voice, 'I will take the disgrace upon myself and even give up my son, but ... but wouldn't it be better to leave it be? But do what you like.'
>
> Turning away from his brother-in-law, so that he could not see him, he sat in the chair by the window. It was a bitter and shameful thing for him; but along with this grief and shame he was experiencing joy and tenderness at the loftiness of his own humility [*pred svoei vysotoi smireniia*].[44]

As we have noted, Levinas (in *Otherwise than Being*) says that vulnerability 'is a having been offered without any holding back and not the generosity of offering oneself, which would be an act'.[45] Karenin's experience of 'joy and tenderness at the loftiness of his own humility' bears ironic witness to the incompleteness of his transcendence before the face of Anna. Tolstoy is here subtly but clearly mocking Karenin's exalted sense of his own humility, of his own generosity, of which he is abundantly and proudly conscious. Hardly true humility, or true vulnerability!

Karenin recants his generous offer of divorce under the influence of his socialite friend Lidiia Ivanovna, who introduces Karenin to the cult of an emotive "spiritualism" that was the rage in Petersburg high society at the time, and who despises Anna. '[F]rom an indifferent and lazy believer', Lidiia Ivanovna turns Karenin

> into an ardent and firm supporter of that new interpretation of the Christian doctrine which had spread of late in Petersburg. Alexei Alexandrovich was easily convinced of this. [...] He saw nothing impossible or incompatible in that notion that death, which exists for nonbelievers, did not exist for him, and that since he possessed the fullest faith [...] then there was no sin in his soul now, and he was already experiencing complete salvation here, on earth. [...] Alexei Alexandrovich needed so much to think this way, so needed in his humiliation to have that loftiness, however fabricated, from which he, despised by all, might despise others, that he clung to this salvation, this mock salvation.[46]

For the spiritualists, 'faith' counts for more than 'works'. In fact, for the believing spiritualist to attain salvation, 'works' mean nothing at all. 'For the believer, there is no sin', Lidiia Ivanovna remarks at a spiritualist séance to which she has invited Stiva Oblonskii in order to introduce him to the charlatan who will seal Anna's fate by proclaiming, after allegedly consulting spirits, that Karenin must refuse the divorce. 'Yes, but faith without works is dead', Stiva remarks, remembering this phrase from the catechism, to which Karenin replies:

> 'There it is, from the Epistle of James the Apostle,' said Alexei Alexandrovich, turning to Lydia Ivanovna with a certain reproach, evidently about a topic they had already spoken of more than once. 'How much harm the false interpretation of this passage has done! Nothing so repels a man from faith as this interpretation. "I have no works, I cannot believe," since nowhere is this said. What is said is the opposite.'[47]

Karenin, in the end, anchors his religious faith in a resistance to vulnerability. I will conclude this second section by contrasting the believer Karenin, whose Christianity has cut itself off from a vulnerable love of the neighbour, with the nonbeliever Levin, with whose epiphany the novel ends. I began by citing Levinas's comment that 'only a vulnerable I can love his neighbor'.[48] Levin's wife Kitty, herself a believer, has never been bothered by her husband's unbelief. For Kitty, Levin's actions speak for themselves:

> What kind of nonbeliever is he? With his heart and his fear of disappointing anyone, even a child! Everything for others, and nothing for himself. [...] All these peasants who come to see him every day, as if he were obligated to serve them.[49]

At the end of the novel, Levin recognizes that he had been taught, through his early religious education that he came to reject in favour of science, to love his neighbour. '"Was it by reason"', Levin asks, '"that I arrived at the idea that one must love one's neighbor and not strangle him?"'.[50] No, Levin concludes, he did not arrive at this principle through reason, which Spinoza (and Tolstoy tells us elsewhere in the novel, that Levin had been reading Spinoza!) refers to as the *conatus essendi,* the striving of each living thing to persist in its being, to be at the expense of, rather than for, other beings. In the passage from *Otherwise than Being* I discussed with reference to Karenin, Levinas refers to Spinoza's notion of the *conatus essendi.*[51] The *conatus essendi,* as both Levin and Levinas make clear, protects itself, at all costs, from vulnerability.

'The Russian novelists ceaselessly wonder,' Levinas remarks in *Ethics and Infinity*, about 'the philosophical problem understood as the meaning of the human, as the search for the famous "meaning of life" [*sens de la vie*]'.[52] Levin, as he says at the end of *Anna Karenina*, finds this meaning not in faith, which he is still not sure he truly possesses, but rather in embracing the feeling of being a vulnerable I who, in striving for goodness, is loving towards his neighbour:

> This new feeling has not changed me, has not made me happy, or suddenly illuminated things as I had dreamed. [...] But faith—not faith—I don't know what it is [*A vera—ne vera—ia znaiu*]. [...] —but my life now, my whole life [*vsia moia zhizn'*], regardless of whatever may happen to me, each minute of it, is not only not meaningless [*ne bessmyslenna*], as it was before, but possesses the undoubted meaning [*smysl'*] of that goodness [*dobra*] I have the power to put into it![53]

Are we not presented, at the end of *Anna Karenina*, with an anticipatory portrait of Levin as Levinas?

Thinking God on the Basis of Ethics: Tolstoy's Resurrection

Anna Karenina concludes, as I have just proposed, with an anticipatory portrait of Levin as Levinas. Levin, like Levinas in his late work, approaches the meaning of God through ethical obligation rather than through faith.

Tolstoy's late novel *Resurrection* (1899) is a rewriting both of Dostoevsky's *Notes from the House of the Dead* (*Zapiski iz mertvogo doma*, 1860–62), Tolstoy's favourite work by Dostoevsky, and of *The Brothers Karamazov*, by which Tolstoy claims to have been bored and which he says he never finished and which lay by his bed when he left Iasnaia Poliana for the last time. Like Dostoevsky in *The Brothers Karamazov*, in *Resurrection* Tolstoy, or rather his protagonist Prince Dmitry Ivanich Nekhliudov, makes the case that 'Each of us—before the faces of everyone and for everything—is responsible, but I more than all the others'.[54] In his youth, Nekhliudov had seduced a servant, Katiusha Maslova, then in the employ of his aunt. Years later, as a member of the ruling aristocratic elite, Nekhliudov is a juror at a trial in which a prostitute is accused of poisoning a client. Nekhliudov is shocked to recognize the accused as the once innocent young woman he had seduced and who, as a consequence of that seduction, went on to become a prostitute. Nekhliudov sees Katiusha's face and is overwhelmed with guilt and the betrayal of his own responsibility for her:

> Yes, this was she. He now clearly saw in her face that strange, indescribable individuality which distinguishes every face from all others; something peculiar, all its own, not to be found anywhere else. In spite of the unhealthy pallor and the fullness of the face, it was there, this sweet particular individuality; on those lips, in the slight squint of her eyes, in the voice, particularly in the naïve smile and the expression of readiness on the face and figure.[55]

After the guilty verdict, which is a travesty, Nekhliudov is determined to follow Katiusha to Siberia and to devote himself to her and to the other prisoners, whom he comes to see more as victims of a cruel political system than as evil criminals.

Resurrection

Unlike Dostoevsky in *The Brothers Karamazov,* Tolstoy in *Resurrection* is not encumbered by insisting on a literal understanding of resurrection or of salvation. Nor is Tolstoy burdened by what Dostoevsky described as his own unquenchable 'thirst to believe'.[56] In *Resurrection* Tolstoy, in anticipation of the later work of Emmanuel Levinas, thinks God beginning with—or on the basis of—ethical obligation, outside the question of faith or belief. Tolstoy equates true religion with ethical responsibility, and he creates, in *Resurrection*, a work of literature that embodies what Tolstoy, in *What is Art?* (*Chto takoe iskusstvo?*, 1897), defines as 'religious art'.[57]

Anna Karenina, written just before Tolstoy's conversion to a religious consciousness (a process described in *A Confession* (*Ispoved'*, 1882)), is more artfully written than *Resurrection* and its characters are more three-dimensional. But redemption through literary greatness was not enough for the later Tolstoy, who came to believe that his own moral life had been corrupted by the thoughtless privilege that, once glimpsed and acknowledged, brought his final literary alter ego, Prince Dmitrii

Ivanich Nekhliudov, to his knees. Tolstoy's novel is titled *Resurrection,* but the resurrection of which he speaks is more precisely an awakening of the moral consciousness.

In *What I Believe* (*V chem moia vera,* published in 1884, four years before the publication of the final version of *Resurrection*), Tolstoy argues that, in the New Testament, 'there are thirteen passages which are understood as being predictions by Christ of his resurrection,' but, in truth, '[i]n none of these passages in the original does the word "resurrection" even occur.' Of the two Greek verbs (ἀνίστημι and ἐγείρω) that are conventionally translated as meaning 'to resurrect,' Tolstoy insists, '[o]ne of these words means "to upraise"; the other means "to awaken," and, in the middle voice, "to wake up," "to rouse oneself." But neither the one nor the other can ever, under any circumstances, mean "to raise from the dead."' Tolstoy insists that '[o]f his own personal resurrection—strange as this may sound to people who have not themselves studied the Gospels—*Christ never spoke at all!*'.[58] Tolstoy understands resurrection as moral regeneration. Sonship to God, for Tolstoy, is not so much a supernatural or miraculous fact of divine inheritance as it is to be morally awake, to love and to be responsible for your neighbour. To be the Messiah, or *a* Messiah, moreover, is not limited to Christ's particular sonship for Tolstoy in *What I Believe.* In Matthew 16.20, Christ warned his disciples not to say that he, Jesus, was the Messiah. Why not? Because, for Tolstoy, it is the disciples' own 'sonship to God' that allows them to participate, on a personal level, in messianic deliverance. When I, like Christ, take responsibility for others, I, too, am a 'son of God'. I am a Messiah.

And here we note a link to a passage from the Talmudic treatise *Sanhedrin,* with which Tolstoy was familiar, a section of which is devoted to rabbinic discussions of the resurrection of the dead as well as to the meaning of messianic deliverance. Two years before he published *What I Believe,* Tolstoy studied Hebrew and the Talmud with the Chief Rabbi of Moscow, Solomon Zalkind Minor. Let us attend to the remarks of Rav Nachman, a Talmudic scholar who died in the year 320 of the Common Era. Some of the rabbis cited in this section (98b) of *Sanhedrin* say that the name of the Messiah is Shiloh (meaning 'a gift [*shai*] to him [*l'o*])'; some say his name is Chaninah ('mercy'); still others say his name is Menachem the son of Chizkiah, for the name 'Menachem' means 'comforter'. Rav Nachman offers a different interpretation: 'If he [the Messiah] is of the living, then he might well be (like) Me,' or 'he may in fact be me' (*kegon 'ana'*). As Levinas remarks of this passage from the Talmud, Rav Nachman is saying 'the Messiah is Myself [*Moi*]; to be Myself is to be the Messiah. [...] The fact of not evading the burden imposed by the suffering of others'[59] is what it means to be a self, to be *Moi*.

The Brothers Karamazov (published as a complete novel in 1881, the year of the author's death) ends with the funeral of the young boy Iliushechka, attended by the boy's young friends. Alesha Karamazov assures the boys that they will all 'certainly' see each other again in the life to come.[60] Here we have a very different response to the meaning of resurrection than that of Tolstoy who, in conversation with his friend the philologist I. M. Ivakin, remarked at virtually the same moment (1881): 'What is it to me if [Christ] is resurrected? If he was resurrected, then God bless him! The questions important to me are: What should I do? How should I live?'[61]

Tolstoy's Rejection of Redemption through Faith

There is a stark difference, for the Tolstoy of *Resurrection*, between faith or belief, on the one hand, and ethical obligation, on the other. Tolstoy continually critiques the idea of the requirement or necessity of religious or dogmatic belief. Towards the end of the novel, Nekhliudov is staying in St Petersburg with an aunt. What has brought Nekhliudov to Petersburg was the opportunity it afforded him to speak with government officials who could alleviate the suffering of the convicts on whose behalf he is now tirelessly working. Urged by his aunt, Nekhliudov attends a dinner party at her stylish house one evening to hear the emotive words of the itinerant German preacher Kiesewetter, who speaks in English, immediately translated into Russian for his audience of aristocratic Petersburgers. Here we have a reprise of Tolstoy's critique of the charlatan spiritualist Landau, whose mutterings in *Anna Karenina* spelled doom for Stiva Oblonskii's plan to secure his sister Anna's divorce from Karenin.

Kiesewetter begins by telling the guests how terribly sinful they—and he—all are, how 'no salvation' is possible for any of them; '"we are all doomed to destruction"'. His tone then changes:

> The orator suddenly uncovered his face, and smiled a very real-looking smile, such as actors express joy with, and began again in a sweet, gentle voice:
>
> 'Yet there is a way to be saved. Here it is—a joyful, easy way. Salvation is in the blood shed for us by the only Son of God, who gave Himself up to torments for our sake. His sufferings, His blood, will save us. Brothers and sisters,' he said, again with tears in his voice, 'let us praise the Lord, who gave His only Son for the redemption of the world. His holy blood—'
>
> Nekhlyudov felt so deeply disgusted that he rose silently, and, frowning and keeping back a groan of shame, he left on tiptoe and went to his room.[62]

For Nekhliudov to seek redemption or salvation as a goal for himself personally, Tolstoy constantly suggests, is a form of egoism, of selfishness. Kiesewetter, in contrast, preaches a praising of 'the Lord, who gave His only Son for the redemption of the world'. Praise of God, with a tacit belief in Him, is enough for Kiesewetter. Here is a 'joyful, easy' way to salvation. True redemption or salvation, however, requires that I spend time in the filth of the prison system listening to those incarcerated there, and that I bear witness to injustice.

Towards the end of the novel, another foreigner—this time an Englishman rather than a German who speaks English—similarly emphasizes the importance of religious belief at the expense of ethical obligation. At this point in the novel, the reader has made the gruelling journey eastward with Nekhliudov across the vastness of Russia to the grim prison in Siberia to which the convicts have been sentenced to spend many years of their lives in exile. An Englishman who claims to be studying Russia's carceral system asks Nekhliudov, a well-educated aristocrat whose English is excellent, to show him around the prison. It is only towards the end of their tour that the Englishman's true motives are revealed.

Nekhliudov and the Englishman, accompanied by a prison official, pass through a corridor where they witness two prisoners urinating on the floor. They then enter the first of several wards. This first ward houses those sentenced to hard labour. Two of the prisoners are clearly very ill but they go untreated because 'the infirmary was overfull'.[63] The Englishman now announces that

> he would like to say a few words to these people, and asked Nekhliudov to interpret. It turned out that besides studying the places of exile and the prisons of Siberia, the Englishman had another object in view, that of preaching salvation by faith and the Redemption. 'Tell them,' he said, 'that Christ pitied and loved them and died for them. If they believe in this they will be saved.' While he spoke all prisoners stood silent with their arms at their sides. 'This book, tell them,' he continued, 'tells us all about it. Can any of them read?'[64]

Of course, most of the prisoners could not read. But what good would it have done them if they could? The Englishman was preaching 'salvation by faith and the Redemption'. The miserable convicts will, he believes, be saved through their *belief* in salvation and redemption. Their belief will, apparently, make it unnecessary for those in power to confront their own betrayal of responsibility that has resulted in this display of man's inhumanity to his fellow man, in which 'Everywhere men—cold, hungry, idle, diseased, degraded, and confined—were shown off like wild beasts'.[65]

The Religious Discourse Prior to Religious Discourse: 'Here I Am'

Several chapters later, Nekhliudov comes upon a strange, nameless man who bears witness to the moral horrors of the prison system that had been glossed over by the evangelizing Englishman. Nekhliudov had originally encountered this strange man while traversing a broad river on a raft towards the end of his journey to the prison in Siberia. As they prepared to set off, the men on the raft all took off their hats and crossed themselves except for this strange, disheveled old man, who asked:

> 'Who's one to pray to?'
> 'To God of course,' said the driver witheringly.
> 'And you just show me where He is—this God?' [...]
> 'Where? In heaven of course.'
> 'And have you been up there?'
> 'Whether I've been or not, everyone knows that one must pray to God.'

> 'No man has ever seen God at any time. The only begotten Son, who is in the bosom of the Father, He hath declared Him,' said the old man in the same rapid manner, and with a stern frown.
> 'It's clear you are not a Christian, but a hole-worshipper. You pray to a hole,' said the driver.[66]

And how does this declaring occur, we might ask? Is it by saying 'I believe in God'? Apparently not, as in response to one of the passengers asking the nameless man what his 'faith' is, the stranger replies, '"I have no kind of faith, because I believe no one—no one but myself."'[67] Who is 'myself'? What does it mean to be 'me'? What does it mean to believe 'myself'? This is the same 'myself' that Nekhliudov comes to realize, to his shame, he had abandoned in his youth and which he is determined to reclaim by devoting his life to Maslova and to so many of the other prisoners. As Levinas writes in his late essay 'God and Philosophy',

> The sentence in which God comes to be involved in words is not 'I believe in God.' [...] The religious discourse prior to all religious discourse is the 'here I am' said to the neighbor to whom I am given over, and in which I announce peace, that is, my responsibility for the other.

Levinas then quotes Isaiah 57:19: 'I [the Infinite One/the Eternal, i.e. God] create the fruit of the lips [which say], "Peace, peace to him who is far off, and to him who is near," says the Infinite One/the Eternal.'[68] The infinite is in *me*, speaks through *my* lips when I say 'Here I am' before the face of the other in front of me ('to him who is near'), and before all the other others (to those who are 'far off'), for whom I am also responsible.

Let us now turn to the end of the novel, where we meet the strange, nameless man for the last time. He is in prison simply because he has no passport. We have earlier in the novel seen others imprisoned unjustly for the very same reason, and for unconscionably long periods of time. What the stranger bears witness to is 'the Antichrist' in the prison 'who tortures men'. For see here, he says, how the Antichrist has 'locked them in a cage, a whole army of them. Men should eat bread in the sweat of their brow. But *he* has locked them up with no work to do, and feeds them like swine, so that they should turn into beasts'.[69]

But how, the Englishman then asks, '"should one treat thieves and murderers now?"' What are we to do with them? Nekhliudov translates this question from English into Russian for the strange old man:

> 'Tell him he should take the seal of Antichrist off from himself,' the old man said, frowning sternly; 'then he will know neither thieves nor murderers. Tell him so.'
>
> 'He is crazy,' said the Englishman, after Nekhlyudov had translated the old man's words; and shrugging his shoulders he left the cell.[70]

The evangelizing Englishman fails to take account of his own responsibility for the fact that some are labelled thieves and murderers in prison. Instead he himself becomes an Antichrist, judging others while taking no responsibility for the prison system. In this sense, the Englishman, who professes Christianity, has not followed the teaching of Dostoevsky's Father Zosima in *The Brothers Karamazov*. Father Zosima insists that, while 'each of us—before the faces of everyone and for everything—is responsible, but I more than all the others', it is also true, at the same time, that

> no one can judge a criminal, until he recognizes that he is just such a criminal as the man standing before him, and that he perhaps is more than all men to blame for that crime. When he understands that, he will be able to be a judge. Though that sounds absurd, it is true. If I had been righteous myself, perhaps there would have been no criminal standing before me.[71]

What is my role in the phenomenon of crime, and of punitive incarceration? Dostoevsky was haunted by the same question after his experience of serving four years in prison in Western Siberia. 'How much youth', the narrator of *House of the Dead* asks, 'lay uselessly buried within those prison walls, what mighty powers were wasted here in vain!'. The narrator continues,

> After all, one must tell the whole truth; those men were exceptional men. Perhaps they were the most gifted, the strongest of our people. But their energies were vainly wasted, wasted abnormally, unjustly, hopelessly. And who was to blame, whose fault was it (*a kto vinovat*)? And that's just it, who was responsible (*kto vinovat*)?[72]

In his last novel, Tolstoy—through his protagonist Nekhliudov—says 'Here I am'. I, Lev Nikolaevich Tolstoy, am responsible, infinitely responsible for the other in front of me, and for all the other others. Here I am, Lev (Nikolaevich Tolstoy), creator of the fictional character Konstantin Dmitrievich Lev-in, and an anticipatory disciple of Emmanuel Lev-in-as.

Notes

1 Emmanuel Levinas, *Ethics and Infinity: Conversations with Phillipe Nemo*, trans. by Richard A. Cohen (Pittsburgh, PA: Duquesne University Press, 1985), p. 22.

2 On Levinas and Dostoevsky, see Jill Robbins, *Altered Reading: Levinas and Literature* (Chicago, IL and London: University of Chicago Press, 1999); Alain Toumayan, '"I More than the Others,": Dostoevsky and Levinas', *Yale French Studies*, 104 (2004), 55–66, https://doi.org/10.2307/3182504; Peter Atterton, 'Art, Religion, and Ethics Post Mortem Dei: Levinas and Dostoevsky,' *Levinas Studies: An Annual Review*, 2 (2007), 105–32; Jacques Rolland, *Dostoïevski: La question de l'Autre* (Paris: Verdier, 1983); Val Vinokur, *The Trace of Judaism: Dostoevsky, Babel, Mandelstam, Levinas* (Evanston, IL: Northwestern University Press, 2008); and Steven Shankman, *Turned Inside Out: Reading the Russian Novel in Prison* (Evanston, IL: Northwestern University Press, 2017). On Levinas and Tolstoy, see A. B. Hofmeyr, 'Dying the Human Condition: Re-reading Ivan Ilyitch with Levinas', *The International Journal of the Humanities*, 5, 2 January 2007, 129–36, https://doi.org/10.18848/1447-9508/CGP/v05i02/43482; Steven Shankman, 'Levinas i Tolstoi: "Total'nost' i beskonechnoe" kak "Voina i mir"' ['Levinas and Tolstoy: *Totality and Infinity* as *War and Peace*'], in *Lev Tolstoi i mirovaia literature: Materialy mezhdunarodnoi nauchnoi konferentsii* 13, ed. by Galina Alekseeva (Yasnaya Polyana, Russia: Yasnaya Polyana, 2018), 97–105; and Steven Shankman, *Turned Inside Out*, pp. 11, 18, 101–02, 109, 112, 139 n9, 147 n47. Eva Marie Hirschmann says, 'I am certain Levinas picked up a copy of *War and Peace* in his father's bookstore [in Kovno, Lithuania]'. See Hirschmann, 'Ethics and the Face in Levinas and Tolstoy,' https://zauberblume.livejournal.com/2124.html [May 4 2007]).

3 Emmanuel Levinas, *Totality and Infinity*, trans. by Alfonso Lingis (Pittsburgh, PA: Duquesne University Press, 1968), p. 54 [Italics in the original]. *Totalité et infini* was first published in The Hague by Martinus Nijhoff in 1971.

4 Ibid.

5 William Large, *Levinas' "Totality and Infinity"* (London: Bloomsbury, 2015), p. 29.

6 Ibid., p. 30.

7 Ibid.

8 Emmanuel Levinas, *Totalité et infini: essai sur l'extériorité* (Paris: Livre de Poche, 1990), p. 8. Levinas, *Totality and Infinity*, p. 23.

9 See Levinas's essay 'La Signification et le sens', *Revue de métaphysique et de morale*, 69 :2 (1964), 125–56. See also Levinas's lecture on Bloch, delivered on May 7 1976 and included in Levinas' *Dieu, la mort et le temps*, ed. by Jacques Rolland (Paris: Grasset, 1973), p. 118.

10 Tolstoy, *War and Peace,* trans. by Alymer and Louise Maude, revised by George Gibian (New York and London: W. W. Norton & Company, 1966; revised 1996), p. 244.

11 Ibid., p. 253.

12 Ibid., p. 788.

13 Ibid., p. 790.

14 Tolstoy, *War and Peace*, trans. by Richard Pevear and Larissa Volokhonsky (New York: Knopf, 2007), p. 891. Cf. the words, recorded by Svetlana Alexievich, of a former Soviet prisoner in the Gulag who is imagining the thinking of those apparatchiks at whose hands he and so many others had suffered: 'Each of them [was] thinking, "That isn't me." I wasn't the one putting those people on the rack or blowing their brains out, that wasn't me back there putting sharpened pencils through women's nipples. It's not me, it's the system. Even Stalin... even he'd say, "I'm not the one who decides, it's the Party." He taught his son: You think I'm Stalin—you're wrong! That's Stalin! And he'd point to the portrait of himself hanging on the wall. Not at himself, but at his portrait [...]. The flywheel turns, but there's no one to blame' (*Secondhand Time: The Last of the Soviets*, trans. by Bela Shayevich (New York: Random House, 2016), p. 280).

15 Levinas, *Totalité et infini*, p. 28.

16 Levinas, *Totalité et infini*, p. 28; Levinas, *Totality and Infinity*, p. 39. Translation modified.

17 Tolstoy, *War and Peace* (Maudes' translation), p. 794.

18 Ibid., p. 852.

19 Ibid., p. 853.

20 Ibid., p. 856.

21 Levinas, *Totality and Infinity*, p. 54, p. 56, p. 59, p. 105.

22 Ibid., p. 896. In opposition to those who argue in favour of determinism, like Tolstoy himself (!) in *War and Peace*, Levinas insists that the I is independent and separated from history, from totality: 'one may denounce as much as one likes its freedom as already enchained to an

ignored determinism; ignorance is here a detachment, incomparable to the self-ignorance in which things [i.e. inanimate objects] lie. It is founded in the interiority of a psychism; it is positive in the enjoyment of itself. The imprisoned being, ignoring its prison, is at home with itself. Its power for illusion—if illusion there was—constitutes its separation' (*Totality and Infinity*, p. 55; translation modified). Pierre's experience of freedom in *War and Peace*, which Tolstoy narrates so vividly and convincingly, belies the author's own theorizing in favour of determinism in *War and Peace*, especially in the Second Epilogue. In the Second Epilogue, Tolstoy sees history as predetermined and freedom as an illusion that is imagined both during and after the fact. For Levinas, I truly am free, as a separated being enjoying my existence, to do as I like. My spontaneous freedom, which truly is freedom, is, however, put to shame by the Other who, it turns out, truly invests my freedom.

23 Levinas, *Totality and Infinity*, p. 55; Levinas, *Totalité et infini*, p. 47.

24 Tolstoy, *War and Peace* (Maudes' translation), p. 901; the Russian is cited from L. N. Tolstoi, *Voina i mir,* 2 vols (Moscow: Astrel, 2010), II, p. 495.

25 Tolstoy, *War and Peace* (Maudes' translation), p. 902. [Italics added].

26 Levinas, *Totality and Infinity*, p. 111. [Italics added].

27 Tolstoy, *War and Peace* (Maudes' translation), p. 937.

28 Ibid., p. 938.

29 Tolstoy, *War and Peace* (Pevear and Volokhonsky translation), pp. 1063–64, translating '*No P'eru slishkom strashno bylo za sebia*' (*Voina i mir,* II, p. 552).

30 Tolstoy, *War and Peace* (Maudes' translation), p. 940.

31 Ibid., p. 941.

32 Ibid., p. 977.

33 Levinas, *Totality and Infinity*, pp. 34–35; Levinas, *Totalité et infini*, p. 23.

34 Levinas, *Totality and Infinity*, p. 79.

35 Levinas, *Of God Who Comes to Mind*, trans. by Bettina Bergo (Stanford, CA: Stanford University Press, 1998), p. 91. The French is cited from *De Dieu qui vient à l'idée* (Paris: Vrin, 2004), first published in 1982.

36 Levinas, *Otherwise than Being, or Beyond Essence*, trans. by Alphonse Lingis (Pittsburgh, PA: Duquesne University Press, 1998), p. 75.

37 See *Anna Karenina*: 'Alexei Alexandrovich had grown up an orphan. There were two brothers. Their father they did not remember, and their mother died when Alexei Alexandrovich was ten years old. Their inheritance was small. His Uncle Karenin, an important official and once a favorite of the late emperor, had raised them.' Leo Tolstoy, *Anna Karenina*, trans. by Marian Schwartz (New Haven, CT and London: Yale University Press, 2014), p. 464. All translations from *Anna Karenina* will be from this version, which I have sometimes slightly adapted.

38 Ibid., p. 256.

39 Ibid., p. 467.

40 Levinas, *Totality and Infinity*, p. 80.

41 Tolstoy, *Anna Karenina*, pp. 133–34. The Russian is cited from L. N. Tolstoi, *Anna Karenina* (Moscow: Eksmo, 2011), p. 143.

42 Tolstoy, *Anna Karenina*, pp. 256–57.

43 Ibid., p. 384.

44 Ibid., p. 396.

45 Levinas, *Otherwise than Being*, p. 75.

46 Tolstoy, *Anna Karenina*, p. 468.

47 Ibid., p. 669.

48 Levinas, *Of God Who Comes to Mind*, p. 91.

49 Ibid., p. 713.

50 Ibid., p. 724. Translation modified.

51 Levinas, *Otherwise than Being*, p. 75.

52 Levinas, *Ethics and Infinity*, p. 22. The French is cited from Levinas, *Éthique et infini* (Paris: Fayard, 2012), originally published in French in 1982.

53 Tolstoy, *Anna Karenina*, p. 742.

54 Fedor Dostoevskii, *Brat'ia Karamazovy* (Moscow: Eksmo, 2003), p. 297. My translation.

55 Leo Tolstoy, *Resurrection*, trans. by Louise Maude (Oxford and New York: Oxford University Press, 1994), p. 35.

56 Fyodor Dostoevsky, *Selected Letters of Fyodor Dostoevsky*, ed. by Joseph Frank, Richard Goldstein, and Andrew MacAndrew (New Brunswick, NJ: Rutgers University Press, 1987), p. 68; the Russian text is cited from Dostoevsky's *Pis'ma*, ed. by A. S. Dolinin, 4 vols (Moscow and Leningrad: State Publishing House, 1928), I, p. 142.

57 Leo Tolstoy, *What is Art?*, trans. by Richard Pevear and Larissa Volokhonsky (London: Penguin Books, 1995), p. 132.

58 Leo Tolstoy, *A Confession, The Gospel in Brief, and What I Believe*, trans. by Aylmer Maude (London: Oxford University Press, 1940), pp. 437–38.

59 Levinas, *Difficult Freedom*, p. 89; Levinas, *Difficile liberté*, p. 137. Rav Nachman's comments are cited from the Schottenstein edition of *Talmud Bavli*, vol. 49, *Tractate Sanhedrin*, vol. III (New York: Mesorah Publications, third edition, 2008; rpt. 2010).

60 Fyodor Dostoyevsky, *The Brothers Karamazov*, trans. by Constance Garnett, ed. by Susan McReynolds Oddo (New York: W. W. Norton, 2011), p. 646.

61 Tolstoy, *The Gospel in Brief: The Life of Jesus*, trans. Dustin Condren (New York: Harper Perennial, 2011), p. viii. 'Christ denies the personal, the corporeal resurrection,' Tolstoy writes in *What I Believe* (c. 1884), 'but acknowledges a restoration of life in a man who merges his life into God's' (*What I Believe*, p. 435). 'If, as the theologians teach, the basis of Christian faith lies in the resurrection of Christ,' Tolstoy goes on to say (*What I Believe*, p. 436), 'one would think that the least one could wish would be that Christ, knowing that he would rise again and that this would constitute the chief dogma of the Christian faith, should at least once say so clearly and definitely. But not only did he not say so definitely and clearly, he never once, not one single time in all the canonical Gospels, even mentioned it!'

62 Tolstoy, *Resurrection*, pp. 285–86. The Russian is cited from L. N. Tolstoi, *Voskresenie* (St Petersburg: Azbuka, 2012), p. 340.

63 Ibid., p. 474.

64 Tolstoy, *Resurrection*, p. 474; *Voskresenie*, p. 563.

65 Tolstoy, *Resurrection*, p. 475; *Voskresenie*, p. 542.

66 Tolstoy, *Resurrection*, p. 455.

67 Ibid., p. 456.

68 Levinas, *Of God Who Comes to Mind*, p. 75. Translation of the Hebrew modified.

69 Tolstoy, *Resurrection*, p. 476.

70 Ibid.

71 Dostoyevsky, *Brothers Karamazov*, pp. 276–77.

72 Fyodor Dostoevsky, *The House of the Dead*, trans. by Constance Garnett (New York: Barnes and Noble, 2004), p. 302; Fedor Dostoevskii, *Zapiski iz mertvogo doma* (Moscow: Eksmo, 2005), p. 355. Translation modified.

8. From Sky to Sea: When Andrei Bolkonskii Voiced Achilles

Svetlana Yefimenko

The ancient poet lives on in what others make of him.

Nora Goldschmidt and Barbara Graziosi, *Tombs of the Ancient Poets*[1]

Tolstoy's engagement with classical literature, philosophy, and history, both Greek and Latin, lasted throughout his life. His thought drew on the work of Herodotus, Plato, Plutarch, and Stoic philosophers, and his interest in antiquity culminated in a sudden and passionate yearning to teach himself ancient Greek in the 1870s. However, Tolstoy's greatest debt is, arguably, to Homer. To state that Tolstoy's writing is Homeric is not a new insight, and critics like George Steiner[2] and Harold Bloom[3] have famously pointed out the connections between the epic writers. What has escaped notice, however, is the possibility of reversing the direction of influence: perhaps the reach of Tolstoy's writing is so vast that it prodded Homer to pick up his lyre.

This paper presents a comparative analysis of the language of Tolstoy's Andrei Bolkonskii and the language of Homer's Achilles, approaching both characters as warrior archetypes. I will proceed by contrasting the Bakhtinian notion of stable and self-consistent epic heroes with a Tolstoyan epic heroism that is both unstable and self-contradictory. Such comparison will serve to illuminate latent tendencies in Homer's text and will also show us how select passages from the *Iliad* (8th Century BC) and *War and Peace* (*Voina i mir*, 1869) rely on a self-reflexive, at times critical, multiplicity of voices. Reading Homer's Achilles as informed by Tolstoy's Andrei helps us glimpse how what Tolstoy took for granted

 https://doi.org/10.11647/OBP.0241.08

when writing, and perhaps more importantly, what readers take for granted when reading, can retroactively determine the meaning of ancient epic narrative.

The Epic Character

Approaching Achilles as Tolstoyan—or, more precisely, as Andreian—troubles the distinction between epic and novelistic writing put forth perhaps most comprehensively by Mikhail Bakhtin. In his typology of the novel, familiar to most critics in the humanities, Bakhtin characterizes the genre as fundamentally opposed to the epic in a variety of ways. Most relevantly, Bakhtin emphasizes the novel's inconclusiveness and internality. This ambiguity stands in contrast to the epic's external exhaustiveness. By virtue of its historical distance, the world of the epic is complete and knowable: 'In distanced images we have the whole event, and plot interest (that is, the condition of not knowing) is impossible'.[4] Such a monolithic conception of epic, however, cannot account for the ambivalence of Homer's Achilles.

In Book 9 of the *Iliad*, Achilles receives an embassy of beloved and esteemed friends—Odysseus, Phoenix, and Ajax—who attempt to persuade the hero to re-join the battle against the Trojans. With characteristic articulacy, Odysseus begins by describing how the Achaeans are suffering; he appeals to Achilles' love and respect for his father, Peleus; he lists the splendid gifts Agamemnon offers, and finally adds that if these things cannot persuade Achilles, then perhaps he will be tempted by the great glory he will surely achieve. After Odysseus has spoken, Phoenix recalls his own long history with Achilles and recounts the story of Meleager[5] as both an ethical example and a cautionary tale. Finally, seeing that they are getting nowhere, Ajax says the envoys ought to leave. Their visit was in vain, Ajax explains, because Achilles has no sense of camaraderie. The three envoys had appealed to multiple Achaean values: duty, loyalty, friendship, kinship, ethics, tradition, glory, and honour. Paul Friedrich identifies nine honour-linked values for Iliadic heroes: power, wealth, magnanimity, personal loyalty, precedence, sense of shame, reputation, courage, and excellence.[6] Each of these values is present in some way in the offers, concessions, and arguments offered by the envoys.

In rejecting the embassy, Achilles rejects these heroic honour-linked values of warrior society for reasons of his own. These reasons certainly seemed incomprehensible to Odysseus, Phoenix, Ajax, and later even to Patroclus, who are closest to him as comrades and epic heroes. Readers, too, are bewildered by the passage, and the embassy to Achilles remains the most contested section of the *Iliad*.[7] Donald Lateiner writes, 'Akhilleus penetrates the ruse and refuses the "king's ransom". Thus he confounds heroes trained keenly to scent booty (which presumably confers most of the desired honour) and at least eighty-one generations of critics.'[8] Richard Martin and Seth L. Schein comment upon the unusual nature of Achilles' refusal; Schein suggests Achilles inhabits a world he 'qualitatively transcends but cannot leave', existing as 'a hero alienated not only from the world of the poem but from the world celebrated by hundreds of years of poetic tradition and cultural values'.[9] How can Achilles exist within heroic epic and yet defy its ethos?

Describing the epic hero, Bakhtin argues that 'what is complete is also something hopelessly ready-made; he is all there, from beginning to end [...]. He is, furthermore, completely externalized. There is not the slightest gap between his authentic essence and its external manifestation [...] outside of this predetermined fate and predetermined position there is nothing.'[10] Achilles *does* have a predetermined fate, and this is the source of his sorrow. However, Bakhtin is not referring to the inescapable prophecy passed on this hero's short life, but to the inability of heroes of epic narrative to question the validity of their lives in a non-trivial, meaningful way (perhaps even in a philosophical way). In Bakhtin's framework, Achilles has no choice but to reflect epic values because he cannot contradict them. If this is the case, then Achilles' refusal of the embassy's appeal is a fit, a temporary aberration, a brief bend in his familiar course until he knows better and returns to himself, unchanged. His narrative becomes an entertaining story with a moral: do not be angry like Achilles. This is precisely the sort of story Phoenix recounts: do not be angry like Meleager.

For Homer to have implied a deeper and more psychologically and philosophically complex meaning, Achilles would require an individuated, private self that is capable of reflecting on and transcending the epic horizon. If Achilles' tale is different from that of

Meleager, it is because Achilles himself differs from the type of hero Meleager personifies. Thomas Finan writes of Achilles:

> It is so easy to see him as what he has been called, merely 'A magnificent barbarian', in reference to his relentless heart, his savage anger and paroxystic vengeance. Even those who perceive the *Iliad* as a tragedy then find it all too easy to fit the pieces together in the traditional moralistic pattern [...]. Achilles is a great character with one big 'flaw', his 'temper' which becomes the ruination of him – until he 'purges' it [...]. This [...] puts the ceiling of the tragedy too low. It misses the vital centre of Achilles. It mistakes existential torment for a primitive force of nature, a 'restless heart' for a glandular condition, and rage against human finitude for a violent temper and want of virtuous self-control. It explains *away* the character of Achilles.[11]

If concepts such as existential torment and rage against finitude seem like dubious qualities to assign to an ancient hero embedded in a traditional heroic context, it is because they are so thoroughly modern. Approaching Achilles as part warrior, part amateur philosopher who positions himself critically against the Homeric epoch might be regarded as the result of a complacent presentism; Kenneth Haynes notes that some critics[12] 'reject that reading as anachronistically imputing to Achilles modern forms of subjectivity and interiority'.[13] The assertion that Achilles lacks interiority is reminiscent of Bakhtin's position. Justina Gregory, too, argues that such a reading introduces a 'subjective-individualist' concept of self which 'seems intuitive to moderns but is anachronistic in the context of archaic Greece'.[14] However, if Achilles is displaced from his own time, modern readers may not be to blame. Perhaps it is not critics who are guilty of anachronism, but Homer.

Heroes

To treat themes which are not readily available within the bounds of the writer's historical context is to participate in what Pierre Bayard terms 'an effect of dissonance' insofar as a text features a genre, theme, or concept 'used at a time when it had yet to be invented'.[15] If we regard Achilles as a philosophically inclined temporal vagabond, he becomes a textbook case of Bayardian dissonance. How does the ancient warrior express such a historically implausible literary psychology? By borrowing the modern language of Tolstoy's Andrei Bolkonskii.

Andrei, it must be noted, is no hero if by *hero* we imply strict obedience to an internalized heroic code which consists of interdependent elements comprising status, performance, and reward.[16] Heroes, whether on the plain of Scamander or the field of Austerlitz, perform bravely in battle and prudently in the assembly, thereby obtaining renown, admiration, and glory. James Redfield writes: 'In his nature the hero remains like other men, but culture bestows on him a value; he does not survive, but he is remembered [...]. His community sustains him and sends him to his destruction. On behalf of community he must leave community and enter a realm of force'.[17] Andrei's father sends him to war with a weighty injunction:

> 'Remember one thing, Prince Andrei: if you are killed, I—an old man—will suffer... But if I learn that you did not behave as befits the son of Nikolai Bolkonskii, I will be... ashamed!'[18]

Compare how Nestor reminds Achilles of the day Achilles' father Peleus prepared his son for Troy:

> Remember your father's last commands? [...]
> The day he sent you out of Phthia [...]
> 'Now always be the best, my boy, the bravest,
> And hold your head up high above the others!' (*Il.* 2.912–37, p. 322)

As the sons of recognized heroes, Andrei and Achilles are to behave courageously, fight only in the front ranks, and achieve glory for themselves and their families. Their allegiance is to themselves, their fathers, and their community. What does it mean, then, when a hero rejects these obligations to family and community and refuses to fight? After all, this is precisely what Andrei and Achilles do.

First, their refusal separates Andrei and Achilles from typical, run-of-the-mill heroes, such as Prince Sarpedon (a Trojan ally) and the Greek warrior-king Diomedes in the *Iliad*, and the Russian army captains Timokhin and Tushin in *War and Peace*. What unites these latter figures is their fulfilment of martial duty without intellectual or moral deviation. Whether they are sung or unsung, whether they question the legitimacy of war or not, nothing interferes with their uncomplicated loyalty and their acquiescence to the way things are. It is such commitment that wins battles, as Andrei points out in the following passage, a notion Tolstoy surely seconded:

> 'Success never depended, and never will depend, on position, or equipment, or even on numbers, and least of all on position.'
> 'On what, then?'
> 'On the feeling that is in me, in him, [...] in every soldier.'[19]

It is this 'feeling' that prompts Prince Sarpedon's famous address to his captain Glaucus on the meaning of heroism in Book 12 of the *Iliad*. Sarpedon is no fanatical youth like *War and Peace*'s Petia Rostov, inexperienced yet eager to fight the enemy. The Trojan ally has already glimpsed the brutal heart of war and so would much rather *not* be fighting. However, Sarpedon also understands that he must die one day, regardless, so there is no sense in cowardice now:

> Ah my friend, if you and I could escape this fray
> and live forever, never a trace of age, immortal,
> I would never fight on the front lines again
> or command you to the field where men win fame,
> But now, as it is, the fates of death await us,
> thousands poised to strike, and not a man alive
> can flee them or escape—so in we go for attack!
> Give our enemy glory or win it for ourselves! (*Il.* 12.374–81, pp. 335–36)

Sarpedon is open to the possibility of the enemy's triumph partly because he has no illusions about justice favouring either side. Tushin is the heroic equal of Sarpedon; he calmly remarks, '*pokorit'sia nado*' ('one must submit').[20] Like Sarpedon, Tushin's attitude is not one of resignation but of acceptance. He resembles the Anatolian Trojans when he sits squatting 'Turkish-style';[21] in his own imagination, he identifies with epic heroes: 'He pictured himself as an enormously tall, powerful man, hurling cannon balls at the French with both hands'.[22] Tushin's vision of himself is truer to his nature than his deceptively feeble appearance, and those who are also heroic, such as Andrei, see him this way, too.

Sarpedon, Timokhin, and Tushin do not challenge the justice of war because they do not challenge the justice of mortality; even if they do, they submit to both nonetheless. An unwillingness to submit is part of what separates Achilles and Andrei from typical heroes; it makes them worthy subjects of inquiry. It is also what makes epic character decidedly less one-dimensional than Bakhtin allows. F. T. Griffiths and S. J. Rabinowitz write:

> Heroism manifests itself faster and more interestingly by its deformations than by its triumphs, which, narratively, must always be rare and climactic [...]. The normative hero being normatively heroic [...] plays no more than a supporting role in epic [...]. There is just no story in it.[23]

While Homer's hearers and Tolstoy's readers respect and admire Sarpedon and Tushin, their story of quiet constancy is not the central story that one wants to read or hear. Readers of epic may expect the heroic, but readers of literature expect unique voices and the familiar made strange. We want to be surprised. Achilles surprised his comrades and continues to surprise readers today precisely because of his inconstancy, a quality I suggest he acquired from Andrei Bolkonskii.

Deformed Heroes

The recalcitrant and arrogant Andrei certainly fails to observe Tushin's maxim that 'one must submit'. Andrei has never submitted to the general mood:

> 'Why are you so gloomy?' Nesvitskii asked, noticing Prince Andrei's pale face and glinting eyes.
> 'There's nothing to be happy about,' answered Bolkonskii.[24]

This exchange occurs early in the novel but might well have happened at almost any point, because Andrei's eyes are usually glinting feverishly and he broods often. Yet it is not his sullenness that marks Andrei as out of place. He is described in terms of his excesses—he is more intense, angrier, and more relentless than others. Overwhelmed by his impressions, he rejects a friendly gesture from Prince Nesvitskii:

> Grown even paler, Bolkonskii, with a malicious expression on his face, pushed him away [...]. That nervous irritation the sight of [the Austrian general] Mack had caused him, the news of his defeat, and thoughts of what awaited the Russian army, found their outlet in exasperation at [junior officer] Zherkov's inappropriate joke.[25]

Such 'nervous irritation' (*'nervnoe razdrazhenie'*) is not unusual for Andrei:

> With an expression of nervous irritation [...]. His serious face trembled with nervous animation in every muscle; his eyes [...] now shone with

> a bright, radiant glitter [...]. [It could be seen that] the less lively he seemed ordinarily, the more energetic was he during moments of sickly irritation.[26]

The nervous energy which manifests itself in Andrei's gleaming eyes and sudden rages can be useful, too:

> ...[A]nxious, but not tired ([...] Prince Andrei could endure physical exhaustion much better than the strongest people) [...].[27]

Andrei can endure more than the strongest people because he *feels* more. This well of feeling is not mediated intellectually—its source is primal. As with his passionate predecessor Achilles, Prince Andrei's greatest fear is dishonour. Yet this purely social fear is overwhelmed by the excess of powerful energy which is responsible for his outbursts and characterizes his inner, socially unmediated self. During a minor disagreement with an officer, Andrei becomes disproportionately angry:

> [Prince Andrei saw] that which he feared most in the world, what the French call *ridicule*, but his instinct urged otherwise. [...] Prince Andrei, with a face disfigured by fury, rode up to him [...].[28]

Andrei's reaction is excessive; a face disfigured by fury (*'izurodovannym ot beshenstva'*) is an elemental, almost bestial thing. These unreasonable reactions never afflict self-possessed heroes who know how to submit. In their excesses of pride, anger, and obsession with honour, Achilles and Andrei can understand one another. In Book 1 of the *Iliad*, in the first of many instances of sudden anger, Achilles reacts violently to an insult from Agamemnon. Like Andrei confronting his brother officer, Achilles is consumed by pride, vacillating between controlling his rage and reaching for a weapon:

> The heart in his rugged chest was pounding, torn...
> Should he draw the long sharp sword slung at his hip [...]
> or check his rage and beat his fury down? (*Il.* 1.223–26, pp. 83–84)

Athena intervenes and prevents Achilles from harming Agamemnon, yet Achilles remains furious:

> But Achilles rounded on Agamemnon once again,
> lashing out at him, not relaxing his anger for a moment. (*Il.* 1.262–63, p. 85)

Achilles' father, companions, and even Athena regularly remind him to control his pride and temper; Andrei receives a similar scolding from his sister, Mar'ia. Such admonitions are in vain because the defect of ill-humour is implicit in these warriors' superiority. Achilles' anger is disproportionate because everything about him is disproportionate—like Andrei, he is stronger and stranger than his fellows. Andrei and Achilles feel more intensely and suffer more deeply because there is more for them to feel and to suffer.

In a certain sense, unusual depth of anger is an asset to a particular type of fighter. Donna Orwin writes, '[t]he spokesman in *War and Peace* for righteous anger as the motivator of the warrior is Prince Andrei'.[29] Anger does not inspire Sarpedon or Tushin; it is a dangerous motivation, both for the warrior and for those who love him. Crucially, it also makes the warrior more complicated by disrupting the nature of his heroism. In their inability to submit and in their emotional and physical excesses, Achilles and Andrei distort the traditional shape of what heroism means. They are deformed heroes in a double sense: they themselves are disproportionate and so they are able to de-form the concept of the heroic.

Without question, however, Andrei *is* a hero. He runs with the standard into the most violent heart of battle, refuses to fall to the ground to avoid cannon fire, and will not let himself be afraid. His father calls him '*voin*' ('a warrior'); [30] the diplomat Bilibin calls him '*un héros*';[31] most tellingly for Tolstoy, General Kutuzov (in the book, an exemplar of what it means to be Russian) claims in a letter to old Bolkonskii that Andrei '*pal geroem*' ('fell as a hero').[32] Later, he praises Andrei nostalgically: '"I remember you at Austerlitz... I remember, I remember you with the standard [...] I know that your path is the path of honour"'. [33] Andrei enters the war expecting glory, and the two men he consistently admires most, his father and Kutuzov, expect him to be courageous and honourable. These expectations exist because, somewhat circularly, Andrei is a warrior and a hero. As with Achilles, heroism is Andrei's social role, determined by birth and by authority: the first as son of the illustrious Bolkonskii, and the second as adjutant to General Kutuzov, who regards himself as Andrei's second father.[34] Andrei's heroic role is then confirmed by practice, namely, success in battle. Andrei's two fathers have pre-determined and delimited the horizon of his possibilities: 'The community asks of some members that they leave the community and enter the anticommunity of combat. There they must overcome mercy and terror and learn to value their honour above their own lives or another's.'[35]

If Andrei's unwillingness to submit to acceptable social mores manifests itself in seemingly trivial ways—a shove here, a hostile remark there—ultimately, the excesses which motivate his insubstantial insubordinations well up into something very substantial indeed: the hero's rejection of his prescribed social role. After Austerlitz, Andrei is a warrior and a hero who renounces both roles. If Sarpedon prefers not to fight, it is because he has a family he misses and because war is cruel and hard. Andrei's withdrawal from the war has very different motivations: he has seen through the illegitimacy of the hero's position in society and the false association with glory that sustains it. Combat may exist outside the boundary of community, but so does freedom, which includes the overturning of conventions established by community. Combat is where Andrei and Achilles learn freedom from convention. In Andrei's brief moments with Napoleon, the warrior ethos collapses for him:

> At that moment, all the interests preoccupying Napoleon seemed so insignificant to [Prince Andrei], his own hero appeared to him so trivial [...], that he could not reply to [Napoleon].
>
> Gazing into Napoleon's eyes, Prince Andrei thought of the insignificance of greatness [...].[36]

I began by asking what it means for an epic hero to refuse his role. First, departing from the 'typical' violent heroism of epic forms, a different sort of heroism is elevated to prominence, one which Griffiths and Rabinowitz identify by its deformations from the norm. There is a grandeur in rejecting honours, but only if the rejection is performed by one who has already earned them. Such a narrative implies a sort of virtue ethics: only an Andrei or an Achilles can refuse glory, and this refusal contributes to the deformation of heroism. Within the bounds of this deformed epic, heroes can take on the *novelistic* burden of rejecting the traditional values of epic, and their rejection is legitimized by their position within epic. If an unwarlike, weaker type, like Homer's grotesque Grecian soldier Thersites or Tolstoy's naïve civilian Pierre Bezukhov, concluded that violence is unjustifiable, we would suspect their criticism of cowardice or sloth, no matter how morally justified it might be.[37] In Achilles and Andrei, epic is performing a self-reflexive, critical function which Bakhtin regards as typical solely of the novelistic genre: 'This ability of the novel to criticize itself is a remarkable feature of this ever-developing genre.'[38]

In her writings on *molodechestvo*, Donna Orwin points out that the *molodets* figure is fundamentally positive for Tolstoy, especially because the *molodets* is usually engaged in defending *narodnye* (popular) interests: 'Freed from preoccupation with themselves, soldiers in this state throw themselves into communal activity in a way that mimics and indeed produces self-sacrifice.'[39] Pierre imagines the soldier type as occupying this ethical and almost supernatural height:

> *They*—these people strange and unfathomable for him until now, *they* were clearly and sharply separated in his thoughts from all other people.
>
> 'To be a soldier, just a soldier!' Pierre thought [...]. 'To enter into that communal life with all one's being [...]. But how to throw off all this unnecessary, devilish stuff, all the burden of the outer man?'[40]

What Pierre envies is the self-forgetful commitment so characteristic of Tushin and Sarpedon which, as Andrei understands, determines victory or defeat. Only those who have achieved this kind of self-abnegation can legitimately question it. A life of courage, vitality, and violence can be regarded as its own justification partly because it produces a unique space for sacrifice, of course, but also for the much more prosaic reason Sarpedon points out: such a life is not possible for most of us because it is painful and hard. Few of us, even if we choose it, would be able to endure it. Only after the prescribed and supremely difficult social role has been affirmed by inheritance, authority, and most importantly, successful violent action, can it be rejected. To be legitimate, judgement on violence must be passed by those who are capable of committing violence. An ex-*molodets* is a tragic, admirable figure.

Second, the nature of the hero's ethical rejection of the epic role is reflective, at the level of both authorial and embedded narrative. A work which simultaneously celebrates "typical" heroism in a Sarpedon or a Tushin, but also interrogates war's validity in the deformed heroism of an Achilles or Andrei, is a self-reflective, polyvocal work, equipped to question its own foundations. The self-reflective epic takes the trouble to provide reasons and arguments for rejecting heroism, here articulated by Achilles and Andrei. These reasons do not necessarily echo the reasons Homer or Tolstoy might have articulated, further complicating the multiplicity of voices. Ruth Scodel describes violent moments in the *Iliad* which beget moral disagreement between narrator and narrative:

> When moral judgments appear in such passages, it is impossible to know exactly whose they are. Agamemnon convinces Menelaus not to spare the lives of any Trojans, 'persuading him in accordance with how it should be' (6.62): this is Menelaus' reaction, but by giving his voice to Menelaus' feelings, the poet hints that for Menelaus, the victim of Trojan outrage, this reaction is appropriate. Zeus waits for Hector to fire a Greek ship as the fulfilment of Thetis' 'excessive' prayer (15.598), inviting the hearer's agreement. When Achilles 'cruelly' sacrifices Trojan prisoners on Patroclus' pyre, the poet almost merges their viewpoint with his own. The technique is surprisingly modern.[41]

The conclusions of Achilles and Andrei can, and do, invite the reader's and hearer's disagreement, yet deformation enables them to see farther and more deeply, with a more philosophically nuanced vision motivated by something other than the pursuit of admiration. Tolstoy's autobiographical 1855 story *Sevastopol in May* (*Sevastopol' v Mae*) concludes that seeking traditional heroes is futile:

> Neither Kalugin with his brilliant courage [...], nor Praskukhin, a vacant, harmless fellow although he fell in battle for faith, the throne, and the fatherland, nor Mikhailov with his timidity [...], nor Pest—a child with no firm convictions or rules, can be either villains nor heroes of a tale.
>
> The hero of my novel, whom I love with all the strength of my soul, whom I have tried to represent in all his beauty, and who is, always has been, and will be beautiful—is truth.[42]

This narrator can unite those who participate in battle heroically, faithfully, timidly, or naïvely because a narrative which undermines conventional values—a philosophical narrative—does not distinguish between great and trifling questions. Such a narrative privileges not typical heroism but the pursuit of truth, which involves estrangement and decontextualization. Tolstoyan heroes, who are not privy to the narrator's discourse, can nevertheless arrive at the narrator's assessment. Achilles' deformation of character alienates him from his comrades and enables him to conceptually remove himself from the action and take up a quasi-narratorial perspective. After stipulating that he detests a man who says one thing and means another—in other words, anyone who does not privilege truth—Achilles collapses conventional epic distance between glorious and ordinary: 'The same honour waits/ for the coward and the brave' (*Il.* 9.386, p. 262). There can be no difference in honour between Sarpedon and Thersites when honour is a myth. Achilles' ability to pass such a damning judgement on heroism is one of the ways epic overflows its categories, reaching beyond itself to wonder at, question, and even mock itself. For Griffiths and Rabinowitz,

> In Homer, the glorious past does [...] maintain its absolute superiority over the present; but it is a glory that instructively dismantles, discredits, and analyses itself. If the 'epic age' is pre-philosophical and unreflective, the great epics are its most philosophical and least characteristic part.[43]

However, the dismantling, discrediting and analysis belong primarily not to Homer but to one of his heroes. And thus Achilles is no conventional, Homeric hero—he is a Tolstoyan hero of truth.

Life and Thought

Andrei's and Achilles' unique position results in their mutual dismissal of heroism—for what? If glory and the social capital it brings are not good, what is good? Andrei's answer to this question shifts from an elemental *home* to an intellectual *nothing*. When he awakens on the Pratzen Heights after the Battle of Austerlitz, Andrei is immediately conscious that he is still alive. Then he recalls the sky:

> ... [I]n the exact place where he fell with the standard in his hands, Prince Andrei lay bleeding [...]. Suddenly he again felt alive, and suffering from a burning, tearing pain in his head.
>
> 'Where is it, that lofty sky [...]?' was his first thought.[44]

Andrei's first experience is pre-discursive and somatic: he knows he is alive because he feels it. It feels like pain in his physical body as something is being torn in his head or, more likely, in his mind. The second experience is *thought* (*mysl'*): abstract, distancing, and clearly secondary to spontaneous awareness. After recognizing the voices of Napoleon and his attendants nearby as they inspect the field, Andrei's focus returns to his body, dissolving Napoleon's individual self into a general sense of humanity. Humans—it does not matter which ones—come between Andrei and the sky, and they will help him return to life, which remains precious:

> It made absolutely no difference to him in that moment who stood above him [...] he was simply happy that people had stopped above him, and wished only that these people would help him and return him to life, which seemed to him so beautiful, because he understood it differently now.[45]

Humanity is the intermediary between Andrei and the sky, between the particular and the universal, and humanity's function is to restore the dying back to life, to continue and to contribute to life. Then thought (*mysl'*) returns. *Mysl'* follows the weakening of the body; it measures life against itself, that is, against abstract thought. The outcome of this comparison is a condemnation of life:

> Everything seemed so pointless and insignificant in comparison to that severe and majestic course of thought which suffering, the near expectation of death, and the weakness caused by blood loss had called forth in him. [...] Prince Andrei thought of the insignificance of greatness, the insignificance of a life, the meaning of which no-one could understand [...].[46]

It is important to note that it is not only Napoleonic grandeur that appears hollow to Andrei now; life itself becomes insignificant. There is a dichotomy here between the powerfully *felt* beauty of life, and the powerfully *thought* unimportance of it. Upon losing consciousness again, the solemn *mysl'* is replaced with visions of home and simple joys, which are then immediately subordinated to the thinking, doubting self again:

> He was imagining a quiet life and serene family happiness in Bald Hills. He was already enjoying this happiness, when suddenly a little Napoleon appeared [...] and the doubts [and] torments began, and only the sky promised peace.[47]

The heroism Andrei had previously sought is empty, while ordinary life among beloved family members is precious. However, just as Andrei begins to take pleasure in this prosaic comfort, he is overtaken with intellectual doubt that only the sky can alleviate. The solution of the sky is negative—it replaces doubt with nothingness because for the sky, individual life does not matter. It dissolves Napoleons into generalities, makes all human activity seem pointless (*bespolezno*) and insignificant (*nichtozhno*), and silences communication—in thinking of the sky, Andrei has no need for the mediation of language.[48] The passage implies that Andrei reaches a "correct", Tolstoy-approved conclusion—heroic glory is unimportant—yet he does so for the wrong reasons. This is because the sky is what Jeff Love describes as 'infinite indifference, an equanimity that marks freedom from decision as well as the temptation to narrative that depends on it, indefinite indifference being a cultivation of nothingness as unaware of itself as it is of the need for authority'.[49] Yet life in the midst of this indifference is not possible. If home and family are life, and the majestic silence of the sky is nothingness and even death, then Andrei founders somewhere in between, where the unanswerable questions are.

The disillusioned Achilles follows Andrei in his response to fighting: he too realizes that he wants to live at home instead of dying on a battlefield. The first words Achilles utters in the *Iliad*, long before Agamemnon insults him, are a plea to return home ('Son of Atreus, now we are beaten back, I fear/ the long campaign is lost. So home we sail...' [*Il.* 1.67, p. 79]). However, even after Agamemnon vows to take Achilles' war prize, the girl Briseis, Achilles explains that he is not invested in the battle. He is angry at Agamemnon, of course, but he has obviously long been aware that the reasons for his participation in the war—presumably, the pursuit of glory—mean little to him. After a decade of fighting, Achilles contrasts the fury of battle with the vast expanse not of the sky, but of the peaceful sea, soil, and mountains:

> It wasn't Trojan spearmen who brought me here to fight.
> The Trojans never did me damage, not in the least,
> they never stole my cattle or my horses, never
> in Phthia where the rich soil breeds strong men
> did they lay waste my crops. How could they?
> Look at the endless miles that lie between us...
> shadowy mountain ranges, seas that surge and thunder. (*Il.* 1.179–85, p. 82)

This contrast, with its final emphasis on distance, is borrowed from Andrei, who observed that the vast sky is very different from the chaotic arbitrariness of battle, that untroubled expanse is 'not like how we ran, shouted, and fought; not like how with angry and frightened faces the Frenchman and the artilleryman tugged the standard from one another'.[50]

Achilles then announces that he is returning to Phthia since it is 'better that way by far,/ to journey home in the beaked ships of war' (*Il.* 1.219–20, p. 83). The great warrior's immediate response to injury is desire not for vengeance and power, but for home and the father who waits for him there. Achilles thinks the best use for warships is a homeward journey. He wants to live, glory or no glory. When Agamemnon's insult comes, Achilles' keen perception pierces through the king's authority as Andrei's pierced through that of Napoleon, revealing his power as founded on nothingness: 'King who devours his people! Worthless husks, the men you rule [...] (*Il.* 1.270, p. 85).' By withdrawing from battle, Achilles is trying to shelter himself from pain and from his heroic role, which suddenly seems hollow.

If Andrei's *mysl'* is begotten by the infinite sky with which he has all but become identified, then Achilles' *mysl'* comes from the infinite sea, with which he is in constant communion. After Briseis is taken, Achilles wanders away from his friends:

> Achilles [...] slipping away from his companions,
> far apart, sat down on the beach of the heaving gray sea
> and scanned the endless ocean. (*Il.* 1.413–15, p. 89)

Achilles finds solace in the expanse of sea. To reach the hero, his companions have to journey 'where the battle lines of breakers crash and drag' (*Il.* 2.243, p. 106). Achilles is not only physically situated near the sea, but emotionally akin to it; both qualities alienate him from others. In Book 16, Patroclus laments Achilles' inhuman excesses:

> But *you* are intractable, Achilles! [...]
> You heart of iron! He was not your father,
> the horseman Peleus—Thetis was not your mother.
> Never. The salt gray sunless ocean gave you birth
> and the towering blank rocks—your temper's so relentless. (*Il.* 16.33–40, p. 413)

This passage eliminates precisely that which is personal about Achilles' association with sea—his mother Thetis, who dwells there. It also describes the sea and 'towering rocks', which recall the mountains Achilles mentioned earlier, as bereft of humanity. The nihilistic, inhuman wisdom that Andrei receives from the sky and Achilles receives from the sea prompts the latter to speak for both when he says:

> One and the same lot for the man who hangs back
> And the man who battles hard [...]
> They both go down to Death,
> the fighter who shirks, the one who works to exhaustion. (*Il.* 9.85–87, p. 262)

Achilles has now had time to think. His considered response, so different from his previous emotional one, is the radical and astonishingly modern conclusion that there is no meaningful difference between hero and loser, between himself and 'cowards'. Death—whether represented as sky, sea, or nothingness—is the great leveller. Here Achilles is echoing Andrei's earlier insight that everything is pointless and insignificant. Yet, after a few moments, Achilles has changed his mind again. Maybe going home is the answer, after all, because life among those who love you is more precious than glory or heroic death:

> I say no wealth is worth my life! [...]
> Cattle and fat sheep can all be had for the raiding,
> tripods all for the trading, and tawny-headed stallions.
> But a man's life breath cannot come back again—
> no raiders in force, no trading brings it back [...]
> To the rest I'd pass on this advice:
> sail home now! [...]
> [...] home in the ships with me
> To the fatherland we love. (*Il.* 9.488–520, pp. 265–66)

Achilles explains that his position as hero, as initiator of violence and destruction, cannot beget the kind of life that matters to him now. Having undergone a profound transformation, Achilles is here divided three ways between honour, life, and the perspective of the sea which makes either choice meaningless. Like Andrei, he is hurt and disillusioned, trying to *think* his way out of a deep uncertainty. In refusing the best solution made available to him by his epoch which the embassy proffers, namely, to accept Agamemnon's gifts and fight, Achilles follows Andrei's thoughts until they are both lost. Only one thing is clear to them: Andrei knew after Austerlitz that the honour which comes from human admiration is false, and so Achilles asks rhetorically, 'What do I need with honour such as that?' (*Il.* 9.740, p. 272).

From this socially and personally doomed but philosophically privileged place, Andrei and Achilles glimpse the same reasoning presented by the narrator of *War and Peace*:

> The ancients left us examples of heroic poems in which heroes make up the entire interest of the story, and we still cannot get used to the fact that, for our time, such a history makes no sense. [51]

This is an overt reference to the *Iliad*, and the irony is that it is precisely that heroic poem which informed the scope and themes of *War and Peace*.[52] After presenting a narrative of heroes and powerful individuals, the narrator says that they are unimportant. Yet the narrator does not argue that heroic history is never relevant, only that it is not relevant today. Achilles, however, realized this truth nearly three millennia ago, and the knowledge deformed him. The world for which epic narrative was valid could neither limit nor account for his insights, and he is a stranger to the heroes who are closest to him. Patroclus regrets that Achilles is intractable, and of course he is, but only because he is a novelistic hero in an epic poem.

What They Said to the Ambassadors

Bakhtin wrote that an epic hero cannot obtain critical distance from his epic context: 'He has no face for it, no gesture, no language'.[53] Yet language is precisely what Achilles has in excess. Richard Martin notes that 'the power of Achilles' representation [...] has persuaded readers since Plato that the words of the hero are somehow different from ordinary discourse'.[54] This assertion has been borne out by empirical studies on Homeric diction, which have demonstrated that Achilles' language is distinct from that of other Iliadic heroes. The distinction is not solely one of content, but of diction itself; signifiers as well as signifieds render the speech of Achilles idiosyncratic. Stephen Nimis has argued that, within an oral tradition in which systematic formulas underlie Homeric composition, innovative diction proceeds by a 'rule-governed creativity' which generates new meanings with conventional units, but that Achilles expands the linguistic conventions available to him by means of a 'rule-changing creativity' that utilizes, among other things, the rhetorical devices of poetry.[55]

Such tools of rhetoric and syntax are manifested in Achilles' speeches in ways that are either exclusive to him or qualitatively different from that of the other speakers in the *Iliad*. They include, as Paul Friedrich and James Redfield have shown, repetitions that take the form of an expanding series (instead of the mere verbatim reiterations which other speakers make) and the ability to depict hypothetical images.[56] When Achilles lists Agamemnon's gifts, for example, he begins with those explicitly offered and ends with imagined gifts of which there are first 'ten times as much' then 'twenty times over;' then he moves from a city, to a larger city, to sand, to, finally, all the particles of dust:

> I wouldn't give you a splinter for that man!
> Not if he gave me ten times as much, twenty times over, all
> he possesses now, and all that could pour in from the world's end—
> not all the wealth that's freighted into Orchomenos, even into Thebes,
> Egyptian Thebes where the houses overflow with the greatest troves of treasure,
> Thebes with the hundred gates and through each gate battalions,
> two hundred fighters surge to war with teams and chariots—
> no, not if his gifts outnumbered all the grains of sand
> and dust in the earth—no, not even then [...]. (*Il*. 9.463–71, p. 264)

At a syntactical level, Friedrich and Redfield identify the marked frequency of subjunctive verbs in Achilles' language along with an elaboration of emotive particles and vocative expressions which results in a free use of both terms of affection and terms of abuse. By plotting the syntagmatic and paradigmatic formulas in Achilles' speech,[57] Richard Martin has concluded that the hero's language includes phrases with unexpected juxtapositions and that his use of verbs deviates from traditional patterns used elsewhere in the *Iliad*.[58] Most idiosyncratically of all, Achilles employs what Martin terms the 'expansion aesthetic'[59] which inserts new words and phrases into formulaic patterns or connects them to other patterns. For instance, Achilles' famous retort to Odysseus' entreaties in Book 9—'I hate that man like the very Gates of Death/ who says one thing but hides another in his heart' (*Il*. 9.378–379, p. 262)—was produced by the poet's splitting of the traditional phrase *tetelesmenon estai*, 'and it shall be brought to pass,' which occurs elsewhere in the *Iliad* only in contexts of threat or promise, to insert the completely different material.[60]

Achilles' language follows Andrei's to a surprising extent, with both speakers arriving at similar conclusions. Andrei, whom Gary Saul Morson describes as possessing a unique mastery of language, and as a 'character from another genre (the epic)',[61] utters descriptions of and reflections upon his situation which become useful for an epic hero who must speak beyond the epic to convey his discontent. In the following section, we will examine the discourse both heroes use when their motives are questioned by their comrades and what it means.

Pierre visits Andrei as a sort of ambassador twice. First, at Bogucharovo where Andrei describes himself as being '*na bivakakh* ('bivouacking'),[62] and again at Borodino, where Andrei is literally in a military camp. During the first visit, Andrei tells Pierre that he has become disillusioned with the war that has nearly killed him, that he cannot sleep until morning because of his endless thoughts (*mysli*), and that he seeks only to live near his family in his own quiet corner, busy with humble tasks like gardening:

> 'I lived for glory. [...] Thus I lived for others, and not nearly, but completely destroyed my life. [...] I have become calmer since I began living only for myself.'
>
> 'But how can one live only for oneself?' asked Pierre, growing heated. 'What about your son, your sister, your father?'
>
> 'But that is all also me, that is not others,' said Prince Andrei [...] 'I build a house, I cultivate a garden [...]. [...] I go to bed at three o'clock, thoughts come to me, and I cannot fall sleep, tossing and turning, I do not sleep until morning because I am thinking and I cannot stop thinking [...].'[63]

When Achilles' embassy arrives at his camp to ask him to return to war, Achilles models his reply on Andrei's. He, too, has suffered and seen through the charade of glory which nearly killed him, cannot sleep at night in his bivouac, and wishes only for a quiet life with his father in a fertile land:

> And what's laid up for me, what pittance? Nothing—
> and after suffering hardships, year in, year out,
> staking my life on the mortal risks of war [...]
> Many a sleepless night I've bivouacked in harness [...]
> Ah but now,
> since I have no desire to battle glorious Hector [...]

> once I have [...]
> loaded up my holds
> and launched out on the breakers [...]
> you will see my squadrons sail at dawn [...]
> [...] the third day out we raise the dark rich soil of Phthia.
> There lies my wealth. (*Il.* 9.389–442, pp. 262–63)

While enduring the torment of battle fatigue and insomnia in a military camp (or its equivalent), Andrei and Achilles both wish for the exact opposite of everything a military camp represents. They want to participate in life in its most literal sense, which is why their respective words refer to gardening and fertile soil, both notions associated with peaceful activities of planting and harvesting.

In response to Pierre's query about whether Andrei will return to the army, Andrei rejects the notion in his characteristically extreme manner: '"I vowed to myself that I would not serve in the active Russian army. And I wouldn't, even if Bonaparte stood here, near Smolensk, threatening Bald Hills, even then I would not serve in the Russian army"'.[64] So too, Achilles concludes his reply to his friends by asking them to tell Agamemnon the following:

> I will not think of arming for bloody war again,
> not till [...] Hector
> battles all the way to the Myrmidon ships and shelters [...]
> But round my own black ship and camp this Hector
> blazing for battle will be stopped. (*Il.* 9.795–800, p. 273)

Achilles almost exactly repeats Andrei's promise, but softens its extremism. He will consider returning, but not until that which explicitly belongs to him—*his* shelters, *his* ships, *his* people—is threatened by the enemy. This is because Achilles in his camp, like Andrei in *his* camp, has self-protectively delimited the horizon of his loyalty.

The second time Pierre arrives at Andrei's camp is just before the Battle of Borodino. Predictably, Andrei is in one of his haunted moods, cynically describing the logic of battles. In his attitude to war, Achilles' pride is as great as Andrei's not for the apparent reason of his arrogance, but because it is underwritten by the same keen insight and suffering. On the eve of battle, Andrei realizes that he has been duped and has paid a heavy price:

> 'We played at war, that's what's vile, we act magnanimously and so on. [...] It's all nonsense. [...] [W]e were duped, and we duped others. They rob other men's homes, issue counterfeit notes, and worst of all, they kill my children, my father and they talk about the rules of war and magnanimity to one's enemies. Take no prisoners, but kill and accept death! Whoever reached this conclusion as I did, by means of the same sufferings...'[65]

Reaching a pitch of emotional intensity typical of him, Andrei mocks the arbitrary nature of war:

> Prince Andrei [...] suddenly paused in his speech because an unexpected tremor had seized him by the throat. [...] [H]is eyes glinted feverishly and his lip trembled when he began speaking again.
>
> 'If there were no such thing as magnanimity in war [...] there would be no wars because Pavel Ivanich insulted Mikhail Ivanich.'[66]

A revelation about the cruelty of pillaging and killing, or the foundation of battle as grounded upon petty disagreements, does not astonish Andrei's hearers. However, when Achilles echoes Andrei in questioning the legitimacy of the pursuit of loot and honour upon which his heroism depends, he is doing something extraordinary, especially when he points out the arbitrariness of the battle's cause. Enduring the horrors of warfare because Paris insulted Menelaus is the absurd equivalent of going to war because Pavel Ivanich insulted Mikhail Ivanich. This cynical insight is anticipated by Andrei when he says that it can be achieved only as he achieved it, through suffering. Achilles becomes more and more emotional as he explains that it was through suffering that he glimpsed the foolish credulity of his position, that he has been duped, both by Agamemnon and by the apparent legitimacy of the battle cause:

> Like a mother bird hurrying morsels back
> to her unfledged young [...]
> but it's all starvation wages for herself.
> So for me [...]
> [D]ay after bloody day I've hacked my passage through,
> fighting other soldiers to win their wives as prizes.
> Twelve cities of men I've stormed and sacked from shipboard [...]
> And from all I dragged off piles of splendid plunder [...]
> Why must we battle Trojans,
> men of Argos? Why did he muster an army, lead us here,
> that son of Atreus? Why, why in the world if not

> for Helen [...]?
> But now that he's [...]
> robbed me, lied to me—don't let him try me now. (*Il.* 9.392–418, pp. 262–63)

Whether Achilles' critique is accurate is less important than the fact that it occurs in a world prescribed by the values men like Sarpedon maintain via enthusiasm for battle and submission to hierarchy. Andrei and Achilles are emotionally paralyzed by the contradiction between what they expected from combat and what they found there.

The three sources of Achilles' sorrow—the deeply insulting loss of Briseis, the distance from his father, and the horror of war which leads to the death of Patroclus—find analogies in Andrei's brooding on the night before battle. Andrei is plagued by three very similar tragedies: the loss of Natasha and its implied insult to his honour, the death of his father, and the protracted war. The first of these sorrows is particularly bitter for both heroes as it is a matter of pride, and Andrei reflects on how Anatole seduced Natasha:

> And suddenly he remembered how his love ended. '*He* did not need any of it. *He* [...] didn't understand anything. He saw in her a pretty and *fresh* girl, with whom he did not condescend to link his fate. And I? And he is still alive and happy.'[67]

When Achilles recalls the seizure of Briseis, he, too, is tormented by the gall of the rival as much as by the absence of the stolen girl:

> [W]hen one man attempts to plunder a man his equal [...]
> That's the pain that wounds me, suffering such humiliation.
> That girl [...]
> right from my grasp he tears her [...]
> Treating me like some vagabond. (*Il.* 16.61–66, p. 414)

The 'treating me like some vagabond' is a restatement of Andrei's outraged 'And I?'. Achilles, as quick-tempered and dramatic as Andrei, loves Briseis as much as he is capable of loving, but it is his obsession with his own honour that makes her absence so painful for him (Achilles laments: 'Any decent man/a man with sense, loves his own, cares for his own/ as deeply as I, I loved that woman with all my heart' [*Il.* 9.414–16, p. 263]).

Yet it is their peculiar sense of their own mortality which is greatly emphasized by war that binds the heroes most of all:

> Despite [...] how not needed by anyone and sorrowful his life seemed to Prince Andrei, just as in Austerlitz before the battle, he felt himself nervous and irritated [...]. The three great sorrows of his life commanded his attention. His love for a woman, the death of his father, and the French invasion, which captured half of Russia [...].
>
> He gazed at the line of birches [...] shining in the sun. 'To die, so that I am killed tomorrow, so that I no longer exist [...] so that all of this exists, but I do not.'[68]

What is striking about this passage is the pervasiveness of Andrei's pity for himself and his prophetic doom-consciousness. As he anticipates his death, nervous and irritated as usual, his thoughts are almost grandiloquent, and his own story as he retells it to himself is Iliadic in its epic scope. Before his final battle, Andrei thinks that his life is 'not needed by anyone';[69] he imagines himself dead. Achilles, before *his* final battle in the *Iliad*, repeats Andrei's lament about his own unneeded life while anticipating death:

> I shall not return to my fatherland...
> nor did I bring one ray of hope [...]
> to [...] my steadfast comrades [...]
> No, no, here I sit by the ships...
> a useless, dead weight on the good green earth
> I'll lie in peace, once I've gone down to death. (*Il.* 18.118–43, pp. 470–71)

In a passage that recollects Andrei's gazing upon the sunlit birches while contemplating death, the nymph Thetis repeats the juxtaposition of sunlight and mortality when she says of her son Achilles:

> Never again will I embrace him
> striding home through the doors of Peleus' house [...]
> [L]ooking into the sunlight, he is racked with anguish. (*Il.* 18.513–16, pp. 481–82)

It is significant that Andrei and Achilles reflect on a life that they believe has been of no use to anyone immediately before they return to battle—where they will die. They can neither take refuge in intellectual ambivalence nor return home. Andrei's and Achilles' lives can be useful again only if they fulfil their social role as heroes. This means that they must accept destruction. In their rage at this inexplicable unfairness, they will inflict destruction first. Their attitude to the enemy is hard: considering themselves deeply insulted and awaiting annihilation, they feel no mercy. Andrei explains it like this:

> 'The fact is [...] whoever fights more wickedly and spares himself less, will win'.
>
> [...]
>
> 'I would not take prisoners. What are prisoners? It's chivalry. The French [...] have insulted me and continue to insult me every second. They are my enemies [...]. They must be executed. If they are my enemies, they cannot be my friends [...]'.[70]

It is important to note that Andrei *used to* subscribe to the notion of taking prisoners. However, he has changed. Taking prisoners is not possible for Achilles anymore, either. He, too, is possessed by the same sense of personal injury and so feels neither patience nor mercy. In one of the most oft-quoted passages of the *Iliad*, Achilles echoes Andrei when he mockingly calls the begging Lykaon 'friend' (*Il.* 21.119, p. 523). A Trojan cannot be Achilles' friend any more than a Frenchman can be Andrei's. Achilles, too, used to spare the enemy, but he now follows Andrei in describing the practice as foolish. Achilles has changed for the same reason Andrei has, and he now knows that whoever will fight more meanly and pity himself least, will win:

> Fool,
> don't talk to me of ransom. No more speeches.
> Before Patroclus [...]
> it warmed my heart a bit to spare some Trojans:
> droves I took alive and auctioned off as slaves.
> But now not a single Trojan flees his death [...]
> Come, friend, you too must die [...]
> There will come a dawn or sunset or high noon
> when a man will take my life in battle too. (*Il.* 21.111–26, pp. 522–23)

The changed attitude to sparing the enemy which manifests itself before battle is part of the deformation Andrei and Achilles undergo. As noted above, magnanimity—or '*rytsarstvo*' ('chivalry'), as Andrei mockingly calls it—is one of the honour-linked Iliadic values identified by Paul Friedrich to which Achilles and Andrei once subscribed. As readers or hearers, we are not sympathetic to their deeply unethical logic, and we are likely to take Lykaon's side. However, this might be because we have not endured the suffering of deformed heroes. We are not capable of enduring such violence, so we cannot accept a legitimation for inflicting it. The position of Achilles and Andrei is not knowledge abstractly acquired but is an accretion of bitter experience. They are both hungry to kill while simultaneously accepting that they will die. They seek to follow Andrei's cruel and tragic advice against taking enemy prisoners. There is room in epic to sympathize with this bitterness, and yet encourage its critique. This critique becomes especially apparent when we consider that after the battle, Andrei and Achilles change once again into morally reformed heroes who take great pity on their rivals, in some sense returning to their better selves.

Griffiths and Rabinowitz write: 'The heroism that is the simple, static, ancient thing from which literary theory traces all the interesting variations and debunkings turns out to be [...] a more manageable inspiration than the disruptive heroes of Greek poetry. In epic, a heroic figure can include all manner of contradictions'.[71] In the simplest terms, the static hero is an abstraction and a narrative function. As the centre of epic, he does not exist. Sarpedon and Tushin are introduced as a foil for Achilles and Andrei. Homeric heroes do not merely disrupt their own historical context but can reach into the future and take inspiration from modernity, because epic narrative includes its own contradiction.

Notes

1 Nora Goldschmidt and Barbara Graziosi, 'Introduction', in *Tombs of the Ancient Poets: Between Literary Reception and Material Culture*, ed. by Nora Goldschmidt and Barbara Graziosi (Oxford; New York NY: Oxford University Press, 2018), pp. 1–20 (p. 5), https://doi.org/10.1093/oso/9780198826477.001.0001.

2 George Steiner, *Tolstoy or Dostoyevsky: An Essay in the Old Criticism* (New Haven, CT: Yale University Press, 1996), p. 71.

3 Harold Bloom, *Where Shall Wisdom be Found?* (New York: Riverhead Books, 2004), p. 71.

4 Mikhail Bakhtin, 'Epic and Novel: Toward a Methodology for the Study of the Novel', in *The Dialogic Imagination: Four Essays*, ed. by Michael Holquist, trans. by Caryl Emerson and Michael Holquist (Austin, TX: University of Texas Press, 1981), pp. 38–75 (p. 53).

5 Phoenix compares the angry Achilles to Meleager, the Calydonian boar-hunter and warrior, who withdrew in anger from a war but eventually allowed himself to be persuaded to rejoin the fighting. Homer, *The Iliad*, trans. by Robert Fagles (New York: Penguin Books, 1991), 9.639–729, pp. 269–71. Hereafter, all translations of Homer, unless otherwise indicated, are by Fagles.

6 Paul Friedrich, 'Sanity and the Myth of Honor: The Problem of Achilles,' *Ethos*, 5 (1977), 281–305 (pp. 290–93).

7 Justina Gregory, *Cheiron's Way: Youthful Education in Homer and Tragedy* (New York: Oxford University Press: 2019), p. 92, https://doi.org/10.1093/oso/9780190857882.001.0001.

8 Donald Lateiner, 'The Iliad: An Unpredictable Classic', in *The Cambridge Companion to Homer*, ed. by Richard Fowler (Cambridge: Cambridge University Press, 2004), pp. 11–30 (p. 15), https://doi.org/10.1017/ccol0521813026.002.

9 Seth L. Schein, *The Mortal Hero: An Introduction to Homer's Iliad* (Berkeley, CA: University of California Press, 1984), pp. 107–10, https://doi.org/10.1525/9780520341067.

10 Bakhtin, 'Epic and Novel', p. 55.

11 Thomas Finan, 'Total Tragedy and Homer's Iliad,' *The Maynooth Review/Revieú Mhá Nuad*, 5 (1979), 71–83 (p. 77).

12 Consider, for example, this passage from James Redfield's introduction to his seminal *Nature and Culture in the Iliad*: 'Homeric man, being objective, has no innerness. He expresses himself completely in words and acts, and is thus completely known to his fellows.' James M. Redfield, *Nature and Culture in the Iliad: The Tragedy of Hector* (Durham, NC and London: Duke University Press, 1994), p. 21.

13 Kenneth Haynes, 'Text, Theory, and Reception', in *Classics and the Uses of Reception*, ed. by Charles Martindale and Richard F. Thomas (Malden, MA: Blackwell Publishing, 2006), pp. 44–54 (p. 52), https://doi.org/10.1002/9780470774007.ch4.

14 Gregory, *Cheiron's Way*, p. 94.

15 Pierre Bayard, *Le Plagiat par anticiapation* (Paris: Les Éditions de Minuit, 2009), p. 107, https://doi.org/10.4074/s0336150009214104. My translation.

16 Gregory, *Cheiron's Way*, p. 68.

17 Redfield, *Nature and Culture*, p. 101.

18 Lev Tolstoi, *Polnoe sobranie sochinenii*, 90 vols (Moscow: Gosudarstvennoe Izdatel'stvo 'Khudozhestvennaia Literatura,' 1928–1964), IX, p. 135. Hereafter, Tolstoi, *PSS*. All translations, unless otherwise indicated, are my own.

19 Tolstoi, *PSS*, XI, p. 208.

20 Ibid., X, p. 138.

21 Ibid., IX, p. 167.

22 Ibid., p. 235.

23 F. T. Griffiths and S. J. Rabinowitz, *Epic and the Russian Novel: From Gogol to Pasternak* (Boston, MA: Academic Studies Press, 2011), p. 40, https://doi.org/10.2307/j.ctt1zxshz3.

24 Tolstoi, *PSS*, IX, p. 153.

25 Ibid., p. 154.

26 Ibid., p. 35.

27 Ibid., p. 183.

28 Ibid., p. 203.

29 Donna Tussing Orwin, 'Leo Tolstoy: Pacifist, Patriot and Molodets', in *Anniversary Essays on Tolstoy* ed. by Donna Tussing Orwin (Cambridge: Cambridge University Press, 2010), pp. 76–95 (p. 86), https://doi.org/10.1017/cbo9780511676246.005.

30 Tolstoi, *PSS*, IX, 121.

31 Ibid., p. 200.

32 Tolstoi, *PSS*, X, p. 33.

33 Ibid., XI, p. 173.

34 '"But remember, my young friend, that I am a father to you, a second father..." [said Kutuzov]. Prince Andrei told Kutuzov everything [...].' Tolstoy, *PSS*, XI, p. 172.

35 Redfield, *Nature and Culture*, pp. 104–05.

36 Tolstoi, *PSS*, IX, pp. 358–59.

37 In Book 2 of the *Iliad*, the unattractive Thersites, despised by the Greeks, insults the Achaean heroes and calls for a swift return to Greece:

> The Achaeans were furious with him, deeply offended.
> But he kept shouting at Agamemnon, spewing his abuse:
> 'Still moaning and groaning, mighty Atrides – why now?
> [...]
> How shameful for you, the high and mighty commander,
> to lead the sons of Achaea into bloody slaughter!
> *Sons*? No, my soft friends, wretched excuses –
> women, not men of Achaea! Home we go in our ships!' (*Il*. 2.260–75, pp. 106–07)

38 Bakhtin, 'Epic and Novel', p. 6.

39 Orwin, *Molodets*, p. 87. Orwin defines a *molodets* as 'a youth fine in body and spirit. The word *molodechestvo* with its abstract suffix "-stvo" indicates the essence of such a youth, so it should be, and fundamentally is, positive. Although the concept is applied quite frequently in a broader context, in folk poetry it is associated with war' (p. 78). Alan Forrest describes the French soldiers as reacting positively to what they perceived as the nobility of their Russian enemy since both French and Russian soldiers subscribed to similar codes of honour. Forrest notes: 'Russian molodechestvo was not so very different from French élan.' See Alan Forrest, 'The French at War: Representations of the Enemy in War and Peace', in *Tolstoy on War: Narrative Art and Historical Truth in War and Peace*, ed. by Rick McPeak and Donna Tussing Orwin (Ithaca, NY and London: Cornell University Press, 2012), pp. 59–73 (p. 67), https://doi.org/10.7591/9780801465895-007.

40 Tolstoi, *PSS*, XI, p. 293.

41 Ruth Scodel, 'The Story-teller and His Audience', in *The Cambridge Companion to Homer*, ed. by Robert Fowler (Cambridge: Cambridge University Press, 2004), pp. 45–56 (p. 52), https://doi.org/10.1017/ccol0521813026.004.

42 Tolstoi, *PSS*, IV, p. 59.

43 Griffiths and Rabinowitz, *Epic and the Russian Novel*, p. 31

44 Tolstoi, *PSS*, IX, p. 356.

45 Ibid., p. 357.

46 Ibid., p. 359.

47 Ibid., p. 360.

48 'Although, five minutes prior to this, Prince Andrei could say a few words to the soldiers who carried him, now, directing his gaze straight at Napoleon, he was silent [...]. In this moment all the interests occupying Napoleon seemed so insignificant to him, so trivial seemed to him his hero with this trifling vanity and joy in victory, in comparison to that lofty, just, and kind sky, which he had seen and understood, that he could not respond to him.' Ibid., pp. 358–59.

49 Jeff Love, 'Tolstoy's Nihilism', in *Tolstoy and His Problems: Views from the Twenty-First Century*, ed. by Inessa Medzhibovskaya (Evanston, IL: Northwestern University Press, 2018), pp. 22–38 (p. 28), https://doi.org/10.2307/j.ctv7cjvw6.6.

50 Tolstoi, *PSS*, IX, p. 244.

51 Tolstoi, *PSS*, XI, p. 185.

52 Quoted by Maksim Gorkii in *Reminiscences of Tolstoy, Chekhov and Andreyev*, trans. by Katherine Mansfield, S. S. Koteliansky, and Leonard Woolf (London: Hogarth Press, 1948), p. 57.

53 Bakhtin, 'Epic and Novel', p. 57.

54 Richard P. Martin, *The Language of Heroes: Speech and Performance in the Iliad* (Ithaca, NY and London: Cornell University Press,1989), p. 147.

55 Stephen Nimis, 'The Language of Achilles,' *Classical World*, 79:4 (1985), 217–25 (pp. 219–20), https://doi.org/10.2307/4349869.

56 Paul Friedrich and James Redfield, 'Speech as a Personality Symbol: The Case of Achilles', *Language*, 2 (1978), 263–88 (pp. 272–73).

57 Martin, *Language*, pp. 167–70.

58 Ibid., pp. 170–85.

59 Ibid., p. 206.

60 Ibid., p. 210.

61 Gary Saul Morson, *Hidden in Plain View: Narrative and Creative Potentials in 'War and Peace'* (Stanford, CA: Stanford University Press, 1998), p. 245.

62 Tolstoi, *PSS*, X, p. 109.

63 Ibid., pp. 111–12.

64 Ibid., p. 113.

65 Tolstoi, *PSS*, XI, p. 210.

66 Ibid., p. 211.

67 Ibid., pp. 212–13.

68 Ibid., pp. 203–04.

69 Ibid.

70 Ibid., pp. 209–10.

71 Griffiths and Rabinowitz, *Epic and Russian Novel*, p. 40.

Afterword: But Seriously, Folks.... (Pierre Bayard and the Russians)

Eric Naiman

You talk like a book, Dad.
No, books talk like me.

Vladimir Nabokov, *Lolita*[1]

Pierre Bayard—the Great Liberator

A country with a notoriously unpredictable past, the consequence of its history's frequent rewriting and of its most powerful inhabitants' dismal record of anticipating the future, Russia offers an ideal testing ground for the paradoxical and gloriously anachronistic interpretive practice of Pierre Bayard. It is no coincidence, as the saying goes, that Bayard eventually followed his *Anticipatory Plagiarism* (*Le Plagiat par anticipation*, 2009) with *The Tolstoevsky Enigma* (*L'énigme Tolstoïevski*, 2017), a book based on the premise that Tolstoy and Dostoevsky were the same person, an author whose range was so great that many scholars have been tempted to divide him into two distinct writers. Even readers of Dostoevsky's *The Double* (*Dvoinik*, 1846) couldn't have expected this sort of afterlife for Russia's most famous novelists.

Unlike Tolstoevsky, or another object of Bayard's fascination, Marcel Proust, Bayard refrains from writing loose baggy monsters, books that might be improved by the cutting of digressions. He takes his ideas in unexpected directions and the reader on sudden swerves through an absurdly defamiliarized canon, yet for all the wildness of their content, Bayard's books are creatures of formal and reassuring predictability: an introduction is followed by three parts of four chapters each, totaling

 https://doi.org/10.11647/OBP.0241.09

around 150 pages. Chapters are no longer than a dozen pages; one consumes them like candy (like the fiction of Agatha Christie or, in his heyday, the films of Woody Allen), and even if one might feel dizzy or even queasy afterwards, the conceits are memorable. Bayard describes one of his books as 'dedicated to the experimental construction of a delusional reading'. 'Such a reading', he adds, 'is not intrinsically mad, but is certainly shot through at moments, like all great systemic delusions, with an invisible streak of lunacy'.[2] The contrast between the delusion at the heart of each work and the orderly, concise fashion with which that delusion is elaborated, is a defining feature of Bayard's charm.

Anticipatory Plagiarism begins with a traditional presentation of the concept's pedigree. It was first coined by members of the Oulipo group, and François Le Lionnais in particular, to describe cases where contemporary writers discovered in texts from the past ideas of which they had considered themselves the innovators. The notion of 'anticipatory plagiarism' was a way of crediting predecessors with having first expressed insights the consequences of which they were not in a position to develop. Le Lionnais used the term 'plagiarism' loosely, so loosely that it might be applied to almost any case of literary influence. Bayard calls his bluff and stakes his own claim for originality on his insistence that anticipatory plagiarism must be wilful. He professes that his study will concern itself with 'the deliberate intention to seek inspiration in works to come'.[3]

Bayard does not deliver on this claim, and how could he? Although he reverts to terms like 'embezzlement' (*malversation*) to describe a past writer's anticipation of future work, he allows that the plagiarism need not be 'completely conscious'.[4] In the case of Kafka, he speculates about the writer's amorous affairs with the ghosts of future women writers, some of whom may not yet have been born; a critic intent on uncovering cases of anticipatory plagiarism must thus function not only as a medium but also as a matchmaker with a clientele of spectral brides. In Bayard's hands, a discourse used more normatively for crimes gives way to talk of inspiration and play. A charge of anticipatory plagiarism 'is not bound up in an exclusively condemnatory logic, but equally pays homage to the authors whose methods it calls into question'.[5] Authors who can anticipate the future well enough to steal from it should be credited for having the good sense—perhaps even the genius—of knowing whom to rob. The discourse of inculpation is merely a façade; as we will see, Bayard's work is far more invested in the dynamics of liberation and acquittal.

Bayard insists that we must distinguish 'authentic thefts of ideas' from illusory ones that are based on mere similarities, often arising from our having read the later texts first.[6] T. S. Eliot famously wrote that each new work of art modifies all its predecessors: it is not 'preposterous that the past should be altered by the present as much as the present is directed by the past'.[7] Bayard claims to go beyond Eliot's insight: 'According an excessive place to retrospective influence would thus serve to relativize anticipatory plagiarism, even to exculpate those guilty of it, who would thereby be provided the means of defending themselves by blaming the imagination of readers and the ability of readers to come up with similarities'.[8] He wants to preserve the frisson of transgression, and he fears that without an insistence on *plagiarism*, anachronistic reading might be too easily naturalized. In the absence of a requirement for intentional copying, 'there is a genuine risk, in the overly large conception which the writers of Oulipo often accord to anticipatory plagiarism, of letting the notion dissolve and thus lose its disruptive force'.[9]

As these last words suggest, *Anticipatory Plagiarism* is perhaps less about the promotion of an idea or the identification of culprits than the generous sharing of an emancipatory affect. The book's principal foe is rigidity—in scholarship and in chronology, and also in literary style. Although Oulipo's practice revolved around play with self-imposed 'constraints', Bayard seeks to free his readers from limitations on interpretation absorbed during their professional formation. So much of learning how to interpret and how to present and defend a reading is bound up with mastering how *not* to argue and interpret. Bayard describes school as 'a realm of violence driven by the fantasy that there exists such a thing as thorough reading', and as 'a place where everything is calibrated to determine whether students have truly read the books about which they speak and face interrogation'. Such an aim, he adds, 'is illusory, for reading does not obey the hard logic of true and false, of waving off ambiguity and evaluating with certitude whether readers are telling the truth'.[10] Although Bayard makes this claim in a book entitled *How to Talk About Books You Haven't Read* (*Comment parler des livres que l'on n'a pas lus*, 2007), that book itself establishes Bayard as a very close reader—if only for his ability to find authoritative propositions in passages which many actual readers of those books easily forget—and which Bayard now renders emblematic.[11]

For all his talk about plagiarism, Bayard is a very forgiving scholar. In the writing of literary history, 'the choice is not between the true and the false but between diverse modalities of error.'[12]

> To accept a margin of imprecision in scientific work is thus not simply a mark of humility, but the recognition—as the entire history of sciences tends to show—that there can be a *fecundity of error* and that the creative detours that error incites can lead us sometimes to an original vision.[13]

'Reading otherwise' can expose a scholar to ridicule. Appearing ridiculous is a risk Bayard endorses, and in a philological version of the Passion he is prepared to assume the consequence of that sin, so that others may find the courage—often productively—to err and play.

Vladimir Nabokov described the experience of appreciating—and analyzing—a work of art as the cultivation of 'a tingle in the spine'.[14] That tingle is in part a result of our education and is not easily developed, yet much of what we are trained to do is to discipline that excited response when it occurs. A great deal of that disciplining comes from respecting chronology. Aesthetic appreciation, the starting point of literary scholarship, is bound up with sensory reactions, while history, that fetishist of chronology, is more strictly an intellectual field, working on the body most when the historian borrows from the armory of literature. Bayard encourages literary scholars to struggle against chronological repression. Even those of us who believe that linear time exists should be willing to concede that too often literary scholarship submits to history at too early a stage in the interpretive work that precedes the outlining and writing of a scholarly contribution.

In this respect Bayard echoes—or inspires—the work of Mikhail Bakhtin, the absence of whose name in Bayard's work—i.e. those books of his that I really have read—is reminiscent of the missing letter 'e' in Perec's *The Disappearance* (*La Disparition*, 1969). Bakhtin's celebrated essay on the chronotope follows a roughly chronological structure—albeit with several important deviations—but it begins with the words 'the process of the mastering in literature of real historical time'—a phrase that is less the beginning of an assertion about a historical fact than an invocation of a creative muse. The entire first paragraph of Bakhtin's famous essay on the chronotope is worth quoting:

> The process of the mastering [*osvoenie*] in literature of real historical time and space and of the real historical man unfolding in them has flowed in complicated and erratic ways. Isolated aspects of time and space accessible at a given historical stage of human development have been mastered [*osvaivalis'*], and corresponding generic techniques have been elaborated for the reflection and artistic reworking of mastered [*osvoennykh*] sides of reality.[15]

Both Bakhtin and Nabokov, as we shall see, are potential and perhaps even repressed interlocutors for Bayard, and what Nabokov said about the word *dom* [home] at the opening of *Anna Karenina*—'this ponderous and solemn repetition, *dom, dom, dom,* tolling as it does for doomed family life [...] is a deliberate device on Tolstoy's part'—applies with equal force to the start of Bakhtin's essay.[16] *Osvoeniia, osvaivalis', osvoennykh*: Bakhtin's extraordinarily creative and extremely influential contribution to the study of literature begins, like Bayard's, with the conquest, subordination, and reworking of time.

The essays in this volume seek to apply Bayard's concept of anticipatory plagiarism to works of Russian literature. That tack already introduces a certain amount of dissonance, because Bayard himself is less interested in literature for its own sake, than for what literature can tell us about the human mind and the process of literature's psychic consumption. The application of psychoanalysis to literature, he admits, is essentially reductive, finding only what it already knows will be there. The use of literature and reading for psychic modelling, literature's application to psychoanalysis, is Bayard's principal concern. Sometimes, as in his reading of Agatha Christie's *The Murder of Roger Ackroyd* (1926), Bayard's analysis can transform our understanding of an entire genre, but for the most part his underlying hypotheses about particular writers or texts don't aim specifically to be true to those texts. Instead, they seek to put those texts to work to produce new models of thinking about literary evolution, reading, or even the structure of the psyche. In disciplinary terms, this is psychoanalysis embracing counter-transference.

How useful a tool is anticipatory plagiarism for the understanding of specific literary texts? One of the problems with applying Bayard's notion of anticipatory plagiarism to works of literature is that it is difficult for a scholar to maintain the pretence of taking this idea sufficiently seriously all the way through to the end of an article, let alone a book. Doing so may give the impression that we are producing an influence study in drag, with the travestying of chronology merely serving to reaffirm linear time's inescapability. Speaking about influence backwards can begin to resemble a kind of scholarly pig-Latin, an exercise in translation more cute than acute, reminiscent of a game show where all the answers have to be phrased as questions.

Where the investigation of specific literary texts is concerned, anticipatory plagiarism works best when it functions as a heuristic conceit early on in the conceptualization of scholarship, when it reveals something about the 'plagiarizing' work that we would not have seen if we had not placed it *in extremis* by trying to fit it to Bayard's model. From what future writers, one can ask a class, or oneself, did Gogol or Tolstoy plagiarize? Svetlana Yefimenko sees the value of anticipatory plagiarism as its ability to 'illuminate latent tendencies' in the work of the anticipatory plagiarizer. We force a text out of its latency by administering the interpretive equivalent of growth hormones, making it mature before it would otherwise be ready. The exercise might result in a grotesque version of what the original work has come to stand for, but the original work still exists in its original form, and we may now know something about its nature that we otherwise would not have grasped.

The notion of anticipatory plagiarism, and of the light that can be shed by unabashedly anachronistic methodologies, may be especially important in giving us the confidence not immediately to dismiss a reading when, chronologically speaking, it seems completely improbable. To cite one example, in *Crime and Punishment* (*Prestuplenie i nakazanie*, 1866) Raskolnikov overhears a student and an officer discussing whether they would kill the detested old pawnbroker whose murder Raskolnikov is himself contemplating. The 'superstitious' Raskolnikov becomes 'greatly agitated':

> Of course, it was all the most common and ordinary youthful talk and thinking, he had heard it many times before, only in different forms and on different subjects. But why precisely now did he have to hear precisely such talk and thinking, when ... *exactly the same thoughts* had just been conceived in his own head? And why precisely now, as he was coming

> from the old woman's bearing the germ of his thought, should he chance upon a conversation about the same old woman? ... This coincidence always seemed strange to him. This negligible tavern conversation had an extreme influence on him in the further development of the affair; as though there were indeed some predestination, some indication in it....... .... [*kak budto deistvitel'no bylo tut kakoe-to predopredelenie, ukazanie*...].[17]

The uncharacteristic extended ellipsis at the end highlights the importance of the passage and draws attention to its final words. Reflecting on the uncanniness of the moment, Raskolnikov almost has an insight: shimmering verbally before him, distorted—*predopredelenie, ukazanie*—lies the name of the novel Raskolnikov inhabits [*Prestuplenie i nakazanie*], the narrative that has always controlled his destiny. This isn't the sort of move one expects to find in nineteenth-century realist fiction, let alone in Dostoevsky; it smacks of the poetics of some writers of the next century. We don't have to accept that Dostoevsky has anticipatorily plagiarized this trick from Nabokov, but treating chronological boundaries as porous prevents us from dismissing this insight as meaningless; we can return to Dostoevsky to hunt for similar examples and begin to play with the various interpretive scenarios in which this reading might make sense.

To take one more example, Tolstoy was notoriously careless about time. In *War and Peace* (*Voina i mir*, 1869) Liza Bolkonskaya's pregnancy lasts well over a year. *Anna Karenina* (1878), as Nabokov pointed out, begins on a day that is alternately Thursday and Friday.[18] Moreover, paying close attention to the timeline reveals that in the first half of the novel Vronskii and Anna live through one more year than Kitty and Levin: 'The mated [live] faster than the mateless'.[19] This is a quintessentially performative gesture by the interpreter; Nabokov is trying not so much to show that the off-kilter chronology of the novel makes intrinsic sense as to demonstrate that he, Nabokov, can make it seem to.

There is another, perhaps more important moment, however, that Nabokov misses. (Even someone as protective of his own priority as Nabokov sometimes cannot tell when he is being anticipatorily plagiarized).

In the novel's seventh part, which terminates in Anna's death, her brother Stiva goes to St Petersburg to try to obtain permission from Anna's husband for a divorce. Stiva's plans are thwarted largely because the husband has fallen under the influence of a French mystic, Landau, formerly a salesman in Paris, who has been adopted by a princess and is now, ludicrously, accepted by Petersburg society as a prophet. Stiva himself falls asleep when Landau goes into a trance, whereupon the Frenchman orders Stiva out of the room: '"*Que la personne qui est arrivée la dernière, celle qui demande, qu'elle sorte! Qu'elle sorte!*" "*C'est moi, n'est-ce pas?*"' Stiva asks, and leaves in a state of terror, 'forgetting about his sister's business'.[20] Stiva's abandonment of his sister's mission is both comic and contemptible, but, ironically, most readers themselves probably forget about this episode in the following tense chapters that lead up to Anna's throwing herself on the tracks.

Remembering that séance might be important, however, because three chapters later Vronskii and Anna receive a telegram from Stiva which subtly indicates—'Decisive answer promised in a day or two'—that in returning the narrative to Moscow, Tolstoy has gone back a day in time, without explicitly telling the reader that he has done so.[21] There is an odd specificity in the pages to follow about the timing of Anna's final moments. Tolstoy tells us the exact hour of her train's departure (8:02 pm), and he emphasizes that her final moments are lit by 'bright evening sunlight.'[22] If the reader recalls the details of Stiva's visit to Petersburg, she might remember that even though he arrives a little late for his evening appointment with Landau and Anna's husband, 'it was still broad daylight outside'.[23] In other words, it is likely that the séance with Landau and Anna's death are occurring at roughly the same time on the same day, and that Landau's final words '"*Qu'elle sorte*"' are directed not only at Stiva (gendered as feminine by being the last person—*la personne*—to enter the room) but, more crucially, at Anna, who, after all, is *the* 'she' of the book. Simultaneously Landau is ordering the brother out of the room and the sister out of the book. He may even be the novel's final incarnation of the fatidic muzhik of Anna's nightmares, who, we should remember, also speaks French.

This sort of subtle narrative trickery is not typical of Tolstoy. For Tolstoy to have planned this parallel would make him a different author from the one we think he is. This synchronization might well be random, and if I had noticed it twenty years ago I would have dismissed it as a curiosity. With an awareness that Tolstoy may have roots in the twentieth century, however, and with an inkling that he may even have intuited the content of the lectures Nabokov would deliver about him eighty years later at Cornell, I hold on to this discovery, seek others like it, and begin to imagine more comprehensive readings into which it might fit.[24]

The essential questions for those primarily invested in a specific author or a specific work of literature are the point at which we should remove the Bayardian scaffolding, and whether we should even admit that it was there in the first place. Should the scholar who uses anticipatory plagiarism as an exploratory device worry about the evidence so gained being tainted, the way a court might hesitate before admitting for the jury's consideration an illegally obtained confession?

Here is where Bayard's affect comes in handy. He dispels the anxiety of influence by muddying the question of influence's vector. This is no less true for scholars than it is for writers. One imagines future reviews and convention cocktail party chatter: 'Your new book is a marvel; I must admit that I began stealing from it long ago'. Rarely will an assertion of priority have seemed so gracious. The doctrine of anticipatory plagiarism—like all of Bayard's work—is actually a celebration of readerly originality, and of Bayard's in the first instance, but it also removes some of the pressure to pretend to be saying something original in the first place. If Bayard were given a home in the syllabi of literature departments, would the result be more plagiarism, less plagiarism, or *better* plagiarism that would raise this fundamental academic crime to a form of art?

The joyousness of the world of Bayard's scholarship is particularly striking. He speaks of 'ghosts', 'revenants', 'survenants' and occasionally of 'haunting', but fear takes the day off. The game of anticipatory plagiarism is not an ego-bruising sport, even though it might not be flattering to all the players involved. One of the take-aways from Muireann Maguire's inspired discovery of the reciprocal plagiarism between Tolstoy and Hall Caine is that she has provided documentation for just how bad *Resurrection* (*Voskresenie*, 1899) is. (The author of *Anna Karenina* could certainly not have engaged in such a relationship with *this* partner, but by the time he wrote his last novel, Tolstoy was no longer the same person who had written that earlier book). Bayard, to be sure, provides the scholar with the tools to step in and help rather than castigate; in another work of 'interventionist criticism' he has suggested how a critic might improve 'failed works'.[25]

The downside of this release from professional panic is that we may lose some of the sense of political and social engagement with which, for better or worse, so many Russian writers have been concerned. Enmeshing a writer like Andrei Platonov in the game of anticipatory plagiarism might deprive his work of its most powerful features, without providing a corresponding pay-off in new insight into his prose. (For Platonov, the jury is still out: does his intense involvement on so many levels with the Soviet project limit his survival as a meaningful writer once the relevance of the Soviet Union subsides?). Can writers who lived through eras of transformative violence find any place in a methodology so invested in the 'play' of ideas?

Pierre Bayard's Nose

It may well be that Bayard's various conceits, including anticipatory plagiarism, work better for authors whose writing has come to be appreciated as timeless, speculative and playful rather than those enmeshed in the social questions of their day—among the Russians, that group would include Gogol, Krzhizhanovsky, Kharms, and, above all, Nabokov. Other Russian writers, such as Tolstoy and Dostoevsky, can fit into that group only with great effort (through, as the French would say, a willingness to *se couper en quatre*).

As Timothy Langen and Ilya Vinitsky demonstrate, Gogol offers a terrific match for Bayard's methodology. Gogol's stories furnish much fodder for traditional psychoanalysis, and they have been subjected to repeated reductive readings. In a psychoanalytic context Gogol's stories need not be read, however, as parables about castration anxiety or fantasies about a return to the womb; on the contrary, Gogol provides fertile territory for Bayard's practice of applying literature *to* psychoanalysis. Let's look at the potential for such an approach in 'The Nose' (*Nos*, 1836) that comedic nightmare about a body part which liberates itself from its owner and takes over the whole of his existence.

We begin with one of Freud's most famous cases. After his analysis with Freud came to an end, Sergei Pankejeff, otherwise known as the Wolf Man, sought treatment with another analyst, Ruth Mack Brunswick, who would also write up his case. Pankejeff had produced one of the most celebrated dreams in the history of psychoanalysis: his vision of wolves sitting in a walnut tree, which Freud interpreted as a reflection of the primal scene, the witnessing by a child of his parents' coitus. When he came to Brunswick, Pankejeff was suffering from what she termed a 'hypochondriacal *idée fixe*'.[26] This was a constant preoccupation with his nose, which he examined every few minutes in a pocket mirror and which he took to several doctors for various forms of unnecessary treatment. At times, he was troubled by the shape of his nose; at others, he complained of a pimple or a hole in it.

During the period of his analysis with Freud, the Wolf Man had been treated as well for the obstruction of his sebaceous glands. Both therapeutic interventions had concluded with apparent success. The glands had begun to function properly and the Wolf Man's unconscious had given Freud enough material to produce insight into the patient's unconscious. Now both mind and nose were perceived by Pankejeff as needing treatment once more, but the two problems had become explicitly conjoined. Brunswick was impressed by 'the monosymptomatic nature of the psychosis. The patient when talking about anything except his nose was entirely sane. The mention of that organ made him act like the classic lunatic'.[27]

Brunswick confidently asserted that 'the nose is, of course, the genital'.[28] Reductively, she saw her patient's desire to inflict a wound on his nose as a castration fantasy, and the hostility he had developed towards dermatologists as a reaction against it.

The Wolf Man had one more symptom which Brunswick found difficult to incorporate into her analysis: he had developed an inability to read fiction. This was due to his refusal to 'identify himself with the hero of a book, because that hero, created by the author, was wholly in the power of his creator; on the other hand, his sense of creative inhibition made it impossible for him to identify with the author'.[29]

Brunswick had great difficulty in forcing her patient to discuss his nose. He did, however, bring her dreams to analyze, including the following one:

> He is standing at the prow of a ship, carrying a bag containing jewelry—his wife's earrings and her silver mirror. He leans against the rail, breaks the mirror, and realizes that, as a result, he will have seven years of bad luck.[30]

Pankejeff told Brunswick that he realized that his nose was present here in the boat's prow, since in Russian '*nos*' means both a nose and the front of a ship. The jewels were objects which in real life Pankejeff had not told Freud about because he feared that if Freud knew about them, he would cease giving him money. Brunswick read the dream as bound up with the patient's refusal to acknowledge his own unscrupulousness (towards Freud), as well as with his adoption of the feminine habit of looking frequently at himself, which she later linked to sexual ideation aligned with the patient's domination by his wife: 'The passivity formerly directed entirely towards his father and even here masked as activity, had now broken its bounds and included in its sweep both homosexual and heterosexual relations'.[31] The seven years were the elapsed time since her patient's analysis with Freud, during which time he had begun concealing his jewels. Pankejeff's hiding his wealth from Freud had resulted in this dream about punishing himself: 'when one breaks a mirror one simultaneously breaks one's own reflection. Thus the patient's own face was damaged along with the mirror'.[32]

Had Brunswick paid more attention to her patient's difficulty with literature, she might have realized that the key to this dream and to his symptoms rested elsewhere than in already ossifying psychoanalytic theory. Brunswick did not speak Russian, and so she did not grasp the linguistic (and conceptual) linkage between Pankejeff's nasal problems and his need for further psychoanalysis. Both the sebaceous glands and the unconscious needed to be unblocked, so that they might give up their *sekrety*, a word which in Russian means secrets and secretions. (Here Ilya Vinitsky's reference in this volume to Gogol's 'secretics' acquires additional significance). More importantly, she does not seem to have read much Russian literature, because if she had, she would have seen the connection between the Wolf Man's predicament and Gogol's famous story. Gogol's intended original Russian title for that tale was '*son*' (a dream)—which. as many of the story's readers realize, is nose spelled backwards.[33] Looking at his nose repeatedly in a mirror, Pankejeff was obsessively contemplating his famous dream.

This dream had come to define Pankejeff and would continue to do so for the remainder of his life. He became, in effect, a ward of the psychoanalytic community. As George Dimock has observed:

> In his later years, the Wolf-Man collaborated within such a mire of vacillation and conflicting interpretations, actively solicited by him from many different psychoanalytic quarters, as to make a mockery of the traditional therapeutic relationship. In interpreting the patient's

> difficulties, indecisiveness, and ambivalences (most often concerning heterosexual erotic entanglements), it becomes impossible to distinguish finally between the patient's struggle for mental health and a mode of existence organized subtly yet effectively around exploiting his place in the early history of psychoanalysis as a test case whose outcome remained forever in doubt.[34]

Pankejeff had become a prisoner of his dream, which his monomaniacal obsession with his nose had turned into his principal symptom. Freud's reading of Pankejeff's dream was based on the dynamics of reversal—the wolves in the dream are still because in reality his parents were engaged in violent coital motion; the beasts are watchful because the dreamer was originally watching them, etc.[35] So it makes perfect sense that Pankejeff's later dream would employ an even more explicit form of visual reversal: spelling backwards. Brunswick may have been right about the dream's aggressivity towards Freud, but that hostility was connected not (or not only) with the analysand's repressed awareness of his own duplicity but with his desire to shatter Freud's reading and the character into which Freud had made him.[36] In this dynamic the earrings also play a role. A *serezhka* is not only an earring, but a diminutive form of the dreamer's first name, the name that would have been used to address Pankejeff as a child and thus his identity at the time of his famous dream. To pursue this reading further, the wolf dream had become a sign of Serezhka's infantilization by psychoanalysis; smashing his dream, Pankejeff was rebelling against his status as Freud's son (i.e. the *son* [dream] that made him Freud's *sohn* [son]) and, perhaps, insisting on recovering the Russian element of his unconscious from its German captivity.[37] His dream about the mirror and the earrings was a meta-dream, less about castration anxiety than about the relationship between patient and analyst.

From this perspective it makes perfect sense that Pankejeff's inability to read literature would be bound up with his nasal preoccupations. He was disturbed by the dynamic of a protagonist finding himself completely controlled by his author, as though the hero had a prior identity that had been lost in the process of storytelling. Here is where Gogol's story comes in. What was once a part of the principal character appropriates his entire identity. Like Pankejeff, Kovalev, the principal figure in Gogol's story, inspects himself frequently in the mirror, and he initially suspects that the absence of his *nose* [*nos*] may be a *dream* [*son*], but he doesn't connect those two words to see that it is his dream that has replaced him in the world of the story. Pankejeff was fond of Russian literature and had probably read Gogol's story, but that likelihood is of less consequence than Gogol's anticipation of what might be considered one of the central dynamics of psychoanalysis: this usurpation of the conscious subject by a suddenly rampant part or product of his identity.[38] Freud himself later observed that after the conclusion of his initial treatment, the Wolf Man 'had been seized with a longing to tear himself free of my influence'.[39] Gogol's story allegorizes an analysand's fear of subsumption by his symptoms and serves as a nightmarish realization of the patient's wish to be free of them. To steal Dimock's phrase, Gogol 'makes a mockery of the traditional therapeutic relationship'. After all, the primal scene of psychoanalysis has nothing to do with parental coitus but is, rather, the analyst's interpretation of the patient's dream.

Pankejeff regarded himself as Freud's partner in the analysis of his own psychopathology, and by this point he had presumably grasped the psychoanalytic penchant for portraying the analysand as, in Peter Brooks' words, 'mak[ing] raids on a putative masterplot in order to remedy the insufficiencies of his own unsatisfactory plot'.[40] It is thus not surprising that his unconscious would turn to literature to represent his psychic plight, although it is unexpected that he would displace Oedipus and the sphinx with Kovalev and his nose, filling in what Freud called the 'gaps in individual truth', not with 'prehistoric truth', as did Jung and Freud, but with Gogol.[41] What *is* astonishing is that long before *Anticipatory Plagiarism,* the Wolf Man had at least unconsciously understood that Gogol had foreseen, or, in nineteenth-century terminology 'prophesized', one of the potential pitfalls of psychoanalysis.

Gogol went into the future to capture the analysand's predicament. It might even be that many of Gogol's mature works of fiction, and, in particular, the Petersburg tales, are anticipatory parables of different aspects of the psychoanalytic situation. (The next step would be to determine what aspects of Gogol's poetics allowed him to so compellingly foresee psychoanalytic practice.) Pankejeff's irrational hatred of tailors during his analysis with Freud might lead us to have a look at 'The Overcoat' ('Shinel'', 1842) in which the predicament of the 'Certain Significant Person', an initially powerful figure haunted at the story's end by the ghost of the pathetic Akaky Akakievich, might function as an exemplary representation of the analyst undone by counter-transference. And as for *Dead Souls...* (*Mertvye dushi*, 1842). We will stop here; Bayard has taken us far enough.

Pierre Bayard—Ivan Karamazov

Bayard's boldest engagement with Russian writers comes in a recent book, *The Tolstoevsky Enigma.* He begins by arguing with critics who have based their work on the far-fetched hypothesis that Tolstoy and Dostoevsky were different people. As everyone knows, one author, Tolstoevsky, is responsible for the single body of work that some have wanted to distribute between two writers.

> It is certainly difficult to admit that *Anna Karenina* and the *Brothers Karamazov* might be products of the same pen, the question of unity is posed in [all of Tolstoevsky's] novels. How else to explain that the same author could have set before us characters as different as Anna and Kitty, or Alyosha and the Karamazov father?[42]

There is a long tradition of treating these two writers as part of a dyad, or, as in Allen's *Love and Death* (1975), as the most important contributors to a common Russian cultural storehouse from which items can be drawn for a variety of philosophical or comic purposes. Bayard lumps them together for a novel reason: he uses Tolstoevsky to argue for a theory of multiple personality that could challenge the Freudian notion of the unconscious.

Although multiple personality is considered a psychiatric disorder, like many such pathologies the disease represents an exaggerated state of a normal aspect of the human condition. Bayard shows how Tolstoevsky's characters act inconsistently in the course of each book. It isn't that Prince Andrei or Natasha change, but that they become "other"; within each of them are several personalities capable of taking control at a given point. This division of a subject into several selves explains how Natasha can simultaneously love two men or Myshkin two women:

> [...] if it is possible to fall simultaneously in love with several people, it is because we are several, and there should be no cause to be astonished by the coincidence in us of parallel loves, something no stranger than if two of our friends fall at the same time for two different women.[43]

As this insight suggests, Tolstoevsky is teaching his readers a message that has been hitherto missed: 'All of Tolstoevsky's work, as well as his life, suggests that we are multiples'.[44] 'The entire oeuvre of Tolstoevsky', Bayard concludes, 'never stops proclaiming: we are not a being divided into distinct parts, we are several persons who fight or sometimes unite, and it is this division which makes us suffer so'.[45]

Towards the end of the book, Bayard implicitly nods to the Tolstoevsky scholar who, apparently, must not be named explicitly: 'It is necessary to think less in terms of [the characters'] psychic evolution than in terms of an internal polyphony that remains active until the end; vanquished personalities or those who have remained discrete do not disappear but seek a chance to seize power up to the very last moment'.[46] In effect, Bayard transforms Bakhtin's notion of polyphony from a serious ideological aspect of Dostoevsky's formal poetics into a semi-comic psychic principle underlying Tolstoevsky's work. The result is not only a parody of Bakhtin's *Problems of Dostoevsky's Poetics* (*Problemi poetiki Dostoevskogo*, 1963) but also an *anticipatory parody* of Yuri Corrigan's *Dostoevsky and the Riddle of the Self* (2017), which appeared the same year as Bayard's book and which argues that Dostoevsky's work is about the suffering produced by 'invasive intimacy' and the porousness of the human personality:

> Behind such examples of feverishly intersecting personalities looms the foundational riddle of Dostoevsky's writing, perhaps the most confusing, contradictory, and agonized aspect of his philosophical worldview, namely, his simultaneous advocacy for and rejection of the notion of an individual self. As an enemy of individualism, Dostoevsky categorically rejected the concept of a self that was not inherently integrated into other selves.[47]

(The category of anticipatory *parody* merits its own chapter and raises the question for Slavists of how Bayard's work might enrich Iurii Tynianov's work on literary parody in particular and the work of the Russian Formalists in general, enabling us, for example, to catch the hidden double pun underlying Boris Eikhenbaum's famous article 'How Gogol's *Poli*chinelle Was Made').[48]

The Tolstoevsky Enigma has additional parodic targets. It also takes as its object the work of both Dostoevsky and Tolstoy themselves. Bayard notes that Tolstoevsky's oeuvre consistently concerns itself with the ethics of judgment, and he focuses on *Resurrection* and *The Brothers Karamazov* (*Brat'ia Karamazovy*, 1881), where the morality of judging comes under particular attack. Disregarding each novel's superficially Christian framing of this issue, Bayard reveals that the biggest problem with passing judgment on another is that judgment relies on the 'illusory' assumption that man is stabilized 'around a univocal essence':

> The dissolution of the 'I' in Tolstoevsky leads to the greatest caution in the evaluation of others, and especially in the project of punishing them. [...] The hypothesis of multiple personalities [...] supposes the existence in us of several subjects in conflict and delineates on this basis a psychic universe that is largely uncontrollable, leading to a society where every act is pardonable from a certain point of view, since the unity of people which would allow for the organization of the collective has disappeared.[49]

While in the *Brothers Karamazov* the problematic of judgment is linked to a message of universal culpability—'each of us is guilty in everything before everyone'[50]—in Bayard's reading, the moral conflictedness of judging is born of a realization that we are all at least partly, or even mostly, innocent. This insight has relevance not only for criminal law but also for the regulation of marriage: 'The legal status of unions between human beings should take into consideration the plurality exemplified by polyamorousness and should leave open the possibility of multiple unions among persons, permitting each of the many that we are to lead an autonomous life with the beings of our choice'.[51] Most of all, Tolstoevsky urges us all to be less hard on ourselves. The theory of multiple personalities so evident in his work 'calls on us to be more attentive to our own person, since it leads us to pay attention to our own selves and to those of our multiple inhabitants, and, as we develop a feeling of *empathy towards ourselves*, to avoid uselessly inculpating ourselves for acts we have not committed'.[52]

Not since D. H. Lawrence explicated 'The Legend of the Grand Inquisitor' has reading Tolstoevsky been so uplifting.[53] One puts down Bayard's book feeling like a better person. He urges us to be more attentive to others, to look, amidst the diversity of personalities offered to us in another as an interlocutor, for the one most likely to engage with us in productive dialogue. Bayard finds the best in every character, too, as in the scene where Andrei forgives Anatole when they simultaneously undergo surgery in the same field hospital. It isn't so much that either of them has been transformed as that a previously-existing person in each of them has now become dominant:

> It would be wrong to say that Andrei has changed, since he is not the same man as the one who was abandoned by Natasha, and it is almost absurd that he keeps the same name and that we use the pronoun 'he' to talk about 'him.' The passage from one personality to another has occurred in him progressively, and the war was the element that triggered this alternation. Coming face to face with the horrors of the front has played a role in what is less an evolution than a substitution.[54]

This is a charitable reading of the scene, which is far darker—and more susceptible to a Freudian interpretation—than Bayard admits. Andrei awakes from his abdominal surgery with a feeling of unexplainable bliss. Anatole is lying on a nearby table—his leg has been removed while Andrei slept:

> 'Show me ... Oooh! oh! oooh!' his moaning, broken by sobs, was heard, frightened and resigned to his suffering. Hearing those moans, Prince Andrei wanted to weep. Whether it was because he was dying without glory, or because he was sorry to part with life, or from those memories of long-lost childhood, or because he was suffering, others were suffering, and this man was moaning so pitifully before him, he wanted to weep childlike, kind, almost joyful tears.
>
> The wounded man was shown his cut-off leg in a boot caked with blood!
>
> 'Oh! Oooh!' he sobbed like a woman. The doctor, who was standing in front of the wounded man, screening his face, stepped away.
>
> 'My God! What is this? Why is he here?' Prince Andrei said to himself.
>
> In the unfortunate, sobbing, exhausted man whose leg had just been removed, he recognized Anatole Kuragin.[55]

Anatole weeps like a woman, because by the logic of castration he has become one. The amputation, occurring while Andrei was under anesthesia, might be read as the consequence of the fantasy of the vengeful Prince's potent unconscious. In any case, the conscious Andrei can forgive Anatole, not because the Prince realizes that he, too, is guilty, or that Anatole was partly innocent, but because someone ('My God!')

has punished Anatole already. Those who are without sin do not have to cast the first stone; Tolstoy will do it for them. This moment is not like the gentle epiphany of Mitia Karamazov's dream of 'The Babe', which emphasizes universal responsibility for the ills of the earth; rather it anticipates the epigraph—'Vengeance is mine [sayeth the Lord], and I shall repay'—which will soon open *Anna Karenina*.[56]

The third object of the Tolstoevsky book's parody (after Bakhtin/Corrigan and Tolstoy/Dostoevsky) is Pierre Bayard himself. In an earlier article, Bayard has summed up the diverse strands of his scholarly work under the rubric of 'regressive criticism'. By this term he means several things, including not only a stylistic return to an early era, a time predating French humanistic writing of the 1970s (*The Tolstoevsky Enigma* might for several reasons have been entitled *Anti-Anti-Oedipus*), but also a return to unconscious and pre-rational modes of thought, where criticism owes much to the logic of dreams, in which identities can be swapped or condensed. A concomitant part of regression is its return of the critic to an infantile view of the world. 'My texts can convey the feeling that they have been written not by a rational adult, but by a child who knows no limits and is animated by a feeling of omnipotence'.[57] The critic becomes a 'demiurge' capable of intervening in a text and bestowing autonomous life on the characters. The resulting 'incompetent criticism' also presses against and even ruptures one of the fundamental boundaries of writing, 'the line which separates theory from fiction'.[58] If scholarship and fiction begin to merge, there is no reason why the critic, like a writer of fiction, cannot employ a narrator who would be different in each scholarly work, or why he could not employ several narrators in the same work:

> The narrators of my theoretical texts are for me characters from whom I maintain a rather large distance even if they resemble me in more than one aspect. I would say that they incarnate certain mad parts of me, but not more, just as an author of detective fiction seeks in himself the criminal impulses to which he only rarely yields in real life.[59]

In the light of these earlier methodological statements, it becomes clear that in *The Tolstoevsky Enigma*, Bayard's narrator has pulled out all the stops, letting his impulses go as far as they can take him. In effect, he treats Russia as an arena for the fulfilment of his demiurgic will, exercising a philological variant of the sense of unlimited freedom that Russians call *volia;* Russia, that stereotypical land of extremes, gives Bayard—like a tourist on an erotic vacation—*carte blanche* for the exercise of his interpretive libido.

Bayard's parodic treatment of Tolstoy and Dostoevsky operates through a dynamic of reversal, as it makes a mockery of their ethical values. Tolstoy's principle of truth and Dostoevsky's adherence to Christ are overthrown, and no absolute principle is installed in their place. The parodic treatment of Bayard by Bayard, however, operates through a different parodic mechanism: acceleration, as though a work like *Anticipatory Plagiarism* were projected (perhaps, backwards) at double-speed. (This is a process practiced in the hysterically funny final chapter of *How to Improve Failed Works* (*Comment améliorer les oeuvres ratées?*, 2000), where Bayard flips the switch to show how easy it is—by accentuating all their faults—to make failed works collapse completely.)[60] A guilt-free Ivan Karamzov takes over, and everything is indeed permitted. Where Bakhtin insisted on the ethical imperative of incarnation, of assuming a place for which one will be responsible, Bayard embraces Bakhtin's *bête noire:* 'an alibi for being'.[61] The scholar can never be reliably located behind his words, from which he always takes his distance. To use a term elaborated in Bakhtin's Dostoevsky book, Bayard always retains a 'loophole'.[62]

Does Bayard's approach to literature have *any* constraints? He suggests in one book that because every literary text represents an incomplete world, the reader is always expected, even entitled, to supplement it, 'for example by consciously or unconsciously imagining a multitude of details that are not directly provided'.[63] In another book, when discussing the plots of *The Third Man*, *Changing Places*, and *The Name of the Rose,* he invents plot details which he reveals as false only much later.[64] Would it be kosher *not* to reveal these changes? (This might explain why in *Tolstoevsky* Bayard has Petr Verkhovenskii execute Kirillov and why he implicates Pierre and the cross-dressing Sonia in an adulterous homosexual relationship.)[65] Would it be permissible to invent quotations, for instance, to supplement phrases used as epigraphs? Are the footnotes, limited as they are, still sacrosanct territory, or may they refer to works of scholarship that should have been written but weren't? If works of literature are allowed to exchange their authors, can texts be reassigned in a bibliography? If the answer to these questions is 'Yes', can scholars liberated by Bayard profit from his insights but still be taken seriously in making original claims about a specific literary text?

Bayard's embrace of dream logic frees the critic from all superficial rapport with the truth, because dreams represent a more profound truth that must be subjectively interpreted to be objectively useful for an understanding of the original texts involved. Is such a combination feasible? Bayard's readers have an advantage over a psychoanalyst, who has access to a text only through the patient's recitation of his dream. Clearly, we don't *need* Bayard to read Tolstoy or Dostoevsky, but we can savour the absurd charm of his *Tolstoevsky* and then return to the original, to which we can apply the fruits of his "fecund" mistakes. Here we see the distance between Bayard and most of the essays in the current collection. Where Bayard's narrator sees in Russia the potential for wild excess, a place where the analyst is freed of all responsibility to the texts under review, the articles in *Reading Backwards* view Russian literature as a place where Bayard's energy can be harnessed. *Enter*, this book says to him, *but please try to behave. We want to exploit you for our purposes, not the other way around.*

Pierre Bayard, Victim of Anticipatory Plagiarism, or The Russian Empire Strikes Back

The idea of multiple personalities is taken from Proust, who 'suggests at many points that we are divided into a multitude of "I"s'.[66] In this respect, *The Tolstoevsky Enigma* is a culturally imperialist project, as though the French were invading Russia once again and appropriating its textual resources. To take a cue from Bayard's other titles, this book might easily have been dubbed *Et si Napoléon avait remporté la campagne de 1812?* (*What If Napoleon Had Won the Campaign of 1812?*), for Russia's defeat seems to be a repeated fantasy underlying Bayard's work. In one chapter of his *What if Works Swapped Authors* (*Et si les oeuvres changeaient d'auteur?*, 2010), Bayard imagines Tolstoy as the author of *Gone With the Wind* (1936), a work that might substitute for *War and Peace*, since it, too, is described as dealing with a vanquished army and a sacked city:

> Born in 1828, Tolstoi had been struck, like all members of his generation, by the debacle of the Russian army and the stories of the Napoleonic invasion. [...] If the historical context of the [South in the American] Civil War is different, it is nevertheless the same story recounted in the two cases: that of a progressive military defeat, which leads to a foreign army taking control of the land on which one lives.[67]

Nowhere does Bayard mention that the Russians eventually defeated and expelled the French (nor that the Russian equivalent of slavery would not be abolished for another fifty years).

Interpretations of Tolstoevsky are not in short supply, and Russianists don't have to corner that market, but we should be particularly wary of—to use Nabokov's phrase—'Proustianizing and Procrusteanizing' readings of Tolstoy.[68] Less than a decade after Proust's death, some Russian writers in France sensed this danger, which arose, oddly, from the very proto-modernist features in Tolstoy that Bayard would see as evidence of anticipatory plagiarism. The Russian poet and critic Georgii Ivanov suggested that Proust could be used as a test to measure the vitality of Russia's greatest writers. Stand Gogol up to Proust, Ivanov wrote, and Gogol remains Gogol, and the same is true for Pushkin, but Tolstoy begins to wither and fade. It is, Ivanov added, 'an unpleasant spectacle'.[69]

In other words, Tolstoy may need our help. The situation demands what Bayard might call 'Counter-Interventionist Criticism'. Instead of accepting the notion that Tolstoevsky's works should be hollowed out and reconstructed in accordance with Proust, mightn't we turn the vector of influence around and point out—graciously but firmly—how in a more traditional but equally unexpected manner Bayard and Proust may have modelled themselves on Nabokov and Tolstoy?

Let's begin with Nabokov. Within the paradigm of anticipatory plagiarism, there is no shame in admitting that much of what Pierre Bayard writes, Vladimir Nabokov stole first. Nabokov's remarks about the topics that so fascinate Bayard are scattered among many works; they rarely become a consistent focus and are, so to speak, consistently exceptional. Thus, it is clear, according to the metrics laid out by Bayard, that this is a case of anticipatory and not classic plagiarism, because Bayard has treated these issues more systematically.[70]

The similarities are numerous and striking. Nabokov's fiction and lectures abound with references to anachronistic reading and backwards influence. In *Lolita* (1955) Humbert Humbert publishes an article entitled 'The Proustian theme in a letter from Keats to Benjamin Bailey'.[71] Nabokov rated Charles Dickens much more highly than Jane Austen, and so he told his students at Cornell when the class moved forward chronologically from *Mansfield Park* (1814) to *Bleak House* (1853) that 'had Dickens come before Austen, we should have said that the Price family is positively Dickensian and that the Price children tie up nicely with the child theme that runs through *Bleak House*'.[72] Nabokov begins his study of Gogol with the writer's death and ended it with his birth, the model for a biography Bayard has envisioned for Oscar Wilde.[73] He concludes his lecture on *Dr Jekyll and Mr Hyde* (1886) with the kind of anecdote Bayard finds irresistible:

> [Stevenson] went down to the cellar to fetch a bottle of his favorite burgundy, uncorked it in the kitchen, and suddenly cried out to his wife: what's the matter with me, what is this strangeness, has my face changed?—and fell on the floor. A blood vessel had burst in his brain and it was all over in a couple of hours.What, has my face changed? There is a curious thematical link between this last episode in Stevenson's life and the fateful transformations in his most wonderful book.[74]

Some of Nabokov's anachronizing fantasies are bizarre. Though he initially resisted the idea of having a child actress play Lolita in a film—'to make a real twelve-year-old girl play such a part in public would be sinful and immoral, I will never consent to it'—he eventually changed his mind: 'a child should play the role. I wish I could turn back the clock on some of our better-known actresses'.[75] Nabokov played with the idea of modelling his novels on works by Tolstoevsky: a student in *Pnin* (1957) dreams of learning Russian so that she can read *Anna Karamazov* in the original, and *Pnin* itself can be read as both a contestation and a mash-up of Tolstoevsky's greatest works.[76] Nabokov's novels often have a circular design; one short story even begins with the words 'In the second place', and ends with a sentence starting 'In the first place'.[77] Like Bayard, Nabokov comes close to effacing the boundary between scholarship and fiction; *Pale Fire* (1962) mirrors Nabokov's commentary (1964) to Pushkin's *Eugene Onegin* (1825–32), *Bend Sinister* (1947) and *Pnin* (1957) contain passages in which analyses of *Hamlet* (1609) and *Anna Karenina* are ingeniously interwoven into the thematics of the novel. Moreover, taking a page from Bayard's book, Nabokov was not averse to describing a non-existent scene when discussing a work of fiction, particularly if that work was his own.[78]

Perhaps most pertinently, Nabokov was fascinated by the theories of John W. Dunne and his 1927 book, *An Experiment with Time*. Dunne, who also interested Borges, viewed dreams not as the road to the unconscious, but as a reflection of the non-linear nature of time. In accordance with Dunne's recommended experimental practice, Nabokov recorded his dreams immediately upon awakening and then, in the days to come, scanned his life as it unfolded for echoing events which, had they occurred before the dream, would have been seen as the source of the dream's content. (Dunne compared this process to holding a book one has already read up to a mirror and rereading it with all the words backwards.) Dunne's idea was that the universe was 'really stretched out in Time, and that the lop-sided view we had of it—a view with the "future" part unaccountably missing, cut off from the growing "past" part by a travelling "present moment"—was due to a purely mentally imposed barrier which existed only when we were awake'.[79] In dreams this barrier gave way; their content was shaped by the simultaneous presence of future and past.

There are many reasons for Nabokov's attraction to Dunne's ideas; Nabokov's model of good reading was to know a text so well that it lost its temporal dimension and became totally accessible all at once, like a painting. Moreover, Dunne's method of reading dreams offered an interpretive paradigm that owed nothing to Freud. While Dunne was uninterested in questions of originality or plagiarism, his idea that dreams pick details out of both the future and the past owes much to one of the explanations offered by Bayard for the phenomenon of anticipatory plagiarism: the Borgesian idea that language is an enormous reservoir (*un gigantesque combinatoire*) from which writers from all times can draw inspiration.[80]

The similarities between Bayard and Nabokov are so striking that a Bayardian model other than anticipatory plagiarism might be put into play: that of parallel universes. In *There Exist Other Worlds* (*Il existe d'autres mondes*, 2014), Bayard devotes a chapter to *Lolita* as part of his heuristic suggestion that the Freudian paradigms of phantasms (repeated libidinal scenarios) and sublimation might be replaced by the conceit that the same writer simultaneously pursues his psychic, creative, and even biographical existences in two or more parallel worlds.[81] Since the universe is infinite, not only life, but specific authors may exist in multiple incarnations, like nearly identical forms of books in an infinite library. One can conceive of this planetary multiplicity in psychic terms; an author's work does not so much body forth or sublimate libidinal desires as imagine alternative paths.

Strangely, Bayard does not perceive that he himself might be an alternative version of Nabokov, that their shared anachronistic fascinations might indicate that one of them has created the other. For Bayard, Nabokov is interesting primarily as an author obsessed with paedophilic desires; Bayard even imagines a parallel Nabokov raping in the woods a school girl attending one of his classes. This crime is presented with such specificity that the reader may wonder if the fantasy is shared by Bayard himself, or, at least, by his narrator.[82] Although its author may not have realized it, the logic of *There Exist Other Worlds* suggests that Bayard and Nabokov, with all their overlapping preoccupations, may actually be the same person. As Charles Kinbote, the ultimate interventionist critic, says at the end of *Pale Fire* (1962):

> God will help me, I trust, to rid myself of [suicidal] desire. I shall continue to exist. I may assume other disguises, in other forms, but I shall try to exist. I may turn up yet, on another campus, as a happy, healthy, heterosexual French intellectual?[83]

Not so fast. *Anticipatory Plagiarism* is based on a rhetoric of similarity, but the differences between Nabokov and Bayard may be more important than the likenesses. Nabokov was more attracted to difference: 'perhaps the less noticeable the difference, the more that difference is divine...'.[84] To name just a few salient points of divergence, Nabokov is far less forgiving, and he certainly does not celebrate the 'fecundity' of mistakes. The concept of 'the bad reader' does not exist in Bayard's gentle universe, while that category haunts Nabokov's lectures, novels and classrooms. (Bayard does admit that there are 'failed works', but he spends an entire book pointing out how they might be improved.)[85] Nabokov is probably the only author ever to write a manifesto in the form of a quiz.[86] The fear of getting caught, or called out for a blunder, and the joy of catching another's 'howlers' subtend the study of Nabokov, who was himself a savage reviewer. In the seven books by Bayard that I've read, and in the dozen or so that I have not, I have yet to find a dismissive or an unkind word for a colleague; since everything is permitted, the world of literary scholarship does not need to be policed. Nabokov's fiction, lectures and scholarship teem with gleeful references to awarding poor marks; returning his midterms on April Fools' Day in 1957, he read aloud two failing exams that he himself had delightedly composed on behalf of a pair of fictitious class members from different economic backgrounds—to show the students that they could *not* convincingly talk about books they hadn't read.[87] I imagine that at Paris VIII, Bayard is a far more indulgent grader.

A final difference comes with Nabokov's insistence on authorial hierarchy and prioritization. Although he could play with anachronistic thoughts, it was very important that innovative artists be given their due. Richard Rorty has explained Nabokov's hostility towards Freud as a case of Nabokov's having discovered that someone had already stolen his best lines.[88] The Oedipal complex aside, Nabokov might have been expected to appreciate Freud's genius for paranomasia, but he claimed that Freud's flair in this regard was but a pale imitation of Shakespeare's talent. Asked by an interviewer what neighbour he would like in heaven, Nabokov responded: 'It would be fun to hear Shakespeare roar with ribald laughter on being told what Freud (roasting in the other place) made of his plays'.[89]

The writer for whom Nabokov made the most affirmative claims of innovation was Tolstoy. He insisted, for example, that Tolstoy had invented stream of consciousness and interior monologue narration long before Joyce.[90] He notes parenthetically in the midst of his lecture on Proust that 'the first homosexuals in modern literature are described in *Anna Karenin*[*a*]'.[91] And he interrupts his Proust lecture once more when he analyzes Proust's device of unfolding extended metaphors. He directs his class's attention to a passage from the first volume of the *Recherche* (1913–1927), where a chain of metaphors enables the author to cover an enormous amount of ground; he pays close attention to the way one Proustian simile unfolds from another, in a potentially endless succession of performatively imagined likenesses. What particularly interests him is the 'peculiar' way in which Proust's narrator 'drifts from the idea of pale light to that of remote music—the sense of vision grades into the sense of hearing'.[92] He then adds an unexpected likeness of his own, in a formulation that will be familiar to any reader who recalls the second paragraph of *Lolita*.[93] He tells his class:

> But Proust had a precursor. In part six, chapter 2, of Tolstoy's *War and Peace* (1864–1869) Prince Andrey stays at the country manor of an acquaintance, Count Rostov. He cannot sleep [....] 'Prince Andrey left his bed and went up to the window to open it. As soon as he had unfolded its shutters, the moonlight broke into the room as if it had been waiting a long time outside on the watch for such a chance. He opened the window. The night was cool and motionlessly luminous. The trimmed trees that stood in a row just in front of the window were black on one side and silvery bright on the other... Beyond them was [some kind of] a roof all shining with dew. On the right stood a great thick-leaved tree, its bole and branches a brilliant white, and overhead an almost full moon was riding the starless spring sky.'
>
> Presently at the window of the floor above him he hears two young feminine voices—one of them belongs to Natasha Rostov—singing and repeating a musical phrase.... A little later Natasha leans out of that window above and he hears the rustle of her dress and the sound of her breathing, and 'The sounds become still like the moon and the shadows.'[94]

Nabokov tells his class to notice three characteristics of this passage as 'foreglimpses of Proust': the 'pathetic fallacy' of the animated moonlight, the 'clearcut quality of the description, and the intermingled sensual perceptions produced by sight and sound'. He directs them to compare this scene to a passage he has read them from Proust: 'Notice the elaboration of the moonlight in Proust, the shadows that come out of the light like the drawers of a chest, and the remoteness and the music'.[95]

In Bayard's terminology this might be called a case of anticipatory plagiarism, but to my mind it is extremely unconvincing. If Tolstoy's attempt was felonious, he was a very poor thief. Unlike the passage from Maupassant that Bayard offers to us in *Anticipatory Plagiarism* as proto-Proustian, the focus on this passage seems to attest primarily to the lengths Nabokov could stretch to assert the primacy of Russian literature. The most one could claim here would be *attempted* anticipatory plagiarism.

But was Nabokov's mistake entirely devoid of fecundity? To my mind, he was onto something very important: this was a moment for Nabokov similar to that experienced by Marcel at Balbec, where he verges on an epiphany that will explain to him the profound beauty of a specific view... but falls short of connecting what he has seen to the cause of its visual echo. Uncharacteristically, Nabokov was thinking purely in terms of similarity, when he should have also been thinking metonymically.

Andrei's gaze out of the window is located just adjacent to a passage in Tolstoy's novel that Proust may have consciously—and crucially—echoed. That scene on the balcony, which becomes a moment of rebirth for Prince Andrei, is the central panel of a triptych. On his way to visit the Rostov family on business, Prince Andrei has seen an old leafless oak that struck him as resolutely impervious to the influence of the new spring:

> 'Spring, and love, and happiness!' the oak seemed to say. 'And how is it you're not bored with the same stupid, senseless deception! Always the same and always a deception! There is no spring, no sun, no happiness. Look, there sit those smothered, dead fir trees, always the same; look at me spreading my broken, flayed fingers wherever they grow [...]. As they've grown, so I stand and I don't believe in your hopes and deceptions' [...].
>
> 'Yes, it's right, a thousand times right, this oak,' thought Prince Andrei. 'Let others, the young ones, succumb afresh to this deception, but we know life—our life is over!' A whole new series of thoughts in connection with the oak, hopeless but sadly pleasant, emerged in Prince Andrei's soul. During this journey it was as if he again thought over his whole life and reached the same old comforting and hopeless conclusion, that there was no need for him to start anything, that he had to live out his life without doing evil, without anxiety, and without wishing for anything.[96]

After returning from the Rostovs and having been enchanted by Natasha, Andrei passes the oak again and at first fails to recognize it, just as Nabokov has failed to recognize this scene's eventual importance for Proust. The oak has been transformed, 'spreading out a canopy of juicy green leaves'.

> 'Yes, it's the same oak,' thought Prince Andrei, and suddenly a causeless springtime feeling of joy and renewal came over him. All the best moments of his life suddenly recalled themselves to him at the same time. Austerlitz with the lofty sky, and the dead, reproachful face of his wife, and Pierre on the ferry, and a girl excited by the beauty of the night, and that night itself, and the moon—all of it suddenly recalled itself to him.
>
> 'No, life isn't over at the age of thirty-one,' Prince Andrei suddenly decided definitively, immutably. 'It's not enough that I know all that's in

me, everyone else must know it, too: Pierre, and that girl who wanted to fly into the sky, everyone must know me, so that my life is not only for myself; so that they don't live like that girl, independently of my life, but so that it is reflected in everyone, and they all live together with me!'[97]

This return to life ostensibly serves as a great communal moment—Andrei's renewed desire to live occurs through a desire for others—even if there is a sneaky admixture of aesthetic narcissism concealed here—the inclusion of his wife's death as one of the best moments in Andrei's life can be read as Tolstoy's self-congratulatory celebration of the best executed moments in his book. It is worth noting that of all Tolstoy's characters Prince Andrei not only is the one who sounds most like his author, but he is also the character most like Proust's Marcel. His initial attraction to Natasha is occasioned by the intolerable idea of Natasha's ignorance of his existence.

For some reason, Prince Andrei suddenly felt pained. The day was so beautiful, the sun was so bright, everything around was so cheerful; and this slender and pretty girl did not know and did not want to know of his existence and was content and happy with some separate—probably stupid—but cheerful and happy anxiety of her own.[98]

The desire that a woman be marked by an awareness of his existence is similar to Marcel's preoccupation with the fisher girls at Balbec: 'I wished that the idea of me, in entering her, in becoming part of her, might attract not only her attention, but her admiration, her desire, and might force it to keep a memory of me against the day when I might be able to benefit from it'.[99] Once Natasha does notice Andrei, indeed, when she has fallen in love with him, Andrei's reaction anachronistically recalls Marcel's insistence that Albertine not kiss him but issue a promissory note for a *baiser* at some point in the future:

'Ah, I'm so happy,' [Natasha] replied, smiling through her tears, leaned closer to him, thought for a second, as if asking herself whether she could, and kissed him.

Prince Andrei held her hand, looked into her eyes, and did not find the former love for her in his soul. Something suddenly turned over in his soul: the former poetic and mysterious delight of desire was not there, but there was pity for her woman's and child's weakness, there was fear before her devotion and trust, a heavy but at the same time joyful consciousness of duty that bound him to her forever.[100]

Everything that happens afterwards in *War and Peace* suggests that this avowed seriousness and joyful sense of duty are suspect. What we would call Marcel's raincheck has its antecedent in the year-long separation imposed by Andrei's father, and accepted by Andrei, before his marriage to Natasha.

So what scene in Proust *was* Tolstoy anticipatorily plagiarizing? Or, to put the question differently, how did Proust manage to spirit this scene out of Russia and melt it down for his own purposes in France?

In the final pages of the *Recherche*'s final volume, Marcel is returning to Paris after a long stay at a sanatorium, depressed about his health and his lack of aptitude for literature, convinced that he will never write anything of value. In the middle of a long paragraph his railway journey comes to a brief halt in front of a row of trees:

> 'Trees,' I thought, 'you no longer have anything to say to me. My heart has grown cold and no longer hears you'. I am in the midst of nature. Well, it is with indifference, with boredom that my eyes register the line which separates the luminous from the shadowy side of your trunks. If I ever thought of myself as a poet, I know now that I am not one. Perhaps in the new, the so desiccated part of my life which is about to begin, human beings may yet inspire in me what nature can no longer say. But the years in which I might have been able to sing *her* praise will never return.' But in thus consoling myself with the thought that the observation of humanity might possibly come to take the place of an unattainable inspiration, I knew that I was merely seeking to console myself. I knew that I knew myself to be worthless. If I really had the soul of an artist, surely I would be feeling pleasure at the sight of this curtain of trees lit by the setting sun....[101]

There are probably other scenes in world literature in which despairing heroes express their melancholy in arboreal address, and if Andrei and Marcel were religious, these moments would read like initially unanswered prayers to pagan deities of the sort with which, as Eve Kosofsky Sedgwick has reminded us, the *Recherche* is strangely and explicitly rife.[102] In Proust's aesthetically charged universe, the most important aspect of this echo is its meta-fictive transposition. The words are spoken not only about the arc of a character's life but about writing itself. The 'heart' mentioned here stands not just for romance but for artistic talent.

But it is what happens next that should interest us most. Having returned to Paris, Marcel goes to a party at the mansion of the Prince de Guermantes, an event at which many of the characters from earlier volumes will be present and which thus assumes an epilogic cast. There he has a series of involuntary memories, the first one produced by a mysteriously familiar sensation of unsteadiness as he steps on a paving stone, a literal pedal note which, as he repeats the motion, eventually recalls to his conscious mind an earlier trip to Venice. The second occurs as he walks into the house. The passage below is long, but if we listen carefully, we can catch not simply unfolding comparisons but distinct reminiscences of Tolstoy:

> [W]hen I had gone upstairs, a butler requested me to wait for a few minutes in a little sitting room used as a library, next to the room where the refreshments were being served, until the end of the piece of music which was being played [...]. And at that very moment a second intimation came to reinforce the one which had been given to me by the two uneven paving-stones and to exhort me to persevere in my task. A servant, trying unsuccessfully not to make a noise, chanced to knock a spoon against a plate and again that same species of happiness which had come to me from the uneven paving-stones poured into me; the sensation was again of great heat, but entirely different: heat combined with a whiff of smoke and relieved by the cool smell of a forest background; and I recognised that what seemed to me now so delightful was that same row of trees which I had found tedious both to observe and to describe but which I had just now for a moment, in a sort of daze—I seemed to be in the railway carriage again, opening a bottle of beer—supposed to be before my eyes, so forcibly had the identical noise of the spoon knocking against the plate given me, until I had had time to remember where I was, the illusion of the noise of the hammer with which a railwayman had done something to a wheel of the train while we stopped near the little wood. And then it seemed as though the signs which were to bring me, on this day of all days, out of my disheartened state and restore to me my faith in literature, were thronging eagerly about me, for, a butler who had long been in the service of the Prince de Guermantes having recognised me and brought to me in the library where I was waiting, so that I might not have to go to the buffet, a selection of petits fours and a glass of orangeade, I wiped my mouth with the napkin which he had given me; and instantly, as though I had been the character in the *Arabian Nights* who unwittingly accomplishes the very rite which can cause to appear, visible to him alone, a docile genie ready to convey him to a great distance, a new vision of azure passed before my eyes, but an azure that this time was pure and saline and swelled into blue and bosomy undulations [...]. And what I found myself enjoying was not merely these colours but a whole instant of my life on whose summit they

> rested, an instant which had been no doubt an aspiration towards them and which some feeling of fatigue or sadness had perhaps prevented me from enjoying at Balbec but which now, freed from what is necessarily imperfect in external perception, pure and disembodied, caused me to swell with happiness.[103]

It is fitting that this scene occurs in a library, because it is not only the start of the character's rereading and writing of his own life but a rereading and rewriting of Tolstoy, who is there not only through that arboreal scene in *War and Peace* but also in that illusion of the noise of the hammer with which a railway man has done *something* to a wheel of the train—a reminiscence of the motif of the French-speaking muzhik from the railway (*'"il faut le battre, le fer, le broyer, le pétrir"'*)—whose indeterminate activity and presence haunt *Anna Karenina*.[104] Both sets of tree scenes end in epiphanies, moments of transcendence for central characters. Note, though, the fundamental difference: where in *War and Peace* the great breakthrough comes through contact, however fleeting, with another human being—Natasha—and promises, illusorily for Andrei, a communal future of interrelated beings, in *Time Found Again* (*Le Temps retrouvé*, 1927) everything takes place within the self. Marcel does not need to meet or communicate with another being to suddenly blossom as an artist. There is no need to return to that wood; indeed, if Marcel were to return there it might be as dead to him as before. Here beauty and art are born in an artistic overcoming of time that occurs within the self. If an 'other' is present, that other is a book. The clink of the hammer is part of an immersion in Tolstoy that provokes the hero to an epiphany about the nature of art. Aesthetic metamorphosis has occurred not in a perceived object but in the subject/viewer.[105]

The candle illuminating the book—the image that accompanies the muzhik's final appearance in *Anna*—will for Proust burst into brighter flame rather than sputter out, because Marcel's epiphany will not only end but begin his book. Epilogue becomes prologue, and Tolstoy has provided the spark that enables Marcel to make this transition, which is also something of an apotheosis of the self. One might even say that—like Lolita for Humbert—Tolstoy has been safely solipsized.

In the course of the past few paragraphs I've backed away from Bayard's model of anticipatory plagiarism for a more old-fashioned notion of traditional inspiration and influence. (Had I remained with that paradigm, I might have been forced to conclude that the fatidic francophone muzhik in *Anna Karenina,* and in particular his penultimate incarnation as Landau, was none other than Marcel Proust!) But Nabokov and his proto-Bayardian 'foreglimpses' have motivated this entire enterprise. And now, covering my Bayardian tracks, I am too much a creature of discipline not to do some of the spade work that Bayard would scorn, or perhaps relegate to a footnote.

I would remind you of how well Proust knew Tolstoy. Proust came late to his appreciation of Russian literature. At the age of twenty-six he wrote to a friend asking him to please find out who had written *The Brothers Karamazov,*[106] although he had begun reading *Anna Karenina* earlier, in the summer of 1894.[107] But he became enamoured of both Tolstoy and Dostoevsky—he once said that if he had to choose the most beautiful novel ever written it would be *The Idiot* (*Idiot*, 1869).[108] Tolstoy he considered, rather oddly, to have been Dostoevsky's student, albeit a talented one: 'In Dostoevsky there's concentrated, still tense and peevish, a great deal of what was to blossom later on in Tolstoy'.[109] Proust read Tolstoy carefully; one friend recalls Proust being able to recite bits of the French translation of *War and Peace* by heart,[110] and he was ready to draw on that knowledge in his analogical poetics, once comparing his friend Robert Dreyfus's description of a little corner of the Parisian sky to Prince Andrei's vision of the sky at Austerlitz. Slightly later, right after Tolstoy's death, Proust wrote that he had found something poetical in Dreyfus's suggestion that Tolstoy would be forever linked to the figure of the simple stationmaster at Astapovo, where he had died: '[Your article on Tolstoy and the stationmaster] pleased me especially since it was as though Tolstoy [had] made this junction between two images without comparable importance—it even made me think of the little muzhik in the train in *Anna Karenina*'.[111]

Proust knew Tolstoevsky not only for his greatest hits, but also for the little ones. Marcel tells Albertine in a creepy scene that is half foreplay, half lecture on literary composition and Russian literature, 'I have talked about the same scene recurring in different novels, but within the same novel scenes and characters can be repeated, if the novel is very long. I could easily give you an example from *War and Peace*'.[112] Proust dug into *War and Peace* the way a miner extracts ore, finding marginal characters who interested him and giving them more prominence. He sent the idiotic diplomat Hippolyte Kuragin to medical school and, allowing him to retain his propensity for impulsive, meaningless utterances, renamed him Cottard. Morel, a member of a military band who is also a virtuoso violinist, the lover of the Baron de Charlus and the son of Marcel's uncle's valet, must be the great grandson of a soldier of the same name, a French officer's orderly in *War and Peace* who is also not without a fondness for music and is forced by the exigencies of war to cross-dress. The writer Bergotte's death, which Bayard sees as prescient of Proust's own demise, was probably modeled on an episode from Tolstoy's second Sebastopol story, translated in 1886 as an excerpt in a French collection of Tolstoy's greatest death scenes.[113]

Most important, though, is that as the *Recherche* began to expand, readers and correspondents began to compare it to *War and Peace*. The similarity surfaces as early as 1913—when Proust discusses his own notion of memory along with those of Tolstoy and Dostoevsky, recalling, in particular, a line from *Crime and Punishment* and adding 'you must understand that if I cite these great names it is not in order to put myself on their level'.[114] We hear the comparison again towards the end of Proust's life, when a correspondent appreciative of the brilliance of his prose cautions him about writing too densely and too much: '*War and Peace* offers itself to the reader as a very long work, but the reader has already been tipped off that it *is* a masterpiece' which is something that the readers Proust wants to acquire don't yet know about the *Recherche*.[115]

All of this, though, would come at the point of revision. I began by pursuing Nabokov's desire that Tolstoy foreglimpse Proust and, infused with the confidence that I could begin collecting evidence to make a case of anticipatory plagiarism, I paused and began rocking one text against another, as though, my forward movement suddenly arrested in a courtyard, I were moving my foot up and down against a paving stone until I arrived at the place where plagiarism suddenly became a gift.

Notes

1 Vladimir Nabokov, *The Annotated Lolita,* ed. by Alfred Appel, Jr. (New York: Vintage, 1991), p. 114.

2 Pierre Bayard, *Who Killed Roger Ackroyd?* trans. by Carol Cosman (New York: The New Press, 2000), p. ix.

3 Pierre Bayard, *Le Plagiat par anticipation* (Paris: Les Éditions de Minuit, 2009), p. 25. My translation.

4 Ibid., p. 28.

5 Ibid., p. 14.

6 Ibid., p. 57.

7 T. S. Eliot, *Selected Essays* (New York: Harcourt, Brace, 1950), p. 5.

8 Bayard, *Le Plagiat,* p. 69.

9 Ibid., p. 28.

10 Pierre Bayard, *How to Talk About Books You Haven't Read,* trans. by Jeffrey Mehlman (New York: Bloomsbury, 2007), p. 129.

11 As Umberto Eco observes, Bayard is such an attentive reader that he must not have read his own book. Eco, 'À propos d'un livre qui n'a pas été lu', in *Pour une critique décalée: autour des travaux de Pierre Bayard,* ed. by Laurent Zimmermann (Nantes: Édition Cécile Defaut, 2010), pp. 39–42 (p. 42).

12 Bayard, *Le Plagiat,* p. 117.

13 Pierre Bayard, *L'Énigme Tolstoïevski* (Paris: Les Éditions de Minuit, 2017), p. 20. My translation.

14 Vladimir Nabokov, *Lectures on Literature* (New York: Harvest, 1980), p. 6.

15 M. M. Bakhtin, *Literaturno-kriticheskie stat'i* (Moscow: Khudozhestvennaia literatura, 1986), p. 121. My translation.

16 Vladimir Nabokov, *Lectures on Russian Literature* (New York: Harvest, 1981), p. 210.

17 Fyodor Dostoevsky, *Crime and Punishment,* trans. by Richard Pevear and Larissa Volokhonsky (New York: Vintage, 1993), p. 66; F. M. Dostoevskii, *Polnoe sobranie sochinenii v tridtsati tomakh,* 30 vols (Leningrad: Nauka 1972–1990), VI (1973), p. 55.

18 Vladimir Nabokov, *Pnin* (New York: Vintage, 1989), p. 122.

19 Nabokov, *Lectures on Russian Literature*, p. 195.

20 'The person who came last, the one who is asking for something, must get out! Get out!' Leo Tolstoy, *Anna Karenina*, trans. by Richard Pevear and Larissa Volokhonsky (New York: Penguin, 2000), p. 738.

21 Ibid., p. 747.

22 Ibid., p. 766.

23 Ibid., p. 732.

24 See 'What if Nabokov Had Written "Dvoinik"? Reading Dostoevskii Preposterously', *The Russian Review*, 64:4 (2005), 575–89, https://doi.org/10.1111/j.1467-9434.2005.00375.x; '"Husband and Wife": An Approach to the Gothic in *Anna Karenina*', in *Critical Insights: Anna Karenina*, ed. by Robert C. Evans (Amenia, N.Y.: Salem Press, 2021), pp. 39–57.

25 Pierre Bayard, *Comment améliorer les oeuvres ratées?* (Paris: Les Éditions de Minuit, 2000).

26 Ruth Mack Brunswick, 'Supplement to Freud's "History of an Infantile Neurosis" (1928)', in *The Wolf-Man and Sigmund Freud*, ed. by Muriel Gardiner (London: Karnac Books, 1989), pp. 263–307 (p. 264).

27 Ibid., p. 300.

28 Ibid., p. 300.

29 Ibid., p. 286.

30 Ibid., p. 281.

31 Ibid., p. 282.

32 Ibid., p. 281.

33 Simon Karlinsky, *The Sexual Labyrinth of Nikolai Gogol* (Cambridge, MA: Harvard University Press, 1976), p. 123. Without using the term 'anticipatory plagiarism', Karlinsky claims Gogol as 'an authentic nineteenth-century surrealist' (p. 124).

34 George Dimock, 'Anna and The Wolf-Man: Rewriting Freud's Case History', *Representations*, 50 (Spring, 1995), 53–75 (p. 55).

35 Sigmund Freud, *Three Case Histories* (New York: Collier, 1963), pp. 219–20.

36 Critiquing Brunswick's treatment of Pankejeff, Robert J. Langs has noted that in her analysis of this dream 'the possible allusions to the Wolf Man's objections to the narcissistic misalliance between himself and Freud, and to the analyst as a mirror, were not considered'. See 'The Misalliance Dimension on the Case of the Wolf Man', in *Freud and his Patients*, ed. by Mark Kanzer and Jules Glenn, 2 vols (New York: Jason Aronson, 1980), II (1980), pp. 373–83 (p. 379).

37 Nicolas Abraham and Maria Torok have identified many interlinguistic homonyms and puns that may subtend the Wolf Man's dreams and analysis, including *son/sohn* and *serega/Sergei*. Though their net is wide, the reversal of *son* and *nos* (sleep/nose) and the place of that reversal in Russian literary history elude them. *The Wolf Man's Magic Word: A Cryptonymy*, trans. by Nicholas Rand (Minneapolis, MN: University of Minnesota Press, 1986), pp. 34–56.

38 On the Wolf Man's interest in Russian literature, see Dimock, 'Anna and the Wolf-Man', pp. 65–67; Eugene Halpert, 'Lermontov and the Wolf-Man', *American Imago*, 32 (Spring 1975), 315–28, and Aleksandr Etkind, *Eros nevozmozhnogo: istoriia psikhoanaliza v Rossii* (St. Petersburg: Meduza, 1993), pp. 97–129.

39 Freud, *Three Case Histories*, p. 316.

40 Peter Brooks, 'Fictions of the Wolfman: Freud and Narrative Understanding', *Diacritics*, 9:1 (Spring, 1979), 71–81 (p. 79).

41 Sigmund Freud, *Three Case Histories*, p. 256, quoted by Brooks in 'Fictions', p. 79.

42 Bayard, *L'Énigme Tolstoïevski*, p. 26.

43 Ibid., p. 50.

44 Ibid., p. 43.

45 Ibid., p. 102.

46 Ibid., p. 157.

47 Yuri Corrigan, *Dostoevsky and the Riddle of the Self* (Evanston, IL: Northwestern University Press, 2017), p. 3.

48 Olga Partan has linked Gogol's 'The Overcoat' ('Shinel'', 1842) to its author's interest in Rome and the Commedia dell'arte, but she notes that for all his attention to Gogol's masks and verbal games, Eikhenbaum, the

author of the famous 1919 article 'How Gogol's Overcoat was Made' ('Kak sdelana shinel' Gogolia'), neglected the possible origin of the story's title in the name of the character Pulcinella/Polichinelle. Partan herself does not see, however, that Eikhenbaum's title may also be a pun (on the basis of the expression '*faire le polichinelle*' ('to play the fool')) and a much better one than that with which she credits Gogol. Bayard helps us resolve this conundrum. The concept of anticipatory plagiarism suggests that Gogol borrowed the title of his story from Eikhenbaum's far more cleverly entitled article about it. See Partan, 'Shinel', Polichinelle, Pulcinella: The Italian Ancestry of Akaky Bashmachkin', *Slavic and East European Journal*, 49:4 (2005), 549–69, https://doi.org/10.2307/20058345.

49 Bayard, *L'Énigme Tolstoïevski*, pp. 150–51

50 Fyodor Dostoevsky, *The Brothers Karamazov,* trans. by Richard Pevear and Larissa Volokhonsky (New York: Farrar, Straus and Giroux, 1990), p. 289.

51 Bayard, *L'Énigme Tolstoïevski*, p. 153.

52 Ibid., pp. 158–9. Emphasis in the original.

53 D. H. Lawrence, 'The Grand Inquisitor', in Fyodor Dostoevsky, *The Brothers Karamazov*, ed. by Ralph E. Matlaw (New York: Norton, 1976), pp. 829–36.

54 Bayard, *L'Énigme Tolstoïevski*, p. 140.

55 Leo Tolstoy, *War and Peace,* trans. by Richard Pevear and Larissa Volokhonsky (New York: Vintage, 2007), pp. 813–14. In the Russian original, there is no exclamation point after 'The wounded man was shown his cut-off leg in a boot caked with blood'. This is a punctuation mark far dearer to Dostoevsky than Tolstoy. By adding it, Pevear and Volokhonsky, who have also produced English translations of *Crime and Punishment* and *The Brothers Karamazov,* affirm the unity of Tolstoevsky's body of work. Their work exemplifies how author-grafting is a feature of literature in translation that is often lost in the original.

56 Tolstoy, *Anna Karenina*, p. xxii.

57 Pierre Bayard, 'Comment j'ai fait régresser la critique', in *Pour une critique décalée: autour des travaux de Pierre Bayard,* ed. by Laurent Zimmermann (Nantes: Edition Cécile Defaut, 2010), pp. 19–37 (p. 32). My translation.

58 Ibid., p. 30, p. 34.

59 Ibid., p. 35.

60 Pierre Bayard, *Comment améliorer les oeuvres ratées?*. This book never uses the word 'parody'. It is as though the narrator is not aware that the concept exists, even though the real author must realize that he is writing a handbook on parodic technique, the practice of which he disguises under the notion of 'interventionist criticism'.

61 M. M. Bakhtin, *Towards a Philosophy of the Act,* trans. by Vadim Liapunov (Austin, TX: University of Texas Press, 1993), p. 42.

62 Mikhail Bakhtin, *Problems of Dostoevsky's Poetics,* trans. by Caryl Emerson (Minneapolis, MN: University of Minnesota Press, 1984), pp. 232–36.

63 Bayard, *Who Killed Roger Ackroyd,* p. 105.

64 Bayard, *How to Talk About Books,* p. 164.

65 Bayard, *L'Énigme Tolstoïevski,* p. 119.

66 Ibid., p. 60.

67 Pierre Bayard, *Et si les oeuvres changeaient d'auteur?* (Paris: Les Éditions de Minuit, 2010), p. 98.

68 Nabokov, *The Annotated Lolita,* p. 283.

69 Georgii Ivanov, comments made in response to a questionnaire on Proust printed in *Chisla,* 1 (1930), 271–78 (p. 273). My translation. Several years earlier, the result had come out differently when Proust himself had placed Tolstoy next to Balzac: 'Balzac manages to give an impression of size; in Tolstoy everything is naturally bigger, like the droppings of an elephant compared to a goat.' Marcel Proust, *Against Saint-Beuve and Other Essays,* trans. by John Sturrock (London: Penguin, 1988), p. 326.

70 Several scholars have linked Bayard and Nabokov, including Jean-Michel Rabaté, who uses their views on Freud to introduce his *Cambridge Introduction to Literature and Psychoanalysis* (Cambridge: Cambridge University Press, 2014), pp. 1–6. Léopold Reigner employs Bayard's notion of the reader's 'inner book' to examine Nabokov's appropriation of Flaubert, in 'Nabokov's Flaubert: Influence, Deviation and Continuity', *Représentations dans le monde anglophone,* 2 (2017), 46–65 (pp. 60–63); René Alladaye has drawn on Bayard to analyse scholars' debates about *Pale Fire,* in *The Darker Shades of* Pale Fire: *An Investigation into a Literary Mystery* (Paris: M. Houdiard, 2013).

71 Nabokov, *The Annotated Lolita,* p. 216.

72 Nabokov, *Lectures on Literature,* p. 56.

73 Pierre Bayard, *Demain est écrit* (Paris: Les Éditions de Minuit, 2005); Vladimir Nabokov, *Nikolai Gogol* (New York: New Directions, 1961).

74 Nabokov, *Lectures on Literature*, p. 204.

75 Vladimir Nabokov, *Think, Write, Speak* (London: Penguin, 2019), p. 245, p. 265

76 Nabokov, *Pnin*, p. 10; Eric Naiman, 'Nabokov's McCarthyisms: *Pnin* in the *Groves of Academe*', *Comparative Literature*, 68:1 (March 2016), 75–95, https://doi.org/10.1215/00104124-3462661.

77 Vladimir Nabokov, 'The Circle', in *The Stories of Vladimir Nabokov* (New York: Vintage, 1995), pp. 375–84.

78 Vladimir Nabokov, *The Defense* (New York: Vintage, 1990), p. 9.

79 J. W. Dunne, *An Experiment with Time* (Charlottesville, VA: Hampton Roads Publishing, 2001), p. 32. For Nabokov's attempts to emulate Dunne, see *Insomniac Dreams: Experiments with Time*, ed. by Gennady Barabtarlo (Princeton, NJ: Princeton University Press, 2018).

80 Bayard, *Le Plagiat*, p. 94.

81 Pierre Bayard, *Il existe d'autres mondes* (Paris: Les Éditions de Minuit, 2014), pp. 99–107.

82 The narrator of this particular book does not seem to be as careful a reader as some of Bayard's other avatars: he makes mistakes about Lolita's age, confuses Lolita's husband with Clare Quilty, and seems to have discovered the existence of *Ada* (1969)—which explicitly deals with parallel worlds and is mentioned in a final footnote—only after the rest of the chapter had been written. Bayard, *Il existe*, p. 101.

83 Vladimir Nabokov, *Pale Fire* (New York: Vintage, 1989), pp. 300–01.

84 Vladimir Nabokov, 'Komnata', in his *Sobranie sochinenii russkogo perioda*, 5 vols (St Petersburg: Symposium, 1999), V (1999), p. 541.

85 Bayard, *Comment améliorer*, passim. To be sure, in order to suggest improvements, Bayard must first dwell on the considerable faults of the works in question, so that an alternative title could have been *Look How Bad Some Great Writers Could Be.*

86 Nabokov, *Lectures on Literature*, p. 3.

87 These invented midterms are still unpublished and can be found in the Nabokov archive in the Berg Collection at the New York Public Library.

88 Richard Rorty, *Contingency, Irony and Solidarity* (Cambridge: Cambridge University Press, 1989), p. 154.

89 Vladimir Nabokov, *Strong Opinions* (New York: Vintage, 1990), pp. 126–27.

90 Nabokov, *Lectures on Russian Literature,* p. 183.

91 Nabokov, *Lectures on Literature,* p. 231.

92 Ibid., p. 220.

93 'Did she have a precursor? She did, indeed she did'. Nabokov, *The Annotated Lolita,* p. 9.

94 Nabokov, *Lectures on Literature,* p. 220.

95 Ibid., p. 221. Ironically, the very passage that Nabokov presents as an example of Proust's quintessential style is singled out by Bayard as one of the particularly "weak" digressions in the *Recherche.* Pierre Bayard, *Le Hors-Sujet* (Paris: Les Éditions de Minuit, 1996), p. 21.

96 Tolstoy, *War and Peace,* p. 420.

97 Ibid., p. 423.

98 Ibid., p. 422.

99 Marcel Proust, *In the Shadow of Young Girls in Flower,* trans. by James Grieve (New York: Penguin, 2005), p. 296.

100 Tolstoy, *War and Peace,* p. 479.

101 Marcel Proust, *Remembrance of Things Past,* trans. by C.K. Scott Moncrieff, Terence Kilmartin and Andreas Mayor, 3 vols (New York: Vintage, 1982), III (1982), p. 886.

102 Eve Kosofsky Sedgwick, *The Weather in Proust* (Durham, NC: Duke University Press, 2011), p. 16.

103 Proust, *Remembrance of Things Past,* III (1982), pp. 900–01.

104 'One must beat the iron, pound it, knead it!' Tolstoy, *Anna Karenina,* p. 361. See also p. 355; p. 722; p. 768.

105 Without focussing on the specific verbal or thematic triggers, Philippe Chardin draws attention to the Tolstoyan character of Proust's creative

epiphanies, including the final ones at the end of the *Recherche*. *Proust, ou le Bonheur du petit personage qui compare* (Paris: Champion, 2006), p. 82.

106 Marcel Proust, *Selected Letters,* trans. by Ralph Manheim and ed. by Philip Kolb (Chicago, IL: University of Chicago Press, 1983), p. 167.

107 Jean-Yves Tadié, *Marcel Proust,* trans. by Euan Cameron (New York: Viking, 2000), p. 178.

108 Henri Bonnet and Pierre Robert, 'Jean de Pierrefeu et Marcel Proust: une correspondance inédite (janvier-décembre 1920)', *Revue d'Histoire littéraire de la France,* 79:5 (Sept-Oct., 1979), 800–23 (p. 812).

109 Proust, *Remembrance of Things Past,* III (1982), p. 387.

110 Walter A. Strauss, *Proust and Literature: The Novelist As Critic* (Cambridge, MA: Harvard University Press, 1957), p. 160.

111 Marcel Proust, *Correspondance de Marcel Proust,* ed. by Philip Kolb, 21 vols (Paris: Plon, 1970–93), X (1983), p. 47, pp. 211–12.

112 Marcel Proust, *In Search of Lost Time. The Prisoner. The Fugitive,* trans. by Carol Clark and Peter Collier (London: Penguin, 2003), p. 350.

113 Léon Tolstoï, *La Mort,* trans. by M. E. Halpérine (Paris: Perrin, 1886), pp. 222–25; Bayard, *Demain est écrit,* p. 102. The importance of this volume for Proust is signalled by Anne Henry in her *Marcel Proust: Théories pour une esthétique* (Paris: Klincksieck, 1981), pp. 34–35.

114 Proust, *Correspondance,* XII (1984), p. 180.

115 Ibid., XVIII (1990), p. 164.

List of Figures

Chapter 2

Chapter 6

Index

About the Team

Alessandra Tosi was the managing editor for this book.

Melissa Purkiss performed the copyediting and indexing, typeset the book in InDesign, and produced the paperback and hardback editions. The text font is Tex Gyre Pagella; the heading font is Californian FB.

Anna Gatti designed the cover. The cover was produced in InDesign using the Fontin font.

Luca Baffa produced the EPUB, MOBI, PDF, HTML, and XML editions—the conversion is performed with open source software freely available on our GitHub page (https://github.com/OpenBookPublishers).

This book need not end here...

Share

All our books — including the one you have just read — are free to access online so that students, researchers and members of the public who can't afford a printed edition will have access to the same ideas. This title will be accessed online by hundreds of readers each month across the globe: why not share the link so that someone you know is one of them?

This book and additional content is available at:

https://doi.org/10.11647/OBP.0241

Customise

Personalise your copy of this book or design new books using OBP and third-party material. Take chapters or whole books from our published list and make a special edition, a new anthology or an illuminating coursepack. Each customised edition will be produced as a paperback and a downloadable PDF.

Find out more at:

https://www.openbookpublishers.com/section/59/1

You may also be interested in:

Twentieth-Century Russian Poetry

Reinventing the Canon

Katharine Hodgson, Joanne Shelton and Alexandra Smith (eds)

https://doi.org/10.11647/OBP.0076

Information and Empire

Mechanisms of Communication in Russia, 1600–1850

Simon Franklin and Katherine Bowers (eds)

https://doi.org/10.11647/OBP.0122

Modernism and the Spiritual in Russian Art

New Perspectives

Louise Hardiman and Nicola Kozicharow (eds)

https://doi.org/10.11647/OBP.0115